ARTS AND TRADITIONS OF THE TABLE
Perspectives on Culinary History

Arts and Traditions of the Table:
Perspectives on Culinary History

ALAN SONNENFELD, SERIES EDITOR

FOOD & FAITH IN CHRISTIAN CULTURE

EDITED BY

Ken Albala & Trudy Eden

Columbia University Press New York

Columbia University Press
Publishers Since 1893
New York Chichester, West Sussex
Copyright © 2011 Columbia University Press
All rights reserved

Library of Congress Cataloging-in-Publication Data

Food and faith in Christian culture / edited by Ken Albala and Trudy Eden.
    p.   cm. — (Arts and traditions of the table)
  Includes bibliographical references (p.   ) and index.
  ISBN 978-0-231-14996-9 (cloth: alk. paper)—ISBN 978-0-231-14997-6 (pbk.: alk.
paper)—ISBN 978-0-231-52079-9 (e-book)
    1. Food—Religious aspects—Christianity—History.   2. Food habits—History.
3. Dinners and dining—Religious aspects—Christianity—History.   I. Albala, Ken,
1964– II. Eden, Trudy.
  BR115.N87F655 2011
  248.4—dc23
                                                                    2011020718

References to Internet Web sites (URLs) were accurate at the time of writing.
Neither the author nor Columbia University Press is responsible for Web sites that may
have expired or changed since the book was prepared.

FOOD
&
FAITH

IN CHRISTIAN CULTURE

Trudy Eden

For many people, the phrase *the lord's supper* may bring forth an image of the Last Supper (such as fifteenth-century mural by Leonardo da Vinci), with Jesus sitting at the center of a dining table and his twelve disciples seated on either side of him. The men are about to share a meal. This images evokes the powerful story of the last hours of Christ's life, depicting the first Eucharist and contrasting the commensal solidarity of those seated at the table with the impending betrayal by one among the group, Judas Isacariot. Betrayal and the love and forgiveness with which Jesus responded to it are, of course, at the center of Christianity. So, too, is the Eucharist. As such, they have been the subject of much study by a wide variety of people, not the least of whom are scholars of numerous academic disciplines.

Another aspect of this image, that of the table laid for a meal, has received little scholarly attention. Yet food and the act of eating, particularly group eating, are potent forces in human culture. No one in any culture sits at a table to share a meal without a complex set of understandings that influence their behavior at the table as well as away from it. It is these understandings and behaviors in the context of Christian culture that this volume seeks. With its focus firmly on the meal, its antecedents, and its consequences, this collection asks the central question: Have Christians used food and its associative practices to shape, strengthen, and/or spread their faith? The answer is a resounding yes. The following essays show that Christians have done so in an astonishing variety of ways from the fourteenth century to the present and around the world. These practices, while retaining a definite Christian character, exhibit a great deal of flexibility. Their rich diversity distinguishes Christian food customs from the more codified traditions of other major religions such as Judaism, Islam, Hinduism, or Buddhism. Food has been, and still is, useful to and powerful for Christians.

This wide array of people, places, and foods in time is woven together by four underlying themes: commensality, fasting, the sacrament, and bodily health. Although modestly defined as "the habit of eating together," commensality entails much more.[1] When a group of people sit together and eat the same food, they create or strengthen physical and social bonds. The type and strength of the bonds varies depending on the circumstances of the meal. Physical bonds arise when people eat the same food, which their bodies metabolize and turn into flesh. They become, if only in part and only temporarily, made one and the same. In earlier times and places, this distinction was important, as it underlay human identity.

Social bonds develop for different reasons. In the premodern and early modern periods in England, for example, people often didn't just "eat together." Depending on the size and nature of the group, eaters were often *arranged* together to eat. The root word *commensal* means eating at or pertaining to the same table.[2] Soldiers, for example, ate with men of the same rank. Nonmilitary diners at banquets sat at tables with people of the same social rank. In both cases the different tables received different kinds and amounts of foods. Commensality, then, ordered as well as bound social groups. Everyone who attended a meal bonded with the larger group but were divided and joined to their smaller group (called the mess) at the same time by the acts of eating the same food and of socializing during the meal.

Commensal has a third definition, as a noun, that developed in the nineteenth century but most certainly has roots in human dining customs. A commensal is an animal or plant which is attached to another and shares its food but is not a parasite.[3] When applied to human activity, this definition suggests the strongest and healthiest of communities, for it is one thing to take from a group and quite another to share with it.

These several meanings of *commensal* and *commensality* appear throughout this volume. Church suppers were, and still are, a common commensal practice, an example par excellence of which are the nineteenth-century love feasts of the Brethren in Christ Church of Lancaster, Pennsylvania, as described by Heidi Lee. Similarly driven by commensal power were the highly successful early twentieth-century efforts of the Missouri-based Unity School of Christianity to first sponsor free vegetarian meals and then build a vegetarian restaurant within the church itself, as analyzed by Trudy Eden. Several essays show that comensal bonds developed among people who, even though they never sat at the same table, adhered to the same philosophy of food. An excellent example is the adherence to the Rule of Saint Benedict. Richard Irvine's twenty-first century monks are bound by their acceptance of the Rule as are Sydney Watts's French monks of the eighteenth century, and both are similarly tied to Salvatore Musumeci's fourteenth-century Italian monastics. Another example is found in the Greek Orthodox practices as described by Antonia-Leda Matalas, Eleni Tourlouki, and Chrystalleni Lazarou. Although adherents were not all seated at the same meal, their strong philosophy on what should be eaten when and by whom created a commensal community of believers and eaters.

The most sacred, and arguably most powerful, commensal activity in both Catholic and Protestant communities is the taking of the sacrament. It produces bonds resulting from group consumption as well as from group beliefs. The "meal" is a simple one: bread and wine. The symbolic and real beliefs attached to both, and to the actual act of consuming them, lie at the heart of Christianity. Several of the following chapters analyze the meaning of the sacrament as a meal. Heather Martel explores its implications for religious identity in her study of the meaning of bread and wine and how Christians in seventeenth-century Spanish America reacted to the sacramental use of native breads, with its attendant fears of the ingestion and assimilation of foreign, not to mention impure, food. While not specifically about the sacrament, Hazel Petrie's chapter on the English missionaries' use of wheat and bread in proselytizing New Zealand Maori relies heavily on the association of bread with the sacrament. The consumption of wheaten bread by the Maori symbolized a new Christian, civilized, and subjected identity for and to those who converted. Highlighting a different approach to the sacrament, Trudy Eden's chapter on the Unity School of Christianity suggests that, although the sect dispensed with the actual ritual of communion, it fully employed the concept of transubstantiation in its belief in the physical and spiritual benefits of vegetarianism.

A vegetarian diet, in the premodern and early modern eras, was a form of fasting. All fasts were believed to have spiritual benefits. Whether recognized or not at the time, they had social benefits as well. Ken Albala describes the role of fasting in religious reformation in Europe as one of individual spiritual cleansing through mortification of the flesh and actual physical cleansing. At the same, fasting by Protestants performed a spiritual cleansing of another type—that of the church itself. Furthermore, fasting as an activity performed by a group, whether formally or informally, proved to be a useful tool for shaping group and personal religious identity. As Johanna Moyer demonstrates in her chapter on the sumptuary provisions of Catholics and Protestants during the Reformation, differences existed between the two groups. Catholics saw fasting as a path to salvation, hence, those who practiced it could live with that assurance. Protestants, assuring their salvation through faith alone, saw their fasting as a marker of group identity. The same was true of Benedictine monks in the fourteenth and twenty-first centuries, who, as Salvatore Musumeci stated of his late-medieval monks, turned the entire year into Lent, a practice, among others, that set them apart from the lay persons in their communities. Fasting of one kind or another provided identity markers for a quickly growing group of "others" who disdained animal flesh. Defining what exactly was meat and what was not, however, could be difficult, as the chapter by Sydney Watts on the scientific debate over whether puffins were fish or flesh in eighteenth-century France shows. The presence of so many chapters from such various backgrounds allows us to see a direct line between fasting in the early modern period to dieting in the postmodern period. Both involved abstention from certain kinds of foods at specific times of the year, for a period of time or for a specific purpose. By the end of the twentieth century, as argued by Samantha Kwan and Christine Sheikh, Christians of varied denominations bound themselves together with their dieting practices, all seeking acceptance and salvation.

Closely connected to the subject of fasting is bodily health. The Rule of Benedict itself, as discussed by Musumeci, Watts, and Irvine, has certain connotations for health. Religious reform through or characterized by fasting, as discussed Albala and Moyer, elided concepts of the ill body and the diseased body politic. Fasting, of course, was thought to cure both. Health, illness, purity, and impurity, as well as the physical and spiritual effects of "dirty" foods, concerned Heather Martel's sixteenth-century Spanish and Catholics in North America just as they did Hazel Petrie's nineteenth-century Maori who regarded wheat with a strong sense of taboo and impurity, the Unity vegetarians examined by Trudy Eden, and the Greek Orthodox adherents who practiced what became the popular, secular Mediterranean diet in the chapter by Antonia-Leda Matalas, Eleni Tourlouki, and Chrystalleni Lazarou. This theme reaches its most complex stage in the late twentieth century with the appearance of the fast-growing and powerful Christian diet phenomena, as told by Samantha Kwan and Christine Sheikh, an elaboration involving the body and its health, Christians versus non-Christians, purity and taboo, sin and redemption, beauty and ugliness, exteriority versus interiority, and the presence or absence of divine grace.

These four main themes—commensality, the sacrament, fasting, and bodily health—intertwine among each other as they bind the following chapters, which are arranged in chronological order. Starting with the culinary life of Italian monks in the fourteenth century, the chapter topics move on to fasting and sumptuary laws in the Reformation, food taboos in early America, and the impact of enlightenment science on lenten food classifications in the eighteenth century. Nineteenth-century topics focus on the use of food by Protestants to proselytize in New Zealand and to solidify congregational bonds in Pennsylvania. Chapters on the twentieth century examine the binding strength of food restrictions from vegetarianism to periodic fasting to dieting in Europe and the United States. Finally, the volume ends as it began, with the culinary life of monks, this time in early twenty-first century England. Altogether these chapters open up for examination the topic of food and Christianity and show how Christians used food and its associative practices to shape, strengthen, and spread their faith.

Notes

1. *Oxford English Dictionary,* "commensality," http://dictionary.oed.com.proxy.lib.uni.edu/cgi/entry/50044904?query_type=word&queryword=commensal&first=1&max_to_show=10&single=1&sort_type=alpha; accessed October 7, 2010.
2. *OED,* "commensal," http://dictionary.oed.com.proxy.lib.uni.edu/cgi/entry/50044902?query_type=word&queryword=commensal&first=1&max_to_show=10&single=1&sort_type=alpha; accessed October 7, 2010.
3. Ibid.

HISTORICAL BACKGROUND TO FOOD AND CHRISTIANITY

Ken Albala

Most of the world's major religions have adopted, if not an explicit code of food taboos, then a conscious attitude toward modes of eating and rituals surrounding consumption and prescribed forms of sacrifice. We find complex rules of kashrut at the core of Judaic worship, veneration of the cow among Hindus, set periods of fasting and forbidden foods among Muslims, and vegetarianism among devout Buddhists. Food prohibitions and celebrations serve many functions: to distinguish believers within defined communities and to cement their social bonds through common ritualized practice, to purify the body and soul through abstinence, or simply to offer up one's own sustenance to the gods as an act of worship. It should come as no surprise that food, being at the center of every human's daily experience of life, should be firmly embedded in every faith's definition of religiosity.

The act of ingestion and digestion involves the incorporation of food into our own flesh. What we eat literally becomes us, and we become it. Logically, therefore, food is among the most powerful expressions of identity, both for the individual and the group. Controlling one's diet and restricting intake can be a direct parallel of the effort to control other aspects of one's life and often comprises an entire ideology of consumption, a regimen or lifestyle that is a direct expression of one's values and worldview. How we eat, what we eat, and with whom are the most fundamental reflections of who we are physically, emotionally, and spiritually. Religions have devised dietary codes based on criteria such as these, defining food as clean and unclean, edible and abhominable, sacred and profane. Such rules may distinguish individuals on the basis of social standing, kinship solidarity, and, of course, religious affiliation. Most importantly, these modes of eating define the relationship of humans to nature as well as to God.

Food has almost always been integral part of religious practice, stemming from the earliest fertility cults to various forms of sacrifice and harvest celebrations; religious rituals are fundamentally agricultural in nature and follow the cyclical rhythms not only of the birth and death of plants and animals but of human life itself. Expressions of faith naturally retain elements of these earliest forms of worship; even after practices are codified and evolve, food remains central to all forms of religiosity.

While Christianity as a whole never espoused a set of explicit and permanent rules governing food, it nonetheless, in the course of its two-thousand-year development struck many varied attitudes toward consumption, ranging from near complete liberty to extreme asceticism, with practically every possible variety of feast and fast in between, including some unique food codes among individual sects or among particular religious orders. Christianity has also set the occasions on which familial celebrations have been held, times for gathering together, sharing traditional recipes, and handing down traditions.

The food ideologies of both early and medieval Christians have received ample scholarly coverage.[1] The present volume has been conceived in an effort to address the relative lack of synthetic studies of the early modern and modern eras, the last five hundred years, especially in comparing developments among varied sects from the Reformation onward, on both sides of the Atlantic and to some extent across the globe. With the splintering of various denominations within Western Christianity, the entire question of the believer's relation to food was opened anew, as it was at the advent of Christianity as an organized religion. Most importantly, the complex laws governing Lent and fasting in the medieval era were reexamined in light of new conceptions of salvation and the role of works in attaining it. The value of self mortification was questioned as well as the panoply of celebrations such as saint's days which filled the medieval calendar with celebratory feasts. These practices were of course investigated with a keen eye to upholding scriptural authority, but also with a sensitivity to the value of traditions, many of which stretched back to practices of the early Church. That is, each denomination carefully reassessed what it took to be its own history and the correct interpretation of food practices as dictated by the New Testament and the Church fathers. That they seldom agreed about how Christians should eat makes this a particularly rich and diverse field of investigation.

Counter to what one might expect, post-Reformation-era attitudes do not shift away from food, they merely redirect attention to other aspects of consumption: toward commensality, bodily image, the nature of self-restraint and control. These, among other issues, will be addressed in this book.

In light of this historically minded reassessment, this collection of essays must open with an overview, albeit brief, of food practices in the first millenium and a half of Christianity and the several strands that influenced Christian attitudes toward food, even when they were rejected. First, it is important to recognize that Christianity was profoundly influenced by both Judaism and Greco-Roman thought. In some respects earlier practices were adopted or continued, in others Christian practice was defined in conscious distinction to what had gone before. This is epecially true of Judaism, from which Christianity sprung.

At the dawn of the common era, Judaism was a sacrificial religion: insofar as Jews had access to the Temple in Jerusalem, they were required by law to make offerings either of animals without blemish or other foodstuffs, portions of which would be burned on the altar within the Temple precincts by priests. This practice stretched back, at least in the biblical account, to Noah who made an offering to the Lord after the flood, being careful to pour out the blood, which was said to belong to God. This practice was formally prescibed in the books of Leviticus and Deuteronomy as part of the Law given to the Jews by God via Moses.[2] Its function was to expiate the sins of the community, the lamb being punished in place of the guilty souls who had transgressed God's commandments. By the time of Roman occupation, however, many Jews lived far from the Holy Land and were scattered in communities throughout the Mediterranean where Temple sacrifice was impossible. In reconsidering ways each community could replace sacrifice, these Jews had already opened the question of what exactly God demanded in terms of sacrifice, in ways that would not only determine Jewish practice after the destruction of the Temple but would, inadvertently, influence Christianity as well. Does God require sacrifice or righteousness? Is food really so important after all? Or can fasting and prayer take the place of sacrifice for the expiation of sins?

Paul devised an ingenious solution to the question of sacrifice by asserting that Jesus dying on the cross was himself the sacrifice, the lamb of God or scapegoat for the sins of humanity. Thus, while the Jewish sacrificial laws were abrogated, they were also in a very real way fulfilled in a different form, now that the era of Grace had superceded the era of Law. Forgiveness comes as a free gift to the faithful, and the outward ritual forms are no longer necessary. Most Jewish rituals were thus reinterpreted in light of this new era of human history.

The complex food prohibitions of Judaism were, however, much more difficult to deal with. Not wanting to restrict Christianity to Jewish converts alone, it is understandable why Paul and others sought to abolish the kosher laws outright. These laws were essentially a way for Jews to avoid eating carnivorous animals and those which appeared to defy the system of classification devised by the Levitical priests. The taboo against pork, for example, was not, as some have contended, a practical solution to avoiding trichinosis, nor a way to maximize economic benefits by focusing on animals well suited to desert conditions.[3] Quite simply the rule to eat only animals which chew their cud and have a cloven hoof was intended to be a short handway of recognizing ruminants, those untainted by murder, which we must recall was forbidden since the time of Eden. The sin of carnivorous animals is unexpiated by sacrifice, and thus they are unclean. The concept of creatures considered unclean extends also to those which appear to either defy classification or move in ways which appear unsuited to their medium. Birds must have feathers, fish fins and scales, land animals four legs. Thus shellfish, snakes, and the like are also unkosher.[4] The concept of clean and unclean thus has little to do with our modern concept of hygiene; locusts, for example, are kosher.

Judaism had several other prohibitions, such as the mixing of milk and meat in the same meal, for one should not eat a "kid boiled in its mother's milk," as well as a prohibition against consuming blood and the ritual slaughter of animals, by severing the jugular vein so they feel the least pain possible, accompanied by a prayer of thanks. There was also one biblically commanded day of ritual fasting on the Day of Atonement or Yom Kippur as well as numerous examples of both personal and corporate fasting to atone for sins or avert God's wrath during impending disaster. The Old Testament also contains examples of miraculous fasting; Moses, for example, fasted for forty days on Mount Sinai.

As the early Christians began to define their practices in opposition to Judaism and in an effort to draw adherents from among Gentiles, they first adopted a position of complete liberty toward food. "It is not what enters into the mouth that defiles the man, but what proceeds out of the mouth" (Matthew 15:11). There are other episodes: when Peter has a dream of a giant net teeming with every imaginable creature, clean and unclean, over which God commands, "Up Peter, kill and eat" (Acts 10:10–16). For these early Christians, this was but another era among several food dispensations demanded of the faithful stretching from fruitarian Eden to the postflood concession, whereby God allowed humans to murder whatever they liked for food, to the era of Mosaic kosher laws. This new dispensation was conceived as the final stage when faithful humans no longer needed complex laws since their sins were forgiven by Grace.

Though the kosher laws had been repealed, there were other aspects of Judaic practice that were retained. One was the ritual celebration of eating together, commensality, or, as the early Christians called it, a love or *agape* feast designed to strengthen social harmony and brotherhood. This was an opportunity to express solidarity as well as a time to exercise charity, although, if the apostolic accounts are accurate, they could also degenerate into luxurious potluck suppers. The practice gradually fell into abeyance, though it was often revived among Protestant sects such as the Moravians and Methodists.

Regarding charity, the practice among Christians was directly analogous to the Jewish performance of good deeds or mitzvot—giving to the needy, especially of food, was carried on directly in the Christian commandment to break bread with strangers. The Sabbath, or day of rest, was another food-related ritual retained, though moved to Sunday, to commemorate the Resurrection. In the Christian tradition, Sunday is thus never a day of fasting.

The Jewish Passover was also retained, but in severely modified form, as the basis for the ritual at the very center of Christian worship—the Eucharist or communion. The rite originates with words spoken by Jesus at the Last Supper, a celebration of Passover. While reclining, drinking the requisite four glasses of wine, and eating unleavened bread, Jesus remarks to his apostles that the bread they eat is his body, the wine his blood, and asks them to remember him when they eat or drink. This statement could be taken literally, as when decided by the Lateran Council in 1215 that the bread and wine miraculously transform into flesh and blood in a process called transubstantiation whereby the "accidents" or external form appear to be bread and wine while the "substance" become Christ's flesh and blood. Or it could be taken metaphorically, the eating of bread to serve only as a memorial or a means whereby grace is infused into the supplicant, a position adopted in the Reformed tradition. In either case, the real presence would be the great dividing issue of sixteenth-century denominations at the start of the early modern period.

The fast as a way to purify the soul and show God one's sincerity and contrition was another practice retained in early Christianity. Jesus and his apostles had fasted, which in this case meant total abstinence from food; Jesus fasted for forty days in the desert. While these forms of abstinence were considered beyond the power of ordinary mortals, the ideal would remain, and in the waves of persecutions among early Christians the fast would also become a communal means of atonement, just as it had been in the Old Testament.

The New Testament is rich with food references and metaphors. Jesus himself, considering his audience, often spoke in terms they could understand, and so we find parables drawn from farming and fishing practices as well as several food miracles. The fact that Jesus himself would provide festivities with loaves and fishes or a wedding with an endless supply of wine is evidence that Jesus and the first Christians' attitude toward food was much like that of other Jews. Sensual pleasures were not in and of themselves suspect; if consumed in the right context under the right circumstances, they were to be considered gifts of God and enjoyed as such. As we will see, in light of subsequent developments, Christians of later eras would have a difficult time reconciling their own urges toward control with what were clearly joyous festivities in the Old and New Testaments.

The last book of the Bible, the Revelations of Saint John, also prompted another unique attitude toward food. Preparation for the apocalypse, the final judgement when sinners would be separated from saints, and humans would return to an era of edenlike peace when Christ would rule on earth, led many Christians to adopt a simple meat-free diet.[5] Eschatological concerns and the coming of a Messiah were equally rooted in Judaism, appearing, for example, in Isaiah and the book of Daniel, but they took a different turn among many Christians who believed that in the New Jerusalem the faithful would no longer need to eat as before. Fruits would become, as they had been in Eden, enough nourishment to survive. Feeding would become more angelic, in a sense, and, just as the lion would lay down with the lamb, man would no longer have to kill for sustenance. In preparation for this new era, if not to actually hasten it, many Christian thinkers espoused vegetarianism—despite the clear passages in the New Testament that allow all foods for the faithful. Vegetarianism was not essentially inspired by concern for animal welfare, at least not among medieval Carthusians, nor among seventeenth-century Boehmenists, or even Seventh Day Adventists in the modern era.[6]

The inheritance of Greco-Roman culture is a little more complex. For one, certain pagan food rituals might potentially conflict with presumably taboo-free Christian food ideology. The pagan Greeks and Romans also performed ritual sacrifices, which served a celebratory function. Citizens were expected to participate in these great communal barbecues, which expressed both the largesse of the state and belonging to a defined group. Opting out, as vegetarians like Pythagoras had done, was in effect a form of social and political protest. But were Christians, as citizens, also expected to partake? Was it all right to consume meat that had been sacrificed to pagan gods? Technically, yes, was the answer Paul gave to the Corinthian community, but, lest one's neighbor be led astray and fall into error regarding the meaning of such a sacrifice, it would be best for Christians to abstain if possible.

More importantly, there was a particular attitude toward eating among many Greeks and Romans that had a long lasting impact on Christianity. Among philosophers of the Stoic school, as well as many Platonists, it was believed that in order to attain virtue the needs of the body should be adequately met but never exceeded. Bodily functions were considered a distraction from the higher operations of the intellect and soul.[7] Thus gluttony, and even excessive feasting on particular occasions, was seen as base and brutish. Rather, the virtuous individual should maintain an abstemious diet, avoiding luxuries, which only weaken and ennervate the mind, and stick to a constant regimen year round. Even the Epicureans, despite the ignominy later attached to their doctrines, maintained that the greatest pleasure could be attained by avoiding suffering, including that derived from not getting those delicacies to which one might be accustomed. Rather than feel the pain of such desire, it is best to live a simple, frugal life, free of excessive needs. The call for a regular frugal diet may be traced directly from classical philosophers to the early Christians, especially in their attacks on gluttony. Stoicism in particular had an impact on the thought of sixteenth-century reformer Jean Calvin, who sought to introduce a sober regime year round, one that has come to be associated with Puritanism.

The concern with gluttony, however, was expressed through all forms of Christian morality. In fact, it was considered the very first sin, stemming from Eve's eating the forbidden fruit in the Garden of Eden. Thence proceed all other cardinal sins as well: avarice, or the failure to practice charity with surplus food; pride, in showing off one's bounty; sloth, in the consequent torpor that derives from overeating; envy, from the desire to obtain luxuries enjoyed by others, and, most importantly, wrath and lust, which were considered the physiological by-products of gourmandism.

Among the early Christians there was a strong medical logic to this call for simplicity and abstinence.[8] The body becomes overtaxed by excesive feeding, the humors become corrupt, and the spirits surrounding the brain foul and thick. Thus the thoughts are disturbed. Moreover, an overly nourished body, especially one fed with meat, was thought to produce a plethora of blood, which would be subsequently converted into sperm (in both males and females), signaling the libido and thus readying the body for procreation. It is precisely for this reason that many early Christian writers counseled their celibate brethren and sisters to eat very sparingly, to avoid flesh, as well as to subject their bodies to various means of cooling off the ardor which leads both to bodily heat and moisture and the proclivity to sin. Among ascetics, this medical logic, ultimately inherited from authors such as Galen of Pergamum, dictated extreme abstinence.

The early Church is rife with examples of asceticism, which originally meant a form of physical "exercise" that was meant to subdue the urges of the flesh so as to strengthen the soul.[9] Rather than a strict dualistic opposition of body and soul, the ancients believed that humans are composed of a systemic psychosomatic whole in which the affections of the mind influence the body, particularly in the production of humors, and the disposition of the body equally influences the mind and soul. For example, an excess of black bile, the cold and dry humor, leads to the psychic condition of melancholy; excess choler leads to wrath: excess phlegm to laziness and apathy. Thus physical distemperatures can exacerbate mental states and incite the individual to sin. These ideas inspired many ascetics to control various aspects of regimen, including food intake, in order to maintain homeostasis but also prevent overnourishment and excessive hot and moist humors. Thus we find cooling and drying regimens for early monastics.

With or without this rationale, there were also what might be called heroic ascetics, those who wandered into the Egyptian desert like Saint Anthony or Saint Simeon atop his column.[10] Such ascetics might live solitary or hermetic lives, but just as often they came into communities as monks, whose food habits were governed by an official rule. That written by Saint Benedict in the sixth century set the pattern for Western monasticism, and, while it provides relatively meager meals, it also makes concessions for the sick and visitors who might be allowed meat or a third dish in a single meal. Most interestingly, in consideration of current habits, and not without certain reservations, Benedict allows his monks a hemina of wine daily (about 10 ounces), though he admits wine is really not for monks. For future generations of ascetics, there was this constant tension between the great heroic examples provided by the early Christians and the practical realities of maintaining health. To willingly damage the body or inadvertently kill oneself was considered a mortal sin, and thus we find constant exhortations to monks and nuns not to fast excessively. This was precisely the trouble Saint Jerome found himself in after the daughter of his friend Paula died from excessive fasting. On the other hand, monastic orders could just as easily grow wealthy, eating and drinking without restraint, as numerous examples of corpulent monks through medieval literature attest. This probably accounts for the recurrent tendency for zealous individuals to break from their lax monastic order to adopt a more austere lifestyle, sometimes forgoing meat altogether, as did the Carthusians, which led their being suspected of heresy.

In the course of the early Middle Ages, the ascetic ideal spread to the lay community as well. Yet, in consideration of the need to work, procreate, and carry on with daily life, fasting was limited to specific days, normally Friday and Saturday and, in some places, Wednesday as well. There were also fasts on the vigils of the most important saint's days, as well as the so-called *quatuor tempori*—four times of the year on solstices and equinoxes. Lent was the most important fast, a forty-day period preceding Easter during which abstention from solid foods was required until sundown, thus partaking in one meal a day for the entire period with the exception of Sundays. Rather than leave the exact dictates of these fasts to parishioners, church officials gradually codified fasting practice in the course of the early middle ages so that all animal products, such as butter, cheese, and eggs, would be forbidden to all healthy adults, with various exceptions made for pregnancy and, in some cases, heavy labor. These regulations would last directly up until the early modern period and thereafter among Roman Catholics until the Vatican II Council in the 1960s. The majority of people for a good proportion of the year subsisted on vegetables, bread, and fish—which were considered cold and moist and suitable for a fast. Individuals might, nonetheless, purchase dispensations, and sometimes whole towns could obtain the right to eat butter or some other animal product.

Before the Reformation for all Christians, and among Catholics thereafter, religion and fast days also directly influenced the development of gastronomy. Chefs were inspired to create elaborate fish and vegetable dishes for their patrons, not perhaps in the spirit of fasting, but technically adhering to the letter of the dietary law. In medieval cuisine, for example, almond milk was widely used as a substitute during fast days, and could even be made into imitation butter and cheese. Other mock meat dishes were made, in fascinating ways prefiguring those of the industrial era.[11]

These fasts days were starkly contrasted with feasts, in particular Carnival, directly preceding Lent. Mardis Gras, or Fat Tuesday, was a day not only to consume all remaining meat before Ash Wednesday but in general a day of licence in food, drink, and bodily pleasures. It was said that the world turned upside down on this day, and inferiors were allowed to openly mock their superiors, albeit masked, in rituals of subversion. Thus there were mock weddings, mock trials, and the lowest person might be crowned king for the day. Rather than pose a threat to the structure of society, it has been suggested that this one day of ritual subversion actually strengthened the social order as a kind of safety valve—allowing people to blow off steam and then return to their proper stations the rest of the year. The closing down of Carnival celebrations in both Protestant and Catholic countries in the sixteenth century suggests that ritual subversion gradually gave way to real violence and disorder. [12]

Protestants, in particular, in keeping with their aim to purge ritual practice of anything not found in Scripture, began to abolish celebrations whose origin they considered too pagan. That is, in the process of conversion centuries before, many pagan holidays had been "accommodated" to Christian worship by renaming for saints or, in the case of Saturnalia, being changed into Christmas. Puritans in seventeenth-century England, for example, abolished it along with many saints' days. In so doing they radically reduced the number of holidays and opportunities for festive communal meals. Similar processes took place elsewhere in Europe. Although many factors were involved, dining became more privatized, along with other ritual celebrations as high culture gradually distanced itself from popular culture. Rather than gathering en masse regardless of social class on set occasions such as church-ales (a variety of traditional feasts), individuals increasingly retired into commerical establishments such as taverns and pubs, while elites ate and drank in their own homes.[13] Holidays such as Christmas were still, of course, celebrated, but the focus increasingly became the family unit rather than the community. The division of the Catholic Church into a multitude of denominations played a large role.

Another perspective from which we might assess the influence of Christianity on foodways concerns the construction of the body in a sociohistorical context. In other words, how did individuals conceive of their own bodies and what foods did they eat or avoid in order to achieve the desired physical outcome? In the ascetic tradition, an outward excess of flesh was seen as a sign of inward moral weakness, yet we might also see the ideal of a slim body and consequent dieting in the modern era as a comparable manifestation of the power of ideas to shape and control intake. Such ideas are not only influenced by medical concerns, but they might also be tempered by social construction of beauty and a conflation of those ideals with holiness and maintaining the Temple of the Body. The practice of dieting has become inextricably entwined with conceptions of bodily purity, and there are many ways in which the modern pathology of anorexia is prefigured by women who starved themselves for Christ.[14] Although the context and milieu may have changed radically over the centuries, the motivation among women to control their own bodies in a world that denied them all access to power is fundamentally, psychologically, tantamount.

This collection is designed to explore the many ways Christian doctrine has influenced consumption patterns and sometimes explicit dietary codes in the past five hundred years in Europe, America, and around the world. Each article addresses a particular way of eating or attitude toward food: vegetarianism, fasting and inedia, weight loss and health regimes, commensality, and so forth. All the chapters also fit into a broader theme: Christianity, no less than any other religion, has, despite its founding tenets of food freedom and the reiteration of this ideal in many reform movements, nonetheless led directly to several unique food ideologies and practices which bear the stamp of religiosity. Christianity continues to influence the way people eat, just as it has done for the past two millennia, as a "civilizing" force among missionaries around the world, as an inspiration for weight loss, as a means of addressing the ethical concerns raised by doctrines of nonviolence and environmental stewardship. That is, Christianity has had a profound impact on what we eat, though how this has happened has never received comparative analysis across the globe and over a long time span.

Notes

1. Feeley-Harnik, *The Lord's Table*; Grimm, *From Feasting to Fasting*.
2. John Cooper, *Eat and Be Satisfied: A Social History of Jewish Food* (Northvale, NJ: Jason Aronson, 1993); Arthur Greene, *Jewish Spirituality: From the Bible Through the Middle Ages* (New York: Crossroad, 1986); Samson Raphael Hirsch, *Horeb: A Philosophy of Jewish Laws and Observances* (New York: Soncino, 1997). For the impact of these practices on modern times, see Leonard Greenspoon, Ronald A. Simkins, and Gerald Shapiro, *Food and Judaism* (Omaha, NE: Creighton University Press, 2005).
3. Harris, *Cows, Pigs, Wars, and Witches*; Simoons, *Eat Not This Flesh*.
4. Jan Soler, "The Semiotics of Food in the Bible," in Carole Counihan and Penny van Esterik, eds., *Food and Culture: A Reader* (New York: Routledge, 1977); Douglas, *Purity and Danger*.
5. Muers and Grumett, *Eating and Believing*.
6. For a good general overview see Spencer, *The Heretic's Feast*.
7. Deane W. Curtin and Lisa M. Heldke, *Cooking, Eating, Thinking: Transformative Philosophies of Food* (Bloomington: Indiana University Press, 1992); John M. Wilkins and Shaun Hill, *Food in the Ancient World* (Oxford: Blackwell, 2006); and Andrew Dalby, *Food in the Ancient World, from A–Z* (New York: Routledge, 2003).
8. Shaw, *The Burden of the Flesh*.
9. Vincent L. Wimbush and Richard Valantasis, eds., *Asceticism* (New York: Oxford University Press, 1998).
10. For the classic primary sources, see Owen Chadwick, ed., *Western Asceticism* (Philadelphia: Westminster, 1958).
11. Fagan, *Fish on Friday: Feasting and Fasting*; and Henisch, *Fast and Feast*.
12. Peter Burke, *Popular Culture in Early Modern Europe* (New York: Harper, 1978); and Mikhail Bakhtin, *Rabelais and His World* (Bloomington: University of Indiana, 1984).

13. Bennett, *Ale, Beer and Brewsters in England*; Richard W. Unger, *Beer in the Middle Ages and Renaissance* (Philadelphia: University of Pennsylvania Press, 2004); and A. Lynn Martin, *Alcohol Violence and Disorder in Traditional Europe* (Kirksville, MO: Truman State University Press, 2009).

14. Bell, *Holy Anorexia*; Joan Jacob Brumberg, *Fasting Girls: The History of Anorexia Nervosa* (New York: Vintage, 2000); Bynum, *Holy Feast and Holy Fast*; and Vendereycken and van Deth, *From Fasting Saints to Anorexic Girls*.

CHAPTER I

THE URBAN INFLUENCE

SHOPPING AND CONSUMPTION AT THE FLORENTINE MONASTERY OF SANTA TRINITÀ IN THE MID-FOURTEENTH CENTURY

Salvatore D. S. Musumeci

The monks of Santa Trinità, in their monastery on the banks of the Arno River in Florence, Italy, participated fully in the universal religious lifestyle of late fourteenth-century monasticism, as dictated by the Rule of Saint Benedict.[1] Santa Trinità, however, had all the benefits of an urban economy and marketplace availability, and its inhabitants took full advantage of this. In theory Santa Trinità's diet was suited to a life of prayer, penitence, and preparation for the afterlife.[2] The Vallombrosans, one of Italy's many traditional religious orders, were dedicated to the Rule and a strict spiritual lifestyle that renounced bodily pleasures, observed perpetual silence, and embraced physical enclosure. Yet their provisioning practices, and the foods eaten by the monks, were similar to those of their secular Florentine neighbors.

Through the use of intermediaries like lay brothers and hired servants, the monks were able to keep to their strict enclosure but also easily and affordably provision their monastery to support the full-time congregation as well as visiting guests and friends. That their diet resembled what the secular Florentines ate is not to say that the monks were decadent or cavalier about the necessity of following Saint Benedict's Rule. Instead, it shows an ability to fit, with resourcefulness and care, what they grew as well as purchased within the strictures and guidelines of their liturgical life.

Santa Trinità's surviving account books, with their highly detailed records of daily expenditure, reveal the tensions between the popular image of monastic life in the middle decades of the Trecento and that life's realities and actual practices, highlighting the fact of just how dependent the monks actually were on the markets and shops of Florence. Since the neighboring families shopped at the same markets and vendors that the monks frequented, it seems clear that the monks ate the same foods as their secular Florentine counterparts. However, they honored the Rule of Saint Benedict that regulated life at Santa Trinità by eating these same foodstuffs in a different manner from their neighbors and by using appropriate foods at the correct times of the year according to the liturgical calendar.

The information in this chapter comes from a *libro di spese,* or book of purchases, kept by Santa Trinità's *camerlengo,* or fiscal administrator, Dom Lorenzo di Guidotto Martini.[3] His purpose was to ensure a careful daily record of what was purchased on behalf of the monastery, its dependents, and guests. Dom Lorenzo's account book runs from January 1360 (1359 in the Florentine calendar) through July 1363.[4] The accounts were not designed to record dinner menus, architectural developments, or musical performances at the monastery. Dom Lorenzo had the inclination, time, and ability to carefully track and annotate institutional expenditures in a manner that was familiar to the many Florentine merchants who kept extensive business records, personal accounts, and *zibaldone* (a mixture of both familial and financial memoranda).[5] Dom Lorenzo, like his secular counterparts, also used these fiscal records to note events that were important in the monastery's history. This was, in part, to justify the expenditure incurred, providing a record that would not be easy to dispute if questions were raised over the accountant's or monastery's probity. Because monasteries were not exempt from secular taxation, Dom Lorenzo carefully recorded the *gabelle,* or taxes, paid for food imported into the city from the monastery's estates outside the city walls. These records permit the analysis of the monastery's self-sufficiency with regard to certain products, as well as justify the need for the monks to engage the markets, shops, and vendors of Florence for the products that were not produced in quantity enough on their lands to allow self-sufficiency. Where items were given as gifts or were exempt (for whatever reason) from taxation, they were not recorded.[6] Dom Lorenzo's text also provides more detail for marketplace purchases, particularly their quantities and prices.

For many scholars the monastic diet was a relatively bland affair and has primarily been viewed against the backdrop of the liturgical year, at times focusing exclusively on the cycle of fasting periods and feast days present in the calendar.[7] Fluctuations in the purchase and consumption of meat, fish, and vegetables are normally understood as signposts for both reverent and irreverent behavior as well as a gauge of the congregation's moral and spiritual health and practices. However, recent studies have established the strong relationship between the diet of the aristocrat and the diet of the religious house, challenging assumptions about an order's relationship to its governing rule.[8] This is not to argue that the liturgical year was not important, only that the argument needs to be made that fasting was only one part of the religious diet in the fourteenth century. Seasonal availability, the skills of the cook, the appearance and frequency of guests, and the obligation to entertain them were also important monastic considerations. Therefore Dom Lorenzo's text can be used to better understand the alimentary habits and consumption patterns of the monastery of Santa Trinità. We would expect, for example, to see fasting clearly delineated in the daily purchases and mealtime preparations rather than through the long-term stores kept at the monastery.[9] Likewise, feast days might be differentiated by the special nature of goods bought for specific occasions or celebrations, such as costly wines, roasted meats, and musical entertainments.[10]

The short period of time covered in Dom Lorenzo's accounts was a relatively peaceful one in Florentine history; the economic and political landscape was mostly stable, providing us a look at what might be considered normative for both secular and ecclesiastic citizens.[11] However, these three and a half years occurred during a longer period of transition between the devastating effects of the Black Death of 1348 (Florence's population dropped from ninety thousand to about fifty-five thousand people) and a great political upheaval in the form of the Ciompi Revolt in 1378.[12] During this time the monastery was embedded within its own long-established religious traditions and key local neighborhood connections.[13] Unlike other monastic orders that were international in scope and ambition, the Vallombrosans were closely connected to the Arno city and its surrounding countryside.[14] The order's founder was a Florentine named Giovanni Visdomini, later known as Giovanni Gualberto, who joined the Benedictine monastery of San Miniato in the early eleventh century.[15] In 1036 he formed a new order just outside Florence in the wooded hills of Vallombrosa, an order that sought to combine the contemplative elements of the Benedictine Rule with a stronger denunciation of material wealth and worldly possessions through the Rule's literal interpretation and application.[16] Gualberto wanted his ideal monastic communities to be self-sufficient.[17] But the need to engage in daily devotions, meditation, and a regular cycle of prayer and praise made the investment of time required for self-sufficiency difficult. Conscious of these contradictions, Gualberto permitted the employment of *conversi,* or lay brothers, and *famiglia,* or hired servants.[18] The lay brothers, along with the hired servants, were meant to serve as a buffer between the outside world, with its secular ideologies, and the secluded sacred world of the fully professed monks.[19]

Using Dom Lorenzo's accounts to identify the actual individuals at Santa Trinità responsible for provisioning the monastery is a complex task, especially in light of the strict observance of Saint Benedict's Rule expected of members of the Vallombrosan order. Three groups at Santa Trinità had interactions with the markets of Florence: the monks themselves, the lay brothers, and the hired servants (employed on a salaried basis by the monastery).[20] Importantly, it becomes clear from the accounts that purchases and orders did not always involve or require actually leaving the monastery.[21] The use of intermediaries, often the merchants themselves, allowed those in charge of a daily shop to bargain effectively without having to compromise their ascetic retreat behind the monastery's walls. The use of intermediaries means that it can be difficult to untangle the distinctions between those leaving the monastery to go out into the markets and shops of Florence and those who simply paid for the requisite items from within the sacred space of Santa Trinità.[22] Entries that record the servicing, purchasing, picking up, or dropping off of items are much more detailed than entries noting transactions taking place within the monastery, and the entries in Dom Lorenzo's text that represent a monk-purchaser lack the detail that physically places the person outside the monastery's walls.[23] Where no one is credited with the purchase, it suggests someone within the monastery simply paid for an item rather than leaving the monastery to purchase it in the marketplace.[24] Indeed, it is plausible that the majority of purchased items noted within Dom Lorenzo's text could have been bought from itinerant sellers or by regular suppliers who brought goods to the monastery door and received their payment via a hired servant or lay brother; thus the fully professed monks of Santa Trinità kept to their enclosure, avoiding contact with the outside world.[25]

The lay brothers played key roles in managing the daily needs and activities at the monastery. Unlike the professed monks of Santa Trinità whose lives were devoted to study, meditation, contemplation, and prayer, the lay brothers (not bound by the rules of enclosure) occupied themselves with a portion of the everyday tasks that were necessary to the smooth and efficient running of the monastery. In addition, and to a lesser extent, they participated in the religious devotions that occurred daily at the monastery.[26] These individuals acted as an important safeguard between the sacred space of the monastery and the secular world of late medieval Florence, a view suggested by the historians Peter King and Clifford Lawrence.[27] Their jobs involved running errands, shopping, picking up, or dropping off items required by the monks. These recorded daily outings into the city center, which in part led the historian Gene Brucker to suspect that the monks had compromised their rule and withdrawal for all the secular attractions that the Arno city had to offer, were in reality simply tasks undertaken mostly by lay brothers to fulfill a specific need which was required by the cook, abbot, or stable boy to benefit visitors to the monastery.[28]

Alongside the monks and lay brothers of Santa Trinità, the hired servants of the monastery assisted with daily routines, undertaking the majority of the work to provision the kitchen and stable. Although both King and Lawrence emphasized the role played by the lay brothers, they largely ignored these secular servants who were the key liaisons between the monastery and the urban community in which it was located.[29] From Dom Lorenzo's entries, we can see that that this group undertook the bulk of the everyday excursions.[30] There were only three servants who were paid on a salaried basis: the cook, the stable boy, and the grammarian— this last individual had little to do with the kitchen. The cook shopped directly for food and occasionally helped the stable boys by purchasing fodder during his daily excursions.[31] In return, the stable boy looked after the animals and their needs but also helped with the purchasing of foodstuffs for the cook and his kitchen.[32]

The Vallombrosans took possession of Santa Trinità in 1092.[33] As a monastery, it was probably one of the wealthiest, largely due to its urban location. While it had been founded outside the original walls of Florence, the construction of new city walls meant that Florence absorbed it into an expanding neighborhood.[34] The piazza that developed outside of Santa Trinità was commonly associated with the church attached to the monastery, and most early fifteenth-century documents refer to piazza Santa Trinità or via di Santa Trinità.[35] However, there were also important secular buildings in this area, and the art historian Kevin Murphy notes references in several 1427 *catasto* declarations to piazza degli Spini rather than piazza Santa Trinità.[36] Indeed, while the chronicler Benedetto Dei names the space as piazza Santa Trinità in 1472, he is also conscious of important local lineages and is careful to list patrician residents of the piazza such as the Gianfigliazzi, Scali, Bombeni, Minerbetti, Soldanieri, Strozzi, Sassetti, and Spini.[37]

Although the cloistered community of Santa Trinità should have stood apart from these wealthy residents, it was, in fact, closely integrated with and increasingly dependent on their support. As with most ecclesiastic buildings, the church's construction was financed by donations and the sale of private chapels.[38] By the fifteenth century the Gianfigliazzi had two chapels and three burial sites for different branches of the family in the church of Santa Trinità.[39] The family held both collective and individual loyalty to the Vallombrosan order during the fourteenth and fifteenth centuries. In part, this could be because two of the Gianfigliazzi became Vallombrosan monks: the brothers Simone di Bertoldo de' Gianfigliazzi and Bernardo de' Gianfigliazzi.[40] According to Murphy, the family provided this level of extensive patronage only to Santa Trinità.[41] This was a gesture that would both justify the Gianfigliazzi's loyalty to the Vallombrosans as well as strengthen the link between the family and the neighborhood within which Santa Trinità was located. The close relationship between the monastic community and its neighborhood is illustrated by the fact that at least two identifiable members of the monastic congregation during Dom Lorenzo's tenure (Dom Jacopo di Bernardo Ardinghelli and Dom Simone di Bertoldo de' Gianfigliazzi) came from local piazza families who contributed to the building and patronage program of the church of Santa Trinità.[42] In fact, Dom Simone and his mother continued to have a close relationship even after he entered the monastery.[43]

Because the monastery was dependent on the city of Florence for so many of its daily needs, as we shall see, we need to briefly consider where sales and purchases of goods took place. Dei described the piazza outside the monastery and church of Santa Trinità as being "full of all the merchants and shops one could want."[44] The accounts do allude to a local open-air market, noting on June 18, 1360, that Dom Lorenzo paid a required tax for a *merchato qui* or "a market here."[45] A later *libro di spese* from Santa Trinità covering the years 1416–1423 mentions the purchase of flour in the piazza itself on a number of occasions.[46] But Murphy's study of the development of the piazza complicates the issue of what the monastery would have been able to purchase in its immediate vicinity. His in-depth study of the piazza's history suggests that it, and the surrounding area, included a high concentration of individuals practicing manual trades such as carpentry or paving as well other nonfood related trades such as moneylending and painting.[47] Murphy concludes that in order for the piazza's residents to secure foodstuffs they would have needed to visit via Porta Rossa or the Mercato Vecchio, literally "the old market."[48]

Historians Maria Bianchi and Maria Grossi, using the *catasti* declarations from 1427 and 1480, concur with Murphy's analysis of the areas surrounding Santa Trinità.[49] Grossi's study deals specifically with the *catasti* declarations of 1427, which Murphy also utilized in his study, and shows that there were a range of places to buy food a short distance from the monastery.[50] For example, within the quarter of Santa Maria Novella the monastery would have found butchers, greengrocers, and bakers.[51] The other quarters bordering Santa Trinità were also well stocked with individuals selling food and wine.[52] Furthermore, itinerant vendors and traveling markets often passed through the area, giving the monks access to the food items they needed, even if the piazza's more established shops did not.[53]

Before we turn to market purchases, let us look briefly at the items Santa Trinità's own farms supplied. Like most traditional monastic institutions, Santa Trinità relied on land holdings that were donated by grateful parishioners, using these lands to garner rental income or provide sustenance in the form of produce or animals.[54] In this way, Santa Trinità would have been closely connected with the surrounding rural economy, husbanding, and overseeing their properties just as other land-owning Florentines would have.[55] During the period in question, the monastery of Santa Trinità owned and farmed a range of properties; indeed, the holdings may have been more extensive than Dom Lorenzo's text indicates.[56] Dom Lorenzo identifies seven farms as distinctive entities in his text: Arcetri, Campora, Ema, Legnaia, Monte, Mugnone, and San Donnino. Paid laborers and farmhands tended each farm (or sometimes two farms), the buildings, and the crops on behalf of the monastery.[57]

The investment in multiple plots of land meant that the monks never had to rely on a single source for their basic provisions. They could ensure themselves against crop failure on one farm by spreading the risks across numerous sites. Looking more closely at what was cultivated and then how the goods were treated and transported gives a sense of the monastery's attitude to the need for self-sufficiency.[58] Imports from the monastery's farms to the monastery's kitchen, pantry, or cellar needed to be well planned and well orchestrated. Fresh foodstuffs would have deteriorated, unless they were used immediately or stored properly, and the monastery no doubt found it difficult to cope with a glut of seasonal produce. Though it is clear that the monastery's farms produced a variety of items they used on a daily basis, and that a variety of products arrived reliably from the monastery's lands, the sheer amounts of some goods produced were not enough to fulfill the monastery's needs.[59] This is in part why the monastery relied so heavily on the markets, shops, and vendors of the Arno city.

The farm at Ema produced beans, chickpeas, and garlic—all items that could be dried and stored.[60] Ema also had an orchard, which provided pears, a variety of apples, figs, walnuts, cherries, plums, grapes, and medlars.[61] All these items were either shipped to the monastery fresh or dried.[62] The farm at Monte also supplied figs, walnuts, and apples.[63] Both Monte and Ema had the ability to dry fruits, especially figs, in their *fornace* or oven.[64] In addition, the farms supplied amounts of pork, poultry, and eggs.[65] However, only three items were supplied from the farms in such quantities that Santa Trinità could be self-sufficient in them: olive oil, grain, and wine.[66] In these items alone the monastery did not rely on the markets to supply their needs. The monks rarely ever purchased olive oil or grain, and though wine was purchased daily, it was in very small quantities and for a very specific purpose.[67]

Olive trees were a long-term investment for the monastery. Of the seven farms recorded in Dom Lorenzo's text, only one piece of land, the farm at Monte, produced olive oil, and in such quantities that allowed for self-sufficiency. Indeed, in 1360, Dom Lorenzo referred to the farm at Monte as a *fattoio da olio* or an oil-producing farm.[68] The same terminology was also used half a century earlier in 1307 when the Commune of Florence sold the property to the monastery.[69]

Enormous quantities of grain were cultivated on five of the seven farms. Dom Lorenzo's text makes it clear that Santa Trinità relied solely upon wheat production and deliveries from its own lands for this essential product. Ema, Monte, and Campora produced wheat, barley, and spelt; the farms at Arcetri and San Donnino only produced wheat.[70] It is likely that the majority of grain was used to make the monastery's bread, since Dom Lorenzo notes the grain was picked up from the monastery, milled, baked, and then delivered back to Santa Trinità in its loaf form.[71] Here the integration of countryside and urban community becomes clearer. For example, the wheat arrived from the farm in an unprocessed state. A miller then collected a small portion of the grain from Santa Trinità's stores on a regular basis, processed it, and sent it on to the monastery's baker. Such a procedure occurs on September 28, 1360, when Dom Lorenzo records two exchanges of wheat between the miller Vespino, who took the resulting flour to the baker Biliotto.[72]

Like the olive groves, vineyards required capital investment and a high level of maintenance and personal attention by the farmhand.[73] But, unlike olive oil, which all came from a single farm, the taxes paid on wine for the monastery indicate a much wider range of grape production. Unfortunately, Dom Lorenzo's text gives us only very basic data: the tax paid on an amount of wine from a certain farm and the date the wine was delivered to Santa Trinità.[74] His records indicate that white wine was delivered only during the month of September, while red wine was delivered primarily in October.[75]

A little over one hundred and twenty-two *some* of red wine were delivered to the monastery of Santa Trinità from its properties, while the records indicate only thirty-nine and a half *some* of white wine were received.[76] The imbalance is unsurprising. White wine required more processing and did not last as long. Trebbiano was the white wine of choice in terms of cultivation and consumption.[77] Trebbiano was a particularly popular Tuscan wine during this period.[78] The popularity of this wine with the members of the congregation and their visitors is further emphasized by the fact that Dom Lorenzo noted several purchases of Trebbiano in addition to deliveries received.[79] When comparing the deliveries of wine recorded by Dom Lorenzo to the purchases of wine made in the city of Florence, we see that wine was bought almost daily, even when there was enough in the cellar to drink.[80] These purchases were usually in small amounts and were most often made when guests were visiting the monastery, suggesting that the wine purchased may have been a high-quality product as opposed to what was served on a regular basis. Bulk purchases of wine, which were still nowhere near the amounts received from the farms, only occurred during the preparations for the annual festival celebrating the feast of the Holy Trinity.[81] Comparison of the amounts delivered and the amounts purchased, therefore, clearly show that the monastery's farms allowed Santa Trinità to be practically self-sufficient with regard to wine production and consumption; questions of quality, however, meant that the monks would turn to local shops when necessary.[82]

The entries that describe wine purchases in Dom Lorenzo's text are interesting in terms of market interaction. Recent research on the *buchette del vino*, or the little windows through which wine was sold in medieval and Renaissance Florence, has shown that Santa Trinità had easy and ready access to a major wholesale wine seller in its very neighborhood.[83] Just steps from the monastery, at palazzo Scali Buondelmonti on *via delle Terme*, those who shopped for Santa Trinità would have been able to secure a portion of wine for their meals as well as for use in topping up and maintaining the barrels in the cellar.[84] Purchases of wine *per minuto*, or literally "by the minute," seem to have been made with daily consumption in mind, especially that of the monks and residents of Santa Trinità, while wine purchased from a shop and given a varietal name, e.g., Trebbiano or Vernaccia, was usually bought for a meal honoring guests.[85] The frequency with which wine was purchased by the monastery is rather deceptive, since the monks received enormous amounts from their farms and yet still saw fit to purchase wine every day or so from the shops in Florence. However, once we examine Dom Lorenzo's actual entries, it is clear that the daily purchases were for very small amounts, perhaps for a special meal or to better honor a visiting abbot or friend. The vast majority of the wine consumed by the congregation was provided by the farms and not by the markets and shops of Florence.

In contrast to the monastery's self-sufficiency in olive oil, grain, and wine, there were many items that the monks got from their lands only in small portions, meaning that they had to supplement these food supplies from the markets of Florence. Let us look now at some of the items the monks purchased. The most popular meat at Santa Trinità was *castrone,* the meat of a young castrated lamb.[86] Lamb seems to have been served regularly and was clearly a reliable market product, whereas veal appeared to be reserved for feast days, including the public celebration of the feast of Holy Trinity, which was held annually for neighbors and friends in the piazza of Santa Trinità. After lamb the next two most popular meats consumed at Santa Trinità were *cavretto*, or kid and pork.[87] The amount of pork purchased from local butchers was much lower, undoubtedly because pigs were being raised regularly on the monastic farms before being slaughtered, salted, and stored.[88]

Purchases of veal averaged about seventy-four *libbre* a year.[89] As already suggested, the appearance of veal on the menu was clearly related to feast days and important meals with visitors; it was hardly ever consumed as part of a daily meal at the monastery. For example, on July 24, 1361, a purchase of veal was made for the feast of Saint Anthony that was celebrated the following day; the abbot of Monte Piano, the prior of San Fabiano, and Nuccio the organ player were to join the monastery for the feast.[90] Veal also figured prominently in the monastery's public celebration of the feast of the Holy Trinity.[91] In 1363, for instance, further purchases of veal meat were made in addition to the live calf that was specifically bought for the occasion.[92] This not only ensured that there would be enough for those in attendance to eat but also indicates that the meat may have been prepared in different ways. This explains why the monastery apparently consumed more veal than pork—it was not that veal was more common, but that it was more appropriate for the extremely large gathering of the one major feast day the monastery subsidized and celebrated with its community.[93]

Poultry was also a very popular item on the monastery's table. The monks consumed several different species of bird and game. In addition to the thrush, hen, capons, and pigeons that the monastery received from its farms and raised on its own grounds, the monks purchased a variety of birds including cocks and goslings.[94] The large amounts and varieties involved may be due to the limited prohibition by Saint Benedict's Rule on the consumption of poultry—though the Rule required abstinence from the meat of quadrupeds, it did not have strictures on the consumption of birds.[95] Along with poultry, eggs were a prominent market purchase. Purchases ranged from 9 eggs in October 1360 to a high of 358 in June 1360.[96]

Cascio or cheese purchases can be found throughout Dom Lorenzo's text.[97] In addition to buying general *cascio*, regional styles of cheese were consumed by the monastery's congregation and guests. The most popular kind of cheese purchased, with an average yearly consumption of forty-four *libbre*, was *cascio di forma*.[98] Purchases of this cheese occur during both feast and fast periods. It appears to have been served at the table as well as incorporated into cooked foods.

Instead of raising it in special ponds, located either on their farms or the monastery grounds, the monks bought fish.[99] As would be expected, purchases spiked during lean months, when it served as the primary food-stuff (along with vegetables) for the morning or evening meal.[100] While tench and eel were the most popular fish, dried sturgeon, *tonnina,* or salami made with the tenderloin of tuna, *sorra,* or salami made from the belly of tuna, salted mullet, fish from the Arno, gilthead, and pike are also noted in Dom Lorenzo's text.[101] The peak months for consumption of fish were March, April, and December, periods of great importance in the liturgical calendar with the celebrations of Lent, Easter, Pentecost, and Christmas. Fresh fish is rarely referred to, which is surprising since the monastery is located only a few yards from the Arno River. Instead, the majority of fish purchased was salted.[102] During the Advent season, tench and other fishes purchased by the monastery normally found themselves prepared in an aspic.[103] So much so that, on December 11, 1361, Dom Lorenzo tells us that Santa Trinità's abbot implored the cook to fry the tench rather than make another aspic out of it.[104]

Surprisingly, the monastery did not grow vegetables on its farms, though some beans, pulses, and legumes were cultivated.[105] Instead, fresh and varied vegetables were readily available in the market and purchased by the monastery on an almost daily basis. Cauliflower, leeks, and fennel, turnips, spinach, and squash frequently found themselves on the daily shopping lists.[106] The consumption patterns of vegetables followed the dietary requirements of the liturgical year, allowing for the incorporation of vegetables, beans, pulses, and legumes into the monastic diet as a way to provide variety during the leaner months.[107] These items not only figured in the menus devised for Advent and Lent but were also part of dishes that appeared throughout the entire year. Primarily serving in the role of side dishes, the vegetables, beans, pulses, and legumes provided a welcome addition to the cook's broths and pottages that were constantly produced from the monastery's kitchen. The monastery did receive shipments of apples, pears, and figs from its farms, but the monks also purchased these same items, and more fruits besides, from the markets and shops of Florence.[108] It was not unusual for complete meals, both lunch and supper, to be composed solely of vegetables and fruits.

Careful analysis of Dom Lorenzo's records indicates that the monks of Santa Trinità were tactful about what they grew or reared themselves. Self-sufficiency was important in terms of essentials: items such as wine, olive oil, and grain. Commodities that could be salted, dried, and then stored for considerable periods, such as pork, beans, and fruits like figs or plums, were also welcome. The farms also provided eggs and poultry in reasonable amounts, and birds were raised within the monastery itself. But, to avoid the danger of perishable products like fruits and vegetables arriving from the farms in large, seasonal quantities, and the expense of the considerable care and pasture that animals such as sheep or cows required, the monks turned instead to the marketplace. There were also very positive impulses behind this choice—the market gave the monastery access to a wide range of imported and more-difficult-to-obtain products such as spices, sauces, and exotic fruits like oranges. The monastery could also save on time and skill by buying ready-cooked meals, roasts, and, above all, fish: these were available from market vendors, itinerant traders, shopkeepers, and innkeepers. Although these market purchases may have grown to resemble that of many of their secular neighbors, important piazza families who were making the same marketplace purchases, the rhythms of the items recorded by Dom Lorenzo fall in line with the liturgical calendar and do not deviate from Saint Benedict's Rule. The studies by Giovanna Frosini and Curzio Mazzi highlight the purchases and meals of the Florentine priors, and, when compared to those recorded by Dom Lorenzo, Santa Trinità's consumption patterns bear witness to the obvious tensions between remaining true to Saint Benedict's Rule and entertaining those who visited the monastery or, more specifically, and ate with the monks.[109]

The previous discussion indicates the enormous variety that was available to the monks in terms of foodstuffs and shows that they took full advantage of what the city of Florence had to offer. This variety was, of course, also enjoyed by the monastery's secular neighbors and the important families in the piazza. However, though the monks enjoyed the same access to and variety of food that their neighbors did, the monastery used this bounty and provision in different ways. While the secular population gave, perhaps, no regard to what they ate and when, the monks were very careful to use their food in a manner appropriate to the Rule. They ate certain foods at certain times, and though there appears to be no difference in quantity, according to Dom Lorenzo's text, there was certainly a difference in the kinds of food the monks ate during periods of religious fasting and feasting. What seems to be remarkable about the monastery of Santa Trinità is that a "fast" for them did not involve not eating— rather, they simply ate less of one kind of food (meat perhaps) and made up for that lack with other types of foods, such as pulses, beans, or fish. That is what Dom Lorenzo's text shows us—the patterns of types of foods consumed, not the pattern of gluttony and feasting during festivals and starvation during periods of the fast. The monks of Santa Trinità appear to have eaten steady portions of food of all varieties, but they certainly followed the letter of Saint Benedict's Rule as to what foods should be eaten when.

Notes

1. I would like to thank Robin Musumeci, Ken Albala, Trudy Eden, and the anonymous readers from Columbia University Press for graciously reading and commenting upon earlier versions of this essay. Translations, unless otherwise noted, are my own.

2. The research for this essay is taken from Salvatore Musumeci, "The Culinary Culture of the Monastery of Santa Trinità in Fourteenth-Century Florence," Ph.D. dissertation, Queen Mary and Westfield College, University of London, 2008.

3. Dom Lorenzo Martini's *Libro di spese* is found in Archivio di Stato di Firenze, Con. Sopp. 89:45 (this essay utilizes this document). A full transcription of the Martini text can be found in Roberta Zazzeri, ed., *Ci desinò l'abate: Ospiti e cucina nel monastero di Santa Trinità, Firenze, 1360–1363* (Florence: Società Editrice Fiorentina, 2003); and Musumeci,"The Culinary Culture," vol. 2, appendix 1.

4. Dom Lorenzo's text covers the Florentine years 1359–1363. The Florentine New Year commenced on March 25, and so each recorded entry before that day counted toward the previous year.

5. On the use of the diary as memoir as well as accounting practices and traditions, see Duccio Balestracci, *The Renaissance in the Fields: Family Memoirs of a Fifteenth-Century Peasant*, trans. Paolo Squatriti and Betsy Merideth (University Park: Pennsylvania State University Press, 1999); Richard Marshall, *The Local Merchants of Prato: Small Entrepreneurs in the Late Medieval Economy* (Baltimore: Johns Hopkins University Press, 1999); and Basil Yamey, *Art and Accounting* (New Haven: Yale University Press, 1989).

6. Musumeci "The Culinary Culture," 56–90, and vol. 2, appendix 2.

7. See especially Bynum, *Holy Feast and Holy Fast;* Bell, *Holy Anorexia*; and Vandereycken and van Deth, *From Fasting Saints to Anorexic Girls.*

8. See, for example, Barbara Harvey, *Living and Dying in England, 1100–1540: The Monastic Experience* (New York: Oxford University Press, 1993), 30–71; Miranda Threlfall-Holmes, *Monks and Markets: Durham Cathedral Priory, 1460–1520* (New York: Oxford University Press, 2005), 34–74; and Mary Hollingsworth, *The Cardinal's Hat: Money, Ambition and Housekeeping in a Renaissance Court* (London: Profile, 2004).

9. Musumeci, "The Culinary Culture," 91–124.

10. Ibid., 177–209.

11. Gene Brucker, *Florentine Politics and Society, 1348–1378* (Princeton: Princeton University Press, 1962), 148–193. See also John Najemy, *A History of Florence, 1200–1575* (Malden, MA: Blackwell, 2006), 124–155; and Christopher Duggan, *A Concise History of Italy* (Cambridge: Cambridge University Press, 1994), 31–59.

12. Brucker, *Florentine Politics and Society*, 15–16, and *Renaissance Florence* (New York: Wiley, 1969), 55; Najemy, *A History of Florence*, 97; Gottfried, *The Black Death*, 45–47; and David Herlihy, *The Black Death and the Transformation of the West* (Cambridge: Harvard University Press, 1997), 39–58. For a list of years that either witnessed plague or famine, see especially David Herlihy, *Medieval and Renaissance Pistoia: The Social History of an Italian Town, 1200–1430* (New Haven: Yale University Press, 1967), 105.

13. See especially Dale Kent and Francis Kent, *Neighbours and Neighbourhood in Renaissance Florence: The District of the Red Lion in the Fifteenth Century* (New York: Augustin, 1982), 48–74; Kevin Murphy, "Piazza Santa Trinità in Florence, 1427–1498," Ph.D. dissertation, Courtauld Institute of Art, University of London, 1997, 271–316; and Roger Crum and John Paoletti, "Florence: The Dynamics of Space in a Renaissance City," in Roger Crum and John Paoletti, eds., *Renaissance Florence: A Social History* (New York: Cambridge University Press, 2006), 1–16. See also Ronald Weissman, *Ritual Brotherhood in Renaissance Florence* (New York: Academic, 1982), 29–30, and "The Importance of Being Ambiguous: Social Relations, Individualism, and Identity in Renaissance Florence," in Susan Zimmerman and Ronald Weissman, eds., *Urban Life in the Renaissance* (Newark: University of Delaware Press, 1989), 269–280, and "Reconstructing Renaissance Sociology: The 'Chicago School' and the Study of Renaissance Society," in Richard Trexler, ed., *Persons in Groups: Social Behavior as Identity Formation in Medieval and Renaissance Europe* (New York: Medieval and Renaissance Texts and Studies, 1985), 39–46; and *Public Life in Renaissance Florence*.

14. George Dameron, *Episcopal Power and Florentine Society* and *Florence and Its Church in the Age of Dante* (Philadelphia: University of Pennsylvania Press, 2005). See also Francesco Salvestrini, *Santa Maria di Vallombrosa: Patrimonio e vita economica di un grand monastero medievale* (Florence: Olschki, 1998).

15. Giuseppe Marchini and Emma Micheletti, eds., *La chiesa di Santa Trinità* (Florence: Casa di Risparmino di Fireneze, 1987), x; see also Federigo Tarani, *L'Ordine vallombrosano: Note storico-cronologiche* (Florence: Scuola Tipographica Calasanziana, 1921), 5–6.

16. See especially Nicola Vasaturo, "L'Espansione della congregazione vallombrosana fino all metà del secolo XII," *Rivista di storia della chiesa in Italia* 16 (1962): 456–485; Ornella Tabani and Maria Vadalà, *San Salvi e la storia del movimento Vallombrosano dall'XI al XVI secolo* (Florence: Consiglio di Quartiere, 1982); and King, *Western Monasticism*, 163.

17. Jean Leclercq, "Western Christianity," in Bernard McGinn, John Meyendorff, and Jean Leclercq, eds., *Christian Spirituality: Origins to the Twelfth Century* (New York: Crossroad, 1989), 128; see also King, *Western Monasticism,* 161–166.

18. On the use of conversi in the West, especially in Italy, see Sara Beccaria, "I conversi nel medioevo: un problema storico e storiografico," *Quaderni medievali* 46 (1998): 120–156; Francesco Salvestrini, "Conversi e conversioni nel monachesimo vallombrosano (Secoli XI–XV)," in Giordano Compagnoni, ed., *"In vice Iohannis primi abbatis": Saggi e contributi per il millenario gualbertiano in onore del Rev.mo Dom Lorenzo Russo in occasione del XXV anniversario di ministero abbaziale* (Vallombrosa: Vallombrosa, 2002), 33–74; and Duane Osheim, "Conversion, Conversi, and the Christian Life in Late Medieval Tuscany," *Speculum* 58 (1983): 368–390.

19. King, *Western Monasticism,* 163–164; and Clifford Lawrence, *Medieval Monasticism: Forms of Religious Life in Western Europe in the Middle Ages* (Harlow: Pearson Education, 2001), 150.

20. Musumeci, "The Culinary Culture," 31–55.

21. Ibid., 125–148.

22. See especially the opening two parts ("Seeing Shopping" and "The Geography of Expenditure") of Evelyn Welch's book for a complete contrast to the scenarios represented in the Martini text. Welch, *Shopping in the Renaissance,* 17–163. James Shaw's work on the fishmonger's guild in Venice also provides a compelling variation from that present in the Martini text. See James Shaw, "Retail, Monopoly, and Privilege: The Dissolution of the Fishmonger's Guild of Venice, 1599," *Journal of Early Modern History* 6 (2002): 396–427, and also "Justice in the Marketplace: Corruption at the Giustizia Vecchia in Early Modern Venice," in Anne Goldgar and Robert Frost, eds., *Institutional Culture in Early Modern Society* (Leiden: Brill, 2004), 281–316.

23. See, for example, how on April 20, 1361, one of Santa Trinità's lay brothers, Francesco, is noted as taking a pair of the abbot's hose that needed mending to the shop of Ghetto, while another of Dom Lorenzo's entries, from April 12, 1363, records Dom Giovanni purchasing a glass flask, but lacks any detail or evidence that places the monk outside the monastery's walls. For Francesco's trip to Ghetto's shop, see Archivo di Santo Firenze (ASF), "89:45," 30r. Entries for Santa Trinità lack the detailed description and complexities that Welch utilizes to analyze and expound upon the shopping practices of Isabella d'Este and her court. See Welch, *Shopping in the Renaissance, 245–273.* In addition, Hollingsworth's study of Ippolito d'Este's quest for a cardinal's hat also employs a set of rich documentation that details the complex process of provisioning, entertaining and up-keeping the archbishop's family as they maneuvered and jockeyed for the ever coveted cardinal's hat. See Hollingsworth, *The Cardinal's Hat,* 25–198.

24. ASF, "89:45," 2v, 3r, 4v, 6r, 12r, 16r, 21v, 23v, 30v, 34v, 39r, 49r, 49v, 50r, 57r, 60r, 69v, 70r, 82v, 83r, 87r. See also Walter Horn, "On the Origins of the Medieval Cloister," *Gesta* 12 (1973): 13–52.

25. Musumeci, "The Culinary Culture".

26. King, *Western Monasticism,* 161–166; Lawrence, "Medieval Monasticism," 149–160; Osheim, "Conversion"; Beccaria, "I Conversi"; and Salvestrini, "Conversi e conversion."

27. See King, *Western Monasticism,* 161–166; and Lawrence, "Medieval Monasticism," 149–160.

28. Brucker, *Renaissance Florence,* 192.

29. King, *Western Monasticism,* 161–166; and Lawrence, "Medieval Monasticism," 149–160.

30. Musumeci, "The Culinary Culture," 130–147. See also Gigliola Fragnito, "Cardinals' Courts in Sixteenth-Century Rome," *Journal of Modern History* 65 (1993): 26–56. See also Hollingsworth, *The Cardinal's Hat;* J. Ambrose Raftis, "Western Monasticism and Economic Organization," *Comparative Studies in Society and History* 3 (1961): 452–469; and David Chambers, "The Housing Problems of Cardinal Francesco Gonzaga," *Journal of the Warburg and Courtauld Institutes* 39 (1976): 21–58.

31. Musumeci, "The Culinary Culture," 141–147.

32. Ibid.

33. Carlo Botto, "Note e documenti sulla chiesa di S. Trinità in Firenze," *Rivista d'arte* 20 (1939): 2; see also Howard Saalman, *The Church of Santa Trinità in Florence* (New York: College Art Association of America, 1966).

34. Murphy, "Piazza Santa Trinità in Florence," 74–75.

35. Ibid., 89–97.

36. Ibid., 90–91.

37. Roberto Barducci, ed., *Benedetto Dei: la cronica dall'anno 1400 all'anno 1500* (Florence: Papafava, 1984), 79; and Murphy, "Piazza Santa Trinità in Florence," 87, 96.

38. Darrell Davisson, "The Iconology of the S. Trinità Sacristy, 1418–1435: A Study of the Private and Public Functions of Religious Art in the Early Quattrocento," *Art Bulletin* 57 (1975): 315–334; and Murphy, "Piazza Santa Trinità in Florence," 200–270.

39. Murphy, "Piazza Santa Trinità in Florence," 225.

40. Ibid., 225–234. Simone di Bertoldo de' Gianfigliazzi arrived at Santa Trinità in 1361 and died after an extended illness in 1363, while his brother Bernardo Gianfigliazzi served as abbot of the monastery at Passignano before becoming head of the order. For information on Simone Gianfigliazzi, see ASF, "89:45." For information on Bernardo Gianfigliazzi, see ASF, Con. Sopp. 89:46. See also Torello Sala, *Dizionario storico biografico di scrittori, letterati ed artisti dell'ordine di Vallombrosa* (Florence: Tipografica dell'Istituto Gualandi Sordomuti, 1929), 263–265; Tarani, *L'Ordine vallombrosano,* 114; and Zazzeri, *Ci desinò l'abate,* xxvi–xxvii.

41. Murphy, "Piazza Santa Trinità in Florence," 226.

42. ASF, "89:45"; and Zazzeri, *Ci desinò l'abate,* xxv–xxviii.

43. ASF, "89:45," 4r, 25v, 27r–27v, 28v, 30r, 38v, 42r, 45v, 48v, 50r, 53r, 63v, 74v, 89v. See also Musumeci, "The Culinary Culture," 48.

44. Barducci, "Benedetto Dei," 79; see also Murphy, "Piazza Santa Trinità in Florence," 272–316.

45. ASF, "89:45," 11r.

46. See especially ASF, "89:46," 2v, 14v, 20v, 25r.

47. Murphy, "Piazza Santa Trinità in Florence," 294–295. Murphy's investigation of piazza Santa Trinità in the period 1427–1498 utilized the declarations from the *catasti* of 1427 and 1480 to recreate what trades and services would have been available to the residents in

and around the piazza. He argues that Santa Trinità would not have been a self-sufficient neighborhood. Murphy's argument is in opposition to that of Weissman, who puts forth the idea that the city of Florence was populated by self-sufficient neighborhoods. See Weissman, "Riual Brotherhood," 29.

48. Again, Murphy bases this statement on a series of entries from a later *libro di spese* that dates from 1416–1423. See Murphy, "Piazza Santa Trinità in Florence," 297. See also ASF, "89:46," 7v, 20v, 31r, 32r, 32v, 33r, 36v.

49. Maria Bianchi and Maria Grossi, "Botteghe, economia e spazio urbano," in Gloria Fossi and Franco Franceschi, eds., *La grande storia dell'artigianato: Il quattrocento*, vol. 2 (Florence: Giunti, 1999), 27–63.

50. Maria Grossi, "Le botteghe fiorentine nel catasto del 1427," *Ricerche Storiche* 30 (2000): 3–55. See also Maria Bianchi, "Le botteghe fiorentine nel catasto del 1480," *Ricerche Storiche* 30 (2000): 119–170.

51. Grossi, "Le botteghe fiorentine nel catasto del 1427," 50–51; see also Bianchi, "Le botteghe fiorentine nel catasto del 1480," 162–167.

52. Grossi, "Le botteghe fiorentine nel catasto del 1427," 41–55; see also Bianchi, ""Le botteghe fiorentine nel catasto del 1480," 152–169.

53. Welch, *Shopping in the Renaissance*, 32–55.

54. See Mavis Mate, "Agrarian Economy After the Black Death: The Manors of Canterbury Cathedral Priory, 1348–91," *Economic History Review* 37 (1984): 341–354. See also Samuel Cohn, *The Cult of Remembrance: Six Renaissance Cities in Central Italy* (Baltimore: John Hopkins University Press, 1992), 42, and "Piety and Religious Practice in the Rural Dependencies of Renaissance Florence." *English Historical Review* 114 (1999): 1121–1142; Brucker, *Florentine Politics and Society,* 18–19, and *Renaissance Florence,* 190–191.

55. This relationship between city and countryside has its roots in ancient urban and rural history and was an important part of daily life and provisioning strategies throughout the Middle Ages and early modern periods. See especially Emilio Sereni, *Storia del paesaggio agrario italiano* (Rome: Laterza, 1961); William Caferro, "City and Countryside in Siena in the Second Half of the Fourteenth Century." *Journal of Economic History* 54 (1994): 85–103; Charles de la Roncière, *Firenze e le sue compagne nel trecento: Mercanti, produzione, traffici* (Florence: Olschki, 2005); and Giuliano Pinto, *Città e spazi economici nell'Italia communale* (Bologna: CLUEB, 1996).

56. Zazzeri, *Ci desinò l'abate,* xxxii–xxxiv.

57. Musumeci, "The Culinary Culture," 56–90.

58. Ibid.

59. Ibid.

60. Salvatore Musumeci, "Per rape et porri et per spinachi: Examining the Realities of Vegetable Consumption at the Monastery of Santa Trinità in Post-Plague Florence," in Susan Friedland, ed., *Vegetables: Proceedings of the Oxford Symposium on Food and Cookery, 2008* (Devon: Prospect, 2009), 146–155. See also Musumeci, "The Culinary Culture," 56–90.

61. Musumeci, "The Culinary Culture," 56–90.

62. The ability to dry fruits and pulses for storage and preservation purposes is mentioned on September 3, 1362. ASF, "89:45," 68v. The same kind of drying apparatus is listed as existing and providing the same service at the farm at Monte. ASF, "89:45," 39v. For deliveries of fruits from the farm at Ema, see ASF, "89:45," 20v–21r, 44v–45r, 46v, 58r, 73r–74v.

63. For deliveries of fruits and nuts from the farm at Monte, see ASF, "89:45," 19v, 47r, 48r, 74r, 79r.

64. See note 62.

65. Musumeci, "The Culinary Culture," 56–124.

66. Ibid.

67. Ibid.

68. ASF, "89:45," 3r.

69. Ibid., 9v.

70. Musumeci, "The Culinary Culture," 86–90.

71. Ibid., 88–89.

72. ASF, "89:45," 18r.

73. See especially Jean-Louis Gaulin and Allen Grieco, eds., *Dalla vite al vino: Fonti e problemi della vitivinicoltura italiana medievale* (Bologna: CLUEB, 1994); and Antonio Pini, *Vite e vino nel medioevo* (Bologna: CLUEB, 1989). See also Zeffiro Ciuffoletti, ed., *Storia del vino in toscana: Dagli etruschi ai nostri giorni* (Florence: Polistampa, 2000).

74. Musumeci, "The Culinary Culture," 82–86.

75. Ibid.

76. Ibid. One *libbra* of weight was equal to twelve *oncie* (once) and was equal to 339.5 grams (about 7/10 of a pound). A *soma* was equal to 91.16 liters (about 20 gallons, or 160.42 pints). The basic unit of measurement for olive oil was the *orcio*. Each *orcio* was equal to 28.86 kilograms (about 63 pounds). Peter Spufford, *A Handbook of Medieval Exchange* (London: Boydell and Brewer, 1986); Iris Origo, *The Merchant of Prato: Daily Life in a Medieval Italian City* (New York: Penguin, 1963); and Angelo Martini, *Manuale di metrologia ossia misure, pesi e monete in uso attualmente e anticamente presso tutti i populi* (Rome: E. R. A, 1976).

77. Red wine is usually referred to as *vino vermiglio* and should not be confused with a type of wine but read as a classification of color. See especially Hanneke Wilson, "Tuscany: Ancient and Medieval," in Jancis Robinson, ed., *The Oxford Companion to Wine* (New York: Oxford University Press, 1999), 721; and Gaulin and Grieco, *Dalla vite al vino,* 59–83.

78. Wilson "Tuscany." See also Redon, Sabban, and Serventi, *The Medieval Kitchen,* 14–16; and Salvatore Musumeci, "'How does it taste Cisti? Is it good?': Authentic Representations of Italian Renaissance Society and the Culture of Wine Consumption in Giovanni Boccaccio's Decameron," in Richard Hosking, ed., *Authenticity in the Kitchen: Proceedings of the Oxford Symposium on Food and Cookery, 2005* (Devon: Prospect, 2006), 331–344. For the popularity of Trebbiano outside of Tuscany, see Pini, *Vite e vino nel medioevo;* and Federigo Melis, "Produzione e commercio dei vini italiani nei secoli XIII–XVIII," *Annales disalpines d'histoire sociale,* 1/3 (1972): 107–133.

79. See ASF, "89:45," 32v, 91r.

80. Musumeci, "The Culinary Culture," 96–101.

81. Ibid.

82. Ibid.

83. Lidia C. Brogelli, *Le buchette del vino a Firenze nel centro storico ed in Oltrarno* (Florence: Semper, 2004).

84. Ibid., 55–58. For a discussion of how buying *per minuto* fit into the larger story of buying and selling wine in medieval and Renaissance Florence, see Paolo Nanni, *Vinattieri fiorentini: Dalle taverne medievali alle moderne enoteche* (Florence: Polistampa, 2003), 41–70.

85. Musumeci, "The Culinary Culture," 96–101.

86. Giovanna Frosini, *Il cibo e i signori: la mensa dei priori di Firenze nel quinto decennio del sec. xiv* (Florence: Presso L'Accademia della Crusca, 1993), 71–72.

87. Ibid., 73–77.

88. Musumeci, "The Culinary Culture," 71–76.

89. Ibid., 105–106.

90. ASF, "89:45," 38r. For other similar purchases see ASF, "89:45," 2r, 3r, 21r, 26v, 45r, 65v, 71v, 74v, 78r, 79r–79v.

91. Musumeci, "The Culinary Culture," 200–208.

92. ASF, "89:45," 90v. For other feast purchases where a live calf and an additional portion of veal is bought, see ASF, "89:45," 10v–11r, 35v–36r, 63v–64v.

93. Musumeci, "The Culinary Culture," 200–208.

94. Ibid.

95. Francis Gasquet, ed., *The Rule of St. Benedict* (Mineola: Dover, 2007), 34. However, in 1336 Pope Benedict XII relaxed the regulations concerning the consumption of meat with regard to Benedictine monks. Though the rules were relaxed, the consumption of meat was still regulated under the pope's proviso. See especially Barbara Harvey, "Monastic Pittances in the Middle Ages," in Woolgar, Serjeantson, and Waldron, *Food in Medieval England,* 220.

96. Musumeci, "The Culinary Culture," 108–109.

97. Frosini, "Il cibo," 136–141.

98. Musumeci, "The Culinary Culture," 109–110.

99. Ibid., 110–113.

100. Capatti and Montanari, *Italian Cuisine,* 69–74.

101. For tonnina, see Frosini, "Il cibo," 100–101, for sorra, see Frosini, "Il cibo," 99. For a complete listing see Musumeci, "The Culinary Culture," 111.

102. Musumeci, "The Culinary Culture," 109–110.

103. On Advent and Lenten menus at Santa Trinità, see ibid., 180–183, 185–186.

104. ASF, "89:45," 49v.

105. Musumeci, "Per rape et porri et per spinachi."

106. Ibid.

107. Ibid.

108. Ibid.

109. Frosini, "Il cibo"; and Curzio Mazzi, "La mensa dei priori di Firenze nel secolo XIV," *Archivi Storico Italiano* 20 (1897): 336–368.

THE IDEOLOGY OF FASTING IN THE REFORMATION ERA

Ken Albala

On a chilly morning in March 1522, in the city of Zurich, the printer Christoph Froschauer sat down with his workers and shared a plate of sausages, in open defiance of the Roman Catholic Church, which forbade the consumption of meat during Lent. Froschauer and his men were dragged before the civil magistrates, where he entered his official plea of not guilty on the grounds that he had a heavy load of printing jobs waiting and his men needed the extra sustenance. Such meals were not unheard of during Lent, and normally for a small fee one could purchase a "dispensation" on the grounds of infirmity, age, or even unusually difficult work. But the printer had never obtained his dispensation and was duly charged. The city rose in protest, street fighting broke out, and, on April 16, the local prelate Ulrich Zwingli preached a sermon defending the printer's actions not on the grounds of necessity but on the basis of scriptural authority. The New Testament, Zwingli pointed out, nowhere mentions food prohibitions of any kind, all of which were merely invented haphazardly by the Church and could in no way constrain the conscience of men.[1] Neither should there be specific times set aside for fasting: "as far as time is concerned, the need and use of all food are free, so that whatever food our daily necessity requires, we may use at all times and on all days . . ."[2] Thus began the Swiss Reformation over a plate of sausages.

The centrality of food to questions of Reform has largely been overlooked by modern scholars who have rightfully seen theological debates as the causative agent in protest, though, at the grass-roots level, fasting and feasting issues played just as great a role in fomenting anticlerical sentiment.[3] Like Luther's outcry against indulgences and other clerical abuses a few years earlier, the arguments over food practices helped create a breach that rent the universal church permanently, and food fights embroiled reformers on all sides for the next few centuries. Food was also involved in most theological debates of the era, primarily because of reformers' attempts to reassess the original intentions of Jesus and his followers and restructure Church practice accordingly.

Despite the conscious efforts of the early Christians to distance themselves from the legalism of Levitical food prohibitions, the complex kosher laws, in the course of a millennium and a half the Church had managed to invent its own intricate food rules—the most important of which was the compulsory fast during Lent. There were also fasts on Saturdays and often Wednesdays, the so-called Quatuor Anni Tempori, equinoxes, as well as on the vigils of saints' days. These might account for up to a quarter of the calendar year, or by some estimates even as many as 150 days. The fast, in this case, stipulated that healthy adults must abstain from the flesh of all animals as well as products derived from them, such as butter, eggs, and cheese. For a six-week period (forty days not counting Sundays) people subsisted entirely on fruits and vegetables, grains, beans, and fish. Furthermore, they were expected to abstain entirely from solid food during the day, breaking the fast with a single meal either at sundown or, in more general practice at Nones, the ninth hour, or 3:00 P.M. There was considerable variation in local observance though, Milan, for example, foregoing the Saturday fast.[4]

For the average parishioner, whose prime understanding of religiosity was in the form of ritual observances or "works," the decision whether to fast was of crucial concern. Morality was not construed as a form of practical ethics in action but rather fulfilling the ritual acts commanded by the Church—participating in the mass, performing works of charity, and abstaining from meat. Yet the reformers raised some serious questions: were the traditional accretions of practice, such as the Lenten fast, necessary for salvation, or was the Bible (and its rejection of dietary legalism) the sole authority dictating worship? Could a person indeed be defiled by "what goes in the mouth" despite Christ's dictum? Even if an individual chose to fast in imitation of Christ, should that not be in the form of complete abstinence from all food, rather than merely animal flesh and derived products? Jesus and the apostles did make lengthy voluntary fasts acts of penitence and purification, but nowhere in the New Testament was any particular time set aside for a fast, nor were any particular foods specified as interdict during these periods. Moreover, if the fast is necessary for salvation, how could there be such a free trade in dispensations, readily available to anyone with money and sometimes sold to entire cities in what was generally construed as a fund-raising effort to finance the new St. Peter's in Rome? Finally, with the new theological emphasis on the exclusive power of faith in gaining salvation, how could such quotidian practices as abstaining from sausages possibly be of interest to the Almighty—and did the Church have the authority to claim it was important in the first place on the basis of tradition alone?

It may seem surprising that through the Middle Ages contestation of the practice of fasting was a rarity. It was taken for granted that physical self-abnegation, mortifying the flesh to bolster the spirit, was among the most praiseworthy acts of devotion possible. Fasting was always to be accompanied by prayer and was construed essentially as an act of contrition, to facilitate forgiveness of sins. There were numerous examples among the early Christian fathers of heroic acts of self-denial. While these were considered beyond the capabilities or obligations of most mortals, a comparable fast, lesser in degree, was thought to purify the body as an act of penance. Meat, conceptually corrupting because inherently pleasurable, nutritious, and invigorating, and linked directly to the libido, was thus excised from the diet as a form of self-punishment. It was not, as we might imagine it, a medically motivated kind of purging of the system, but rather a conscious ritual of intentional undernourishment.[5] As a form of penance (and a sacrament), it washed away sins through suffering. As further justification, the fast was a proactive curb to the cardinal sin of gluttony, which was actually the first of the seven deadly sins, thanks to Eve's apple. Fasting was also, in popular parlance, a good "work" which in a sense *earned* one salvation. On the grand ledger of good works (the book of life), every act of fasting was logged in as a kind of brownie point—the more collected in the course of one's life, the greater the chances of gaining access to heaven. That is, fasting was considered tantamount to other ritual practices such as communion, pilgrimages, venerating relics, and making pious benefactions to the

Church. These all earn salvation in the popular consciousness, without which it is unachievable, unless one's surviving progeny sponsor masses, which truncate one's stay in purgatory.

In sum, eating in a particular way and avoiding certain foods during specific times of the year was considered a devout act of piety. The specific scriptural warrant normally cited was Matthew 9:15: "but the days will come when the Bridegroom shall be taken from them, and then shall they fast."[6] The specific times for fasting and foods to be avoided were solely a matter of tradition and varied widely from place to place and across the centuries. But, as such, it was also a ritual practice that bound the community in common forms of observance, year after year, in a regular and predictable pattern. Food, in this respect, was at the core of the average person's conception of religiosity, and devotion was defined in terms of the things one does, not necessarily the things one believes, as in a creed. Thus, for many people—not only those defending Catholic orthodoxy—the threat to these seemingly timeless rituals was also a threat to community and social bonds. Many reformers, solely on this basis, defended the practical benefits of fasting as useful for inculcating and bolstering faith, which alone gains salvation. This was Luther's position on adiaphora, practices that were not esential to salvation, which, while not harmful in themselves, might help common parishioners strengthen their faith, as long as they understood that they could in no way earn or merit the gift of grace. It was precisely this question which vexed those in the Reformed tradition and in the English Church: what did ordinary people really understand? The danger of continuing a food practice which people might construe as a necessary "work" might outweigh the practical benefits of communal solidarity.

It should not be surprising that when ritual practice was questioned by theologians on the basis of scriptural authority, and when the mechanism of salvation was scrutinized, so too were these quotidian forms of observance. Fasting and feasting, asceticism, the mass itself—are these necessary for salvation? Is this what God demands of us? Are these the things that will get us into heaven? The answer for Protestants was, of course, unequivocally no. But should this then lead necessarily to a ban on fasting, which admittedly might be a useful spiritual exercise? Should it be a private matter, or could there still be public fasts, if not at specific times as prescribed arbitrarily by the "popish" Church, then perhaps as in the Old Testament during times of distress, to avert plague, to repent for sins, and in days of public mourning. This would be the pattern adopted generally by the Reformed tradition, taking their cue from Calvin's *Institutes*, in which the public communal fast became the norm in imitation of Old Testament fasts.

The interaction between the clearly defined theological issues and the daily practice of common people provided the ultimate criteria for enacting policy in all denominations. In other words, since reformers, Protestant and Catholic, were concerned with doctrinal and ecclesiastical uniformity—and they were convinced that most people never fully grasped the deeper theological issues at stake—they were especially anxious about carefully defining the nature and meaning of the fast. And since confrontations erupted primarily over daily practices: tithes, church courts, and especially food regulations, this was one of the most pressing issues, and one that few could adequately address, which probably accounts for the arguments dragging on well into the seventeenth century. Intellectuals and reformers on all sides were forced to define their position on food restrictions, much as had the early Christians in defining their distinction from Judaism and its food regulations, and, as before, this proved no simple task.

The origins of the debates over fasting and Lent in the early modern era are found in the fifteenth century, primarily among Renaissance humanists whose ideas about food were imbued with classically derived concepts of moderation and balance, which was generally antithetical to the fast-and-feast mentality of the Middle Ages.[7] Of course the return to scriptural primacy among reformers was also founded on the humanists' hermeneutics and insistence on interpreting classical texts in historical perspective. That is, they understood precisely why the early Christians rejected official food prohibitions and generally ate a simple, frugal, but regular diet. The humanists also bolstered their defense of a regular diet with ancient medical precepts that, while stressing seasonality, could not defend either abstinence or excess. Even more powerful in their criticism of medieval foodways was the haphazard and hypocritical ways in which these restrictions were applied. Dispensations were easy to obtain for a price and under practically any pretext, practices differed widely from place to place, and regulations were rarely enforced.

These concerns were brought to a head in 1491 when Pope Alexander VI (Rodrigo Borgia) began to both loosen the restrictions on butter and grant extensive dispensations from Lent. This itself was nothing new, but it occurred now on an unprecedented scale to raise money for the Church. Such dispensations were even peddled, much like indulgences, by itinerant papal agents. Beyond these personal exemptions, there were also more lucrative corporate dispensations, especially in northern Europe with butter, witness the impressive Butter Tower on the Cathedral in Rouen, paid for with money collected from dispensations. Some cities or entire regions were exempted from regulation. In the humanists' minds, these were merely part and parcel of the range of clerical abuses (concubinage, simony, absenteeism, clerical ignorance). The ultimate absurdity of declaring such foods as beaver tail or puffin legitimate for Lent, merely because they live in water and are therefore technically fish, gave the humanists further ammunition for ridicule.

While this loosening of restrictions may have contributed to the evolution of culinary arts through the greater incorporation of butter, eggs, and dairy products into cuisine, especially with fish dishes and in sauces, it also directed public attention to the arbitrary way the Church enacted and enforced legislation. Anyone with enough money could basically buy the right to ignore what were ostensibly devout acts necessary for salvation, and if butter could so easily be taken off the list of prohibited foods, why was it there in the first place? Perhaps all restrictions were equally unnecessary.

This climate of opinon is best exemplified by the colloquy of Erasmus published in 1526, even though it postdates the earliest years of the Reformation.[8] In it a butcher and fishmonger argue over the possible consequences should Lent be abolished. The fishmonger contends that meat would not be so highly valued if it were no longer a forbidden food. The butcher thinks it would be healthier for people to eat meat in cold months (which, at least according to contemporary humoral physiology, was absolutely true). The two continue to accuse each other, one that fish stink, the other that butchers sell cat meat. Eventually, however, the argument blossoms into a full-scale debate over food laws instituted by humans versus the essential laws as laid down by biblical authority. In the New Testament, fasts were only voluntary, they could take place any time of year, and they did not exclude specific foods. Erasmus ultimately presents a theological discussion over how the rigorous laws of the Old Testament were abrogated with the new dispensation. Mandatory food regulations are therefore inherently unchristian, and the Church had no right to institute them in the first place. Interestingly though, Erasmus went no further than chiding the Church into a policy change, he was not interested in schism.

Elsewhere in the writings of Erasmus, and among other humanists, were other related concerns bearing on the topic of fasting.[9] Those in the community who should have been most inclined to the rigors of abstinence, monastics, were often themselves gourmands, living richly despite their vows of personal poverty. Likewise any wealthy family could adhere to the letter of the law by eating only fish during Lent, though the most rare and exotic species and garnished so lavishly and presented at such astronomical expense that the entire spirit and purpose of fasting was ignored. A fast should logically involve self-denial, but what kind of suffering was involved in such elaborate fish-based meals? The humanists were also concerned, as would be later reformers, with curbing what they saw as disorderly riot and mayhem in the days preceding Lent, the Carnival or Mardi Gras celebrations. While modern critics have pointed out the valuable function of such celebrations as a social "safety valve"—an opportunity to blow off steam in an otherwise rigidly controlled and hierarchical culture, the threat of real violence, especially in the early sixteenth century, led many elites to ban Carnival celebrations, which in turned open the whole question of whether Lent was also strictly necessary.[10] These were, of course, political expedients to keep a growing population orderly in a period of inflation and rural displacement. But it had the effect of making the fast and feast cycles obsolete. It also did not help that many of these celebrations had their roots in pagan practices, or were so perceived, making them a prime target for those interested in restoring Christianity to its pristine origins.

Among the first Protestant reformers, it is interesting that ritual and food practices do not gain great attention. Luther, like Erasmus, mentioned the absurdity of restrictions. For example, Germans were forced to buy oil rather than use local and plentiful butter. This was oil that the people in Rome "would not use to grease their shoes. But they sell us permission to eat butter and other things in spite of the holy apostle who says that the gospel gives us complete freedom to do everything." "They think that eating butter is a greater sin than lying, swearing or committing fornication."[11] Yet in the end Luther had little deep abiding interest in much beyond the theological doctrine of *sola fidei*, salvation by faith alone. How one worships, what form of church government is put in place, and indeed whether one fasts or not was of no great importance as long as one understands that these are not the means whereby we attain grace. A fast can be useful, but we can not gain merit thereby. Such trivial concerns should be left to magistrates to decide. And, in fact, after the Peasant Wars, magistrates were more interested in not upsetting the fabric of society, so they left Lent in place along with most of the trappings of the Church hierarchy, including bishops. But equally as interesting is the focus on family, marriage, and procreation, which put an end to the ascetic/celibate and monastic traditions in Lutheran regions. There was thus no longer a pious and abstinent ideal outside the family context, and fasting became a private matter, often observed in practice, but not enforced. Gradually, but over centuries, it disappeared.

Ulrich Zwingli, in Zurich, mentioned earlier, was truly the first to make a decisive break from Lenten restrictions as something positively harmful for Christian worship. This was not only fundamentally different from Luther's lax attitude but would set the tone for later Swiss and other Reformed traditions. Here not only was the Bible to be the standard for all practices, but anything not found in the Bible should be decisively abolished, that is, all the traditions of the Church without biblical warrant, including Lent, and of much greater theological import, the very meaning of the central food ritual of Christinity—the literal consumption of the flesh and blood of Christ in the Eucharist by means of transubstantiation. For Zwingli, the entire ritual was nothing more than a memorial. *Hoc est corpus meum* was meant to be figurative, as so much else that Jesus said. Any other interpretation, any kind of real presence, could only be a form of cannibalism. Regarding Lent, in the Reformed tradition (including the Swiss, Dutch, Scots, Huguenots, and Puritans on both sides of the Atlantic) seasonal fasts and fasts on Saturday were abolished solely because they are nowhere mentioned in Scripture.

However, penance remained a sacrament, and fasts could still be undertaken for the purpose of spiritual cleansing, to seek absolution from sins, especially in public form, just as the ancient Israelites had done to avert God's wrath—particularly for Calvinists, who saw God in an active role sending portents and offering rewards and punishments here on earth. What this meant is that, despite the abolition of Lent per se, public fasting and atonement, in this case often complete abstinence from food for an entire day, was declared by political authorities. In England it was Parliament, elsewhere city councils. They saw this as a means of directly communicating with God to gain favor and possibly seek absolution. Moreover, the Calvinists were more strictly concerned with public order and propriety and theologians praised frugality on a year-round basis. How extensively this new attitude was adopted by ordinary people is a matter for debate, and it is too easy to caricature Puritans as dour disciplinarians. But it is true that a regular and frugal diet around the calendar became the cultural ideal, completely replacing the seasonal cycles of medieval Christianity.

The English Church, at least theologically fell in this camp as well, though perhaps stemming from Elizabeth's infamous *via media*, and desire to please a wide array of worshipers, a so-called political Lent remained on the books until the end of the seventeenth century. Ostensibly, this was defended as a means of supporting the fishing industry and maintaining a strong fleet in the event of war. That, at least, was the official explanation lest the retention of Lent upset the more ardent reformers. Among Anglicans of the seventeenth century, however, many were fully committed to the ancient apostolic and legitimately instituted forms of fasting which they believed ought to be retained. Every monarch to follow renewed the statute on fasting upon inheriting the crown, but few people seem to have obeyed it. As in Lutheran lands, fasting gradually became obsolete.

The Radical Reformation took an entirely different tack in regard to fasting. Returning to the "roots" of Christianity along with its pacifism, adult baptism (hence the name *anabaptist*), they also "democratized grace," to borrow a phrase of Sir Christopher Hill. That is, they believed salvation was attainable not only to a select predestined few "saints," as the Calvinists contended, but to everyone and anyone who could attain faith. Thus one could fast as a means of attaining grace; as their detractors so called them, radical reformers became "work saints." And because they were unaligned with any political establishment—in fact consciously apart from them—there was no way they could declare official fasts. They became a matter of individual conscience and an important form of personal penance. Even more important, many of the radical sects were strict millenarians, fully expecting an imminent second coming. Fasting thus became a means of spiritual cleansing in preparation for the return to Edenic purity after the apocalypse. Hence many became not only pacifists, but vegetarians, anticipating the moment when the lion will lay down with lamb. In an entirely unexpected way, the asceticism of the early Church was reintroduced to communities whose descendants would be the Mennonites and Amish,[12] indirectly laying the foundation for many other sects that would adopt vegetarianism as a new form of perpetual fast, most notably the Seventh Day Adventists.

Lastly, the Catholic Church responded to these assaults. Rather than adopt reforms from within, the Council of Trent decided to reemphasize works as a means of attaining grace. Lenten rules stayed in place and observation was enforced. But they also imbued the religion with a new kind of energy and dynamism, using the arts to win adherents back into the fold. New saints appeared, heroic ascetics, and a form of self-starvation that Rudolph Bell has called holy anorexia. The exact parameters of Lent were also debated, most notoriously in Spain where chocolate was taken in the morning during church services at a time when people were not supposed to take any "food" whatsoever. The debate over chocolate hinged on its nutritional classification; if a beverage then permitted, if a nutritious liquid food then highly suspect. There also appeared a whole new literature defending Lent, such as Theodor Peltanus, *De jejunio et ciborum delectu* (1572), Johannis Viringi, *Tractatus de jejunio et abstinentia* (1597), and Paulo Zacchia, *Il vitto quaresimale* (1637). There were also detractors in the Protestant camps—like French Protestant Joannis Dallaeus's *De jejuniis, et quadragesima liber* 1654. The topic remained vibrant and hotly debated long after the initial years of the Reformation.

Why fasting should still have been an ongoing issue a hundred years later is the most interesting question. The polemic, largely between Lutherans, Calvinists, and Jesuits in the seventeeth century, was motivated partly by political threats, as the Counter-Reformation was in full swing and as military violence loomed over Germany and of course erupted in the Thirty Years War. Protestants felt motivated to defend their position on fasting, and Catholics sought to enforce theirs, both with arms and newly invigorated theology, particularly in the writings of Cardinal Bellarmine. In a nutshell, the Protestants cited biblical passages regarding the original intention of fasting as a voluntary act of penance, and the Catholics and Jesuits defended their form of fasting as a rite that did indeed develop over time as a tradition of the Church, was based on apostolic forms, but is not something people may decide to ignore without good cause, and some claimed that it is required for salvation. Nonetheless, there were dispensations available for a fee under various pretexts: infirmity, age, pregnancy, and nursing.

Rather than recount in detail the several dozen texts written in this era, I will focus on just two very important sources from the mid seventeenth century, one Jesuit, the other Calvinist, to offer a specific example of how the aforementioned issues were debated. The first is entitled *Aloe Amari, sed salubris succi Ieiunium* (Bitter aloes, or healthy essences for fasting), written by Jeremias Drexel, who was a convert to Catholicism who went to study at Ingolstadt, joined the Jesuits in 1598, and became preacher at the court of Maximilian I, elector of Bavaria. The book was published in 1637, shortly before his death, and went through many editions: 1638 in Antwerp, 1642, 1650, etc.[13] It is a massive book of about five hundred pages and represents what is truly in the spirit of the Catholic Reformation attempt to gain back converts to Catholicism, not through threats of eternal damnation or physical punishment but by promoting fasts as good and moral in and of themselves. The tactic was different from earlier polemics, which basically made obedience to the Church's commandments a requirement for salvation. This makes a very rational argument—even a gastronomic one—about why fasting is useful.

The other text is by French Protestant theologian Johannes Dallaeus (Jean Daillé), *De jejuniis et Quadragesima liber,* printed in Deventer in 1654,[14] which nicely captures the types of arguments made by the Reformed side in this era, arguing not that fasting should be completely abolished but that they should be undertaken in the spirit in which they were originally intended, as they were in the Bible, particularly in the Old Testament. These are two completely opposed ideological texts, and yet, fascinatingly, they argue in the end the same essential point, that fasts are very beneficial for the body and soul and valuable for maintaining moral integrity.

Beginning with Drexel, the book is a remarkably well-crafted sales pitch promoting fasting. Not only is the author a great storyteller, but he argues convincingly that fasting is a moral virtue, that it is beneficial for health and mental well-being and happiness. The basic idea is that when one feeds the body excessively it makes the spirit weaker and one more easily succumbs to temptation. But by castigating the flesh one makes the soul stronger and better able to fend off sin. "Abstinence and fasting ennervates this enemy, thus however much the flesh is supressed, so greater the spirit is lifted up."[15] People shouldn't fear fasting: exactly the opposite. It is a kind of exercise that makes you stronger, physically and morally. And, although this basic line of reasoning was nothing new, the way he illustrates his argument with poignant vignettes is truly novel and persuasive. For example, he tells about one Macarius Alexandrinus who made a habit of walking around holding bags full of sand to make his arms stronger. Eventually he hardly even noticed them, but then it never bothered him to lift anything thereafter. Fasting is precisely the same, a small hardship at first, but in the end dealing with hunger becomes no burden at all.

Drexel also has a very personable style and addresses his readers directly. He adds anecdotes in ways that connect with the reader. For example, he knows very well the running criticism of Jesuits that they live very lavishly, and, while most people are eating frugally during Lent, the general impression is that Jesuits have rare and delicate fish, fruits, perfumed biscuits, and sweet wines—anything but hardship. Drexel retorts: fine, I'll tell you exactly what we eat—very plain and frugal food. Even on feast days, were you to walk into the refectory, you might find a piece of beef, some cabbage or vegetables, perhaps a minutal (a kind of minced stew with tripe, lung, or liver), or fried eggs and broth. To close the meal, there might be some cheese or fruits such as cherries or apples. But normally there is no meat, but rather fish, such as sole or stockfish, or whole chickpeas. Everything is served in small amounts, and no one would call these meals sumptuous.[16]

The popular impression that Jesuits live lavishly stems largely from the fact that they are an active order, and brothers often serve in princely households. They find themselves at meals where delicacies and fine wines are served. But they do not partake of these, in fact, despite what you read, there are many ascetics among Jesuits who perform proper fasts, flagellate themselves, keep long vigils, and wear a hair shirt.

Drexel also makes an impassioned defense of abstinence as a longevity regimen. One need only look at the thousands of impoverished people who live on so little yet labor long hours and often live to eighty or ninety—even sometimes one hundred years. His words sound startlingly familiar to us: most people overeat and eat too quickly, both of which tax the system. If you want to eat like a dog, expect to suffer many diseases. "There is no doubt that daily many thousands are killed, who if they had eaten less, and moderately, and more frequently sustained hunger, would have lived many more years."[17] As a rule, one should also leave the table before hunger is sated, or, as the saying goes in German, "Stehe vom

Tisch mit lust auff." Likewise one should not eat foods of extreme qualities "such as melons, mushrooms and cucumbers, which are most cold, yet taken as irritants of gluttony."[18]

Apart from all these medical rationales for fasting, Drexel also makes what is a most convincing gastronomic defense as well. He claims that hunger is the best condiment and suggests a little experiment: try going a few days eating a small amount of the lowliest foods, as paupers do. Or try skipping supper on Saturday night and then Sunday food will taste much better to you. In fact, the pleasure we receive from food has more to do with the disposition of the mouth as an organ of taste than with the food itself or as it is transformed by hands of the cook. Everyone knows a constant diet of delicacies soon makes the palate jaded. But, with abstinence, the powers of gustatory sensation are stronger, and thus even simpler foods taste better. Fasting is actually a gastronomic exercise. The vegetables and bread of the laborer taste better than the "stuffed chicken or creamy dessert" to the leisured diner. Only this type of person needs the numerous stimulants to gluttony like olives, capers, mustard, pickles, and sour condiments, which are all irritants for a deranged palate which no longer senses hunger and needs to be artificially deceived. The same goes for pepper, cloves, ginger, nutmeg, and similar aromatics—they ultimately dull the senses.[19]

The timing of these comments in the mid seventeenth century is, incidentally, just at the point that dominance of spices was giving way to purer flavors unsullied by juxtapositions of condiments. It is quite surprising to find it in a theological tract on fasting though. In any case, Drexel offers what appears to be the quintessential Catholic Reformation appeal, not merely commanding obedience to the Church but rather making a logical and impassioned argument favoring the benefits of following the Lenten fast as prescribed as well as fasting in general and living a basically abstemious life. Most important, Drexel stresses fasting for the right reasons: as a form of penance and as a way to help moderate the passions and prevent us from sinning. Here too he is very clear about the ultimate payoff: eternal life.

The book on fasting by Dallaeus comes from a totally different ideological and theological standpoint, though makes much the same arguments. Even though the prescribed Lenten fast is criticized as popish superstition, he still favors a general kind of frugality and simplicity (which of course is typical among Calvinists and Puritans) as well as a proper

Old Testament fast, the serious chest-pounding lamentation with dirt in your hair and rent clothes. Dallaeus argues that the primary reason to fast is to punish your body so as to avert God's wrath. It is much better to punish yourself than to let Him do it. Not that this gains merit or contributes to salvation in any way (for all Protestants that is faith alone). Nonetheless, there is a conception of God very actively intervening in human affairs, and witnessing the faithful in active contrition, confessing their sins, and punishing themselves as a way to show their sincere interest in reforming truly pleases God.

It's also interesting that while the fish days, saints' days, and Lenten fasts were all abolished among Calvinists, they did conduct public fasts, again exactly the kind that were in the Old Testament, either to gain favor in battle, avert some impending disaster or epidemic, or even just to begin some great project auspiciously. The English Parliament, for example, regularly held an official fast before the opening of each session in the seventeenth century.

In any case, Dallaeus, writing in the 1650s, just before the revocation of the Edict of Nantes when Huguenots were expelled from France, is primarily concerned with countering the standard Catholic conception of a fast as abstinence from meat in specifically prescribed days: Saturdays, for various saint's days, and of course through Lent. He approaches the topic as a historian, on the one hand distancing himself from any idea of food somehow being unclean (a Levitical notion), yet promoting the kind of voluntary fasts one finds in the Old Testament, like Moses on Mount Sinai or Joel on Mount Horeb, that were replicated in Jesus's forty-day fast and the fasting among the apostles.

What is particularly striking is that, like Drexel, Dallaeus intimately understood the details of Baroque cookery and the whole battery of roasts, jumbled-up stews, condiments, and delicate wines that are eaten during fast days but simply do not include meat. To him, these defeat the whole purpose of fasting. Can it be called a fast when "we do not taste meat, but every variety of fish, condiments and vegetables are laid out, and the stomach is inundated with wine most generously, which is belched forth in drunkenness."[20] Again this is a matter of following the letter of the law rather than its intended spirit. In place of this, he suggests that year-round frugality is far more virtuous and more appropriately fits the kind of sober lifestyle promoted by Calvinists—because intemperance in food is directly connected to intemperance in other vices.

Dallaeus is extremely insightful on this point: Serving lavish meals leads to the sin of pride—because you're flaunting your wealth. This in turn causes envy among others. Gluttony itself is a sin, because you're eating food that could otherwise feed hungry people—so it leads to the sin of avarice and neglect of charity. Drunkeness obviously leads to loss of control, libidinousness, and a variety of other sins. Who is more holy, the poor peasant or the Apician priest who imagines it's a hardship to linger for "no more than two hours" at his meal of exquisitely prepared fishes?[21] This is not considered a sin, yet to even taste a tiny lump of dry bacon is considered a mortal sin during Lent. Even worse in his mind are the throngs of obedient Catholics who believe that following these arbitrary and capricious rules will somehow count as a good work, as Cardinal Bellarmine claimed, and that his will contribute to their salvation.

The real strength of Dallaeus's argument are the many passages in the New Testament that show no food bad in itself, an idea which even the early Church Fathers condemned as a form of heresy among the Manichaeans and various other vegetarian groups. He shows, rightfully, that the idea that meat corrupts the spirit and increases the libido has no Christian foundation, but is rather medical. It can be traced back to Greek medicine, which posits that meat is the most nutritious substance, best suited to increase our own blood and flesh, and directly converted into sperm, which in turn activates the libido. Dallaeus may have been aware of the shift in medical theory away from orthodox Galenism, but, even if he did not, he claims definitively that one would have to be pretty stupid ("stultus es, si hoc putas") to think that "meat is the seed of the libido, and thus promotes it, and to believe that anyone who tastes a crumb of meat is thus contaminated."[22] It is gluttony and drunkenness, an excess of food elaborately prepared, that corrupts us, not meat itself eaten in moderation.

Strikingly, Dallaeus is not arguing to abolish fasting per se. He merely wants it to be a voluntary act, a kind of exercise, which is useful when accompanied by prayer and undertaken with the right goals in mind. In no way can it be considered a necessary rite, something conducted out of mere obedience to the Church and of course not in the form of elegant fish meals. In the end both Dallaeus and Drexel are arguing many of the same points—decidedly moving away from the whole fast-and-feast mentality of the Middle Ages and arguing for fasting as a means of strengthening body and soul and keeping us morally vigilant. In that respect both are remarkably modern. We can never be sure whether people actually followed their recommendations, but readers, or the congregations to which clerical readers preached, would probably have been made to feel guilty for their eating habits, and the whole idea of year-round frugality and abstemiousness as a moral ideal is certainly something new on the cultural landscape.

In the end, it appears that fasting was considered such an integral part of Christianity, an indispensible component of penance, that theologians, regardless of denomination, were loath to abolish it altogether. In the process of debating the importance of fasting, they changed its nature or at least attempted to make it a conscious and deliberate act of piety rather than a rote habitual practice.

Notes

This essay represents the initial research to be included in a longer monograph on fasting in the Reformation era now in progress.

1. Ulrich Zwingli, "Concerning Choice and Liberty Respecting Food," in *Early Writings*, ed. Samuel Macauley Jackson (Eugene: Wipf and Stock, 1999), 70–112.

2. Ibid., 83.

3. A recent exception is Mentzer, "Fasting, Piety, and Political Anxiety."

4. Anonymous, *The Wonderful Effects of a True and Religious Fast* (London: John Thomas, 1642), 180, n. g, which cites Augustine, epistle 86, among other sources.

5. The primary sources for these ideas are recounted in detail in Grimm, *From Feasting to Fasting*.

6. Take, for example, George Buddle, *A Short and Plaine Discourse Fully Containing the Whole Doctrine of Evangelicall Fastes* (London: Mathew Law, 1609), which focuses on the meaning of this passage.

7. Montanari, *The Culture of Food*; Henisch, *Fast and Feast*.

8. Erasmus, "Ichthyophagia."

9. See especially Erasmus, *Duae Homiliae Civi Basilii de laudibus iejunij* (Friburgum Brisgoae: Ioannes Emmeus, 1532).

10. Mikhail Bakhtin, *Rabelais and His World*, trans. Helene Iswolsky (Bloomington: Indiana University Press, 1984); Peter Burke, *Popular Culture in Early Modern Europe* (New York: Harper, 1978).

11. Martin Luther, "An Appeal to the Ruling Class of German Nationality as to the Amelioration of the State of Christendom," in *Selections from His Writings*, ed. John Dillenberger (Garden City, NY: Anchor, 1961), 456.

12. Kenneth Ronald Davis, *Anabaptism and Asceticism* (Eugene: Wipf and Stock, 1998).

13. Drexel, *Aloe Amari sed salubris succi Ieiunium*.

14. Dallaeus, *De Jejuniis et Quadragemisa Liber*.

15. Drexel, *Aloe Amari sed salubris succi Ieiunium*, 27.

16. Ibid., 49–50.

17. Ibid., 69–70.

18. Ibid., 74.

19. Ibid., 135–144.

20. Dallaeus, *De Jejuniis et Quadragemisa Liber,* 22. "vi in singulorum culinas, ac coenacula irrumpunt, & quid quisque coenet non curiose modo, sed etiam impudenter scrutantur. Homines coeli disciplinam professi Theologiam suam ad lances, & cacabos, & ollas, & patinas demittunt; magnaque & supercilios gravitate de ossis, & condimentis, & esculentorum invenio, atque paratura jus dicunt." It should be noted that the author shows an intimate familiarity with baroque cookery.

21. Ibid., 52–53.

22. Ibid., 108.

CHAPTER 3

"THE FOOD POLICE"

SUMPTUARY PROHIBITIONS ON FOOD IN THE REFORMATION

Johanna B. Moyer

> Que la Religion est le premier et le principal objet
> de la Police . . .
>
> —Nicolas De La Mare, *Traité de la police*

In 1577 the French nobleman François de L'Alouette complained that "sumptuary laws, so well received in the past, are now-a-days held in such great contempt. . . . If these [laws] were well-kept, [the authorities] would not be searching taverns and cabarets for delicious morsels, the people would not ruin themselves on superfluities and great quantities of foods; feasts and banquets would not be so frequent; and the policing of food . . . would not be so difficult to enforce."[1] While L'Alouette was concerned that the legal codes regulating the quantity and type of food French men and women ate were not being enforced, the reality was that in the sixteenth century these sumptuary laws were increasingly included in a variety of plans to reform early modern society.[2]

By L'Alouette's time, the Reformation of Christianity was well underway, and both Catholic and Protestant legislators used sumptuary edicts to interfere in the personal habits of their subjects. Sumptuary statutes restricting the use of luxury clothing, food, banquets, baptisms, weddings, and even funerals were being enacted all over sixteenth-century Europe.

The sumptuary laws on food enacted during the Reformation were the ultimate form of the modern twentieth-first-century notion of a "food police." However, where some modern physicians and legislators argue for legal restrictions on "junk foods" because of concerns with what they see as an increasingly unhealthy public, sixteenth-century legislators were more concerned with what they saw as the spiritual unhealthiness of their subjects. Reformation-era legislators enacted sumptuary legislation to promote religious conformity and affirm the religious practices of their communities. Both Catholics and Protestants enacted sumptuary legislation to ensure that individual members of society did not stray into the religious practices of the rival confession or, even worse, convert to the rival religion.

SUMPTUARY RESTRICTIONS ON FOOD AND BANQUETING

Sumptuary laws had been a regular part of medieval law codes in the centuries before the Reformation. Prior to the sixteenth century, sumptuary edicts had regulated luxuries and conspicuous displays of wealth. Most medieval statutes restricted luxury clothing, such as garments made of silk or luxury furs. In 1294, for example, the French king issued a law which forbade any "bourgeois man or woman" to wear "vair, grey fur, or ermine, . . . nor are they allowed to wear gold, precious stones, or crowns of gold or silver." Other parts of the law restricted the number of garments a person could own by social rank.[3] Less frequently, these laws restricted foodstuffs or even household items. The same thirteenth-century law in France also forbade non-nobles from having "any torches of beeswax" and limited the number of dishes that could be served at any one meal.[4] Sumptuary laws in the medieval period were often enacted to protect the distinctions between the estates or to preserve the wealth of certain social groups.[5] Some medieval laws were tied to Christian notions of morality and were seen as a way to curb the sins of pride, vanity, gluttony, and even lust.

During the Reformation, both Protestant and Catholic areas experienced an upsurge in the enactment of sumptuary laws. This newly enacted body of sumptuary legislation was not only larger than medieval sumptuary law, but some historians argue that it also regulated more items and in more detail.[6] Historians of sumptuary legislation attributed this new interest in sumptuary legislation to Protestant governance of

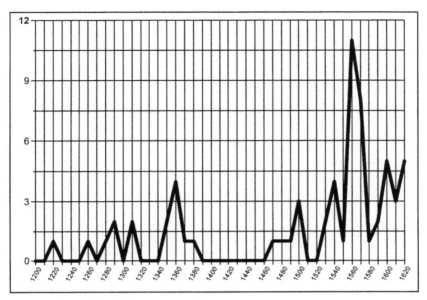

Figure 3.1 Chart of French Sumptuary Law Frequency

morality. These historians also noted a growing number of laws regulating Sabbath observance, gambling, drinking, profanity, and courtship in Protestant countries.[7]

However, more recent studies have disputed this connection. In them historians found little or no change in the content of sumptuary laws. They argue that the *frequency* of sumptuary law enactment followed the same general pattern in both Catholic and Protestant areas during the Reformation. Still, most agree that there was no change in the *content* of sumptuary provisions between the Middle Ages and the end of the sixteenth century. Nevertheless, this interpretation does not present a completely accurate picture of sumptuary law in the Reformation as it ignores the fact that there was an increasing concern within the general body of sumptuary law in Europe in the sixteenth century with what people ate. During the Reformation both Protestant and Catholic governments enacted secular regulations on food and banqueting in increasing numbers.

Food regulations had been a regular part of some medieval sumptuary codes. Yet in the sixteenth century food restrictions were enacted in increasing numbers and made up a greater percentage of the total body of sumptuary laws enacted in some countries. In France, for example, only two laws regulating foodstuffs were enacted between 1229 and 1490, or 2.5 percent of total body of medieval sumptuary laws.[8] What's more, in the sixteenth century, six laws were enacted against food items, with the bulk in the 1560s at the start of the religious wars.[9] This represented 12.5 percent of the total body of sumptuary law in that century. In Scotland no laws regulating food were enacted before 1551. After that date one-third of all sumptuary regulations enacted by the Scottish Parliament in the sixteenth century targeted the culinary excesses of the Scottish population.[10]

Both Catholic and Protestant countries saw an increase in the number of sumptuary restrictions on food during the Reformation of Christianity. However, the sumptuary laws that regulated luxury foodstuffs were not identical in Catholic and Protestant areas. Legislators in Catholic areas tended to focus on the type and amount of food eaten. These provisions frequently restricted meats, especially red meats and wild game. A French royal edict of 1533, for example, forbade the eating of lamb and beef,[11] and was repeated in a series of laws in the mid sixteenth century against luxury apparel "and the eating of certain meats."[12] Although French law targeted the spending habits of an overweening nobility, Catholic countries like Italy, where the hereditary nobility was less important, also restricted meat and game consumption. A Milanese law of 1565 prohibited peacocks, pheasants, and roe deer,[13] while Venetian senators banned similar fowl as early as 1472.[14] A later Venetian statute of 1562 added that "wild birds and animals, Indian cocks and hens, and doves shall be strictly forbidden.[15]

By the mid sixteenth century it was not simply the type of meat eaten that concerned Catholic legislators but also the amount of meat that gluttonous diners consumed. Catholic sumptuary restrictions in this period limited the number of meat dishes that could be legally consumed per meal. The aforementioned Milanese law forbade more than two courses of "flesh/meat" per meal,[16] while in Venice the Senate decreed that at "banquets for public and private parties, and *indeed at any meal of meat* [my emphasis], not more than one course of roast and one of boiled meat may be provided."[17]

Both Catholic and Protestant sumptuary laws discouraged general overeating with limits on the number of courses and plates that could be served. Under Louis XIII, French Catholics "of whatsoever quality and condition" were forbidden "more than three services in all and of one simple rank of courses, not stacked on one another: and none can have more than six pieces per course: whether it is porridge or roast" both "in their houses or in public houses and rooms."[18]

Protestant legislators created different sorts of sumptuary regulations on foodstuffs. Some Protestant lawmakers avoided sumptuary regulations on food altogether. In England, for example, only one sumptuary law on food was enacted in the early modern era. This law was an early proclamation of Henry VIII; the English Parliament never issued any restrictions on food or banqueting. Moreover, Henry's proclamation was enacted in 1517, before his quarrel with the pope.[19] All the sumptuary statutes and proclamations issued after that date in England dealt with apparel or gilding.[20]

When Protestant legislators did regulate food and dining, they were less likely to focus on what a person ate and more likely to restrict how much a person ate. Therefore, Henry VIII allowed his subjects all of the varieties of meats and game birds that were forbidden to the French and Italians, including "cranes, swans, bustard, peacock, and all other fowl of like greatness," however he limited them to "but one dish."[21] Furthermore, each meat had to "stand for one dish."[22] In Calvinist Scotland, consuming meat in general was acceptable in the eyes of the law but was restricted by rank so that "neither an Archbishop, Bishop, nor Earl have at his mess but 8 dishes of meat, nor an Abbot Lord Prior nor Dean have at his meals but 6 dishes of meat, nor a Baron nor Freeholder have but four dishes of meat at his meals, nor a Burgher nor other substantial man spiritual not temporal have at his meals but 3 dishes and but any kind of meat in every dish."[23]

Protestant governments employed the particular strategy of limiting the number of dishes or servings per course to control the amount of food that was eaten at a single meal or banquet. Lawmakers in Basel became so desperate to get wedding banquets under control they actually included a suggested menu in a 1629 statute. The menu limited the nuptial feast to three courses, but allowed entrees like "chopped mutton," "beef, veal, and smoked meat." However, to curb overeating and cost, the dinner "must begin at 12 o'clock and stop at 4, and everybody must leave by 5 o'clock."[24] Protestant legislators were more concerned with the cost of foodstuffs than with what diners ate. Hence many laws in Protestant areas restricted expensive items like rare meats, wines, and, the more recent addition to European celebrations, sweet deserts and sugary confections. A law from Nuremburg forced revelers to give up expensive fowl like heron and peacock in favor of "roast capon on a side table."[25] German legislators, not trusting the judgment of their citizens, often dictated sensible and less expensive alternatives. Oenophiles were forbidden the pleasures of spiced wine, but could have instead "Franconian or Flemish" or a "similar grade" wines.[26] Sumptuary restrictions extended to all sorts of meals and celebrations. A seventeenth-century Swiss law on baptisms and "Christening suppers" forbade any "sweet wine" or confectionary."[27]

As the decades passed, legislators increasingly included suggestions for foods that were acceptable in place of the more expensive luxury item. Earlier sumptuary statutes on bridal dinners and other banquets forbade more expensive "imported drugs,[28] confectionaries and spices brought from the parts beyond the sea and sold at dear prices to many folk that are very unable to sustain that cost."[29] Four decades later, the Scottish Parliament felt constrained to add that "no person use any manner of dessert of wet and dry confections at banqueting, marriages, baptisms/ feasting or any meals except the fruits growing in Scotland.[30] Legislators also worried that the high price and popularity of certain foods led to shortages and increased the price of foodstuffs generally. Others complained that individuals frittered away their fortunes on excessive celebrations.[31]

The desire to limit expense combined with the Christian belief that overindulgence was a sin. Protestant statutes often limited the cost of banquets and amount of food consumed by limiting the number of guests that could be invited as well as the number of meals that could be given for certain celebrations. The strategy was clearly one of the most popular tools in the antiluxury arsenal of sixteenth-century lawmakers. A late fifteenth-century law in Nuremburg restricted weddings. Guests for the nuptial feast were limited to family and visitors from out of town, although anyone could join the celebration after the banquet ended.[32] In 1529, in Zurich, legislators believed that weddings had become "too extravagant" and limited banquet guests to twenty-four, or if you had "a lot" of relations, forty.[33] By 1628, in Basel, guests were limited to "four tables of twelve," and, to ensure compliance, bridal dinners were moved from private homes to "guild houses and public inns."[34] This statute actually limited the cost of the meal per guest.

Wedding customs in Europe were complex in the early modern era. The process of "getting married" included several stages of celebrations, from the betrothal to the removal of the bride to the groom's home. Where our modern marriage ceremony, whether religious or civil, is believed to constitute the moment in time when the couple are actually "married," early modern Europeans saw marriage more as the product of a series of events.[35] Medieval customs had created dinners and banquets for many of the stages of the marriage celebration, leaving legislators hard-pressed to keep up with the regulation of all meals in the marriage process. By the seventeenth century, Swiss legislators simply dealt with the problem by issuing a blanket prohibition allowing "only one meal . . . on the wedding day," fining any additional lunches or dinners on subsequent days."[36] Newlyweds in Protestant Nuremburg were allowed only one "wedding party with seven friends" after they had settled into their new home. [37]

Baptisms were also targeted. The municipal government in Basel outlawed "Christening suppers" altogether in 1612 and even included the now standard prohibition on "sweet wine and confectionary."[38] In later centuries Swiss legislators even banned the number of guests allowed at funeral dinners.[39]

These examples illustrate a larger trend in Protestant sumptuary restrictions on food and banqueting. Virtually all these laws targeted the meal and food served in the context of a celebration or important life event. These meals were public events, important to the life of the Protestant community. Protestant legislators believed that the social function of the meal was as important as the food itself, contending that while excess in eating was bad, public excess was even worse. For the Catholics who enacted sumptuary regulations, however, it was what was eaten and how much was eaten that was important.

THE CASE OF FRANCE

Why was there a difference in the types of sumptuary restrictions enacted against food in Protestant and Catholic areas? The French Wars of Religion (1562–1598) present an excellent opportunity to understand Catholic and Protestant attitudes toward sumptuary regulations. Many partisan treatises on religion, politics, the economy, and the role of the nobility were written during and after the Wars of Religion. Both Catholics and Protestants discuss the ills of France, including overindulgence in luxuries. These texts provide a perfect opportunity to explore opposing ideas about luxury and luxury control.

Catholics

The Catholic side of the debate was presented during the Wars of Religion primarily by members of the Catholic League. The league was founded in 1576 to oppose the ascension of the Protestant Henri de Navarre to the French throne. The Catholic texts diagnosed with the ills of France, speculated on the causes of the Wars of Religion, and of course plied their own candidates for the throne. Many Catholic authors saw the prevalence of luxury, particularly among the French nobility, as one of the chief problems with their kingdom, at once both a cause and effect of the religious troubles in France.

Catholic writers as a group noted the growth in the use of several kinds of luxury before the wars, which they blamed predictably on "heretic and Huguenot rebels."[40] Luxury was rampant in the kingdom, a result of "excess expense on clothing, banquets and superfluity of attendants" as well as large amounts spent on housing and servants.[41] Food and banqueting were a constant source of criticism by Catholic authors. One author lamented the current fashion for "sumptuous banquets,"[42] while another noted that gourmandizing was rampant among those in government and administration.[43] Most authors, however, blamed the upper echelons of French society. The French government and nobility, they complained, spent money and taxes from the French people on luxuries, starving the people and draining money from the poor. Traditionally, excess food and money was supposed to be channeled into charity for the poor. In fact, one of the major reasons for medieval sumptuary laws was to ensure that the wealthy would donate surplus income into charity. Medieval advice manuals for the nobility literally dictated how much income should go for the noble's own table and how much should be directed to charity.

Catholics often associated luxury, especially the overindulgence of luxury foods, with physical sins. In medieval theology, gluttony had been a "gateway" sin leading to more serious transgressions, particularly lust and fornication. Although some Catholic authors during the French Wars of Religion associated excessive luxury with the sin of idolatry—the "worship of wealth,"[44]—others associated luxury with the base physical sins of "carnality and purulence."[45] Worse still, they thought that luxury spread from person to person like a disease, spreading the associated sins and ultimately the most dangerous of all sins, the Protestant heresy.

Luxury not only endangered the soul but also damaged an individual's physical health. Galenism enjoyed a resurgence in popularity in the sixteenth century and was used to justify all sorts of restrictions on food and alcohol.[46] Catholics often employed the medical model of Galen's humors to explain the deleterious effects of overeating and luxury on both the body and the soul. In Galenic humor theory, all food and drink had the potential to cause disease. Sixteenth-century physicians believed that food was incorporated into the body's structure, a kind of medieval version of "you are what you eat." Early modern physicians frequently used dietary strictures to manipulate and even change the physical makeup of the body.

Overeating in traditional Galenic medicine was associated with an increase in the moist humors. Food was used by the body to increase blood, which was then turned into other bodily fluids. Excess blood, however, led to disease. Galen noted on several occasions that overeating led to disease, "an excessive consumption of food, however nutritious and excellent is the cause of cold diseases."[47] It is more likely, however, that those who called for sumptuary legislation in Reformation France were influenced by the large quantity of dietary literature that was published during the Reformation. Ken Albala has noted that the dietary advice manuals published during the period from 1530 to 1570 were particularly influenced by the Galenic revival that was such an important part of medicine in this period. Galen pushed out competing medieval and ancient medical authorities to produce a more detailed and precise body of dietary advice.[48]

Galen's admonition against an excessive and luxurious lifestyle was seconded by a chorus of condemnations of gluttony from the authors of these Reniassance dietaries.[49] Such criticism struck a chord with Catholic authors worried about the transformative powers of food and the role food played as a portal to sin. Moist diseases were caused by excessive lifestyles, Galen argued, including "a surfeit of foods that are moist in power, too many drinks, an excessively luxurious mode of life, sex and frequent baths."[50] Catholic authors saw a direct connection between the "superfluity" of luxury and the "superfluity" of humors in the body that they believed luxury engendered.

Overeating caused illness, but some believed that eating meat, particularly red meat and game in excess, exacerbated the problem. Galen cautioned that meats like beef were not "easily digested" and "generates thicker blood than is suitable." This led to sanguine illnesses like "cachexy" and "dropsies."[51] Not all early modern authors agreed with Galen, however, on the deleterious effects of meat. Many of the authors of Renaissance dietary guides saw meat as one of the substances most similar to the human body and therefore highly nutritious. Several guidebooks advocated meat, even beef, "contrary to the warnings in Galen, Isaac, and Salerno,"[52] Others noted, however, that beef was slow to digest, which could, in fact, destroy some of its nutritive properties.[53]

Game meats also presented similar problems for strict Galenists. Meats like hare and venison, according to Galen, were difficult to digest and generated "thicker blood."[54] Some early modern dietary advice manuals, however, cited the traditional *doctrine of signatures,* which held that foods "looked like" their elemental properties. Red foods, therefore, were hot and generated blood.[55] The disagreement between the authors of the dietary manuals and the proponents of luxury control was whether or not this blood that was generated posed a health problem for the diner. Many early modern nutritionists argued that darker-fleshed meats were more nutritious, though some thought harder to digest. Nevertheless, the amount of blood that was engendered by meat eating was the amount the body needed to regenerate. Luxury opponents believed that the blood engendered could be excessive and therefore dangerous. The authors of the dietary manuals did note, however, that dark-meated game birds and swans, banned in some sumptuary laws, might generate choler and melancholy in the body of those who consumed them. Lighter-colored chicken, recommended in some laws, was therefore a better choice.[56]

No matter how early modern nutritionists recast the value of red meat, it could not overcome the long-standing Christian strictures against meat eating. Since the Middle Ages, sumptuary legislation had been motivated by the Christian association of gluttony, meat eating, and illicit sexuality. Some aspects of Renaissance dietary theory reinforced this doctrinal association. Extremely nutritious foods, including meat, often created more blood than the body needed to replenish itself. The surplus was then converted to sperm. The greater the amount of surplus blood, the greater the quantity of sperm, which in turn increased the sex drive.[57]

Whether early modern diners followed Galen strictly or followed the strictures of a favorite sixteenth-century dietary advice manual, the advice to readers was always to eat a moderate diet.[58] For strict Galenists, persistent overindulgence at the table led to illness, which could only be treated by having a physician drain off the excess humor. Joannitius observed that "phlebotomy [bloodletting] is proper in all the cases named above, for if a man eats much meat and drinks much wine . . . he is not safe: sanguine illness may be generated in him, or perhaps he may drop dead suddenly. But if he is bled, his health can be preserved longer."[59] A patient who persisted untreated, however, ended up obese and diseased, their bodies and souls transformed.

For Catholic League member Nicolas Rolland, the physical dangers of overeating and the luxury of the table could not be separated from the dangers gluttony posed to the soul. The greatest of these dangers was the evils of the Protestant "heresy." Luxury and Protestantism had taken over foreign governments, Rolland noted, with disastrous consequences. The "poster boy" for these dangers was the English Protestant king, Henry VIII. Rolland described what he believed had happened to the English king after he left the Catholic Church.

> He had been at the start of his reign, the most handsome and agreeable Prince who was well regarded, but since he separated from the Church, he became strangely voluptuous; he was so gluttonous and gourmandized beyond measure. This rendered him so large and so fat, that he became in a short period of time completely deformed, he could no longer pass through the small doors of the bedrooms and loos, nor himself climb the height of the stairs to go to the rooms of his palace, which made it necessary to lift him in the air with machines and artifices; they sat him in a chair.[60]

Overeating had horribly transformed Henry's physical body, but ultimately it was the sign of a diseased soul. For Rolland and other Catholics, luxury was a physical symptom of heresy; the sinful state of the soul apparent in the diseased state of the physical body.[61]

The damage caused by luxury and overeating to the bodies of individual sinners mirrored the larger damage done to the greater body politic of France. The metaphor of the body politic became more popular in the sixteenth century, especially with the growth of new theories on rational government and absolutism in France. Each organ or member of the human body had a specific function, and all of the other parts of the body depended upon that function for life. Early modern thought linked the specialized functions of each part of the body to the different but interdependent functions of society. The social classes, economic functions, and even religion needed to be balanced and regulated, just as the members and humors of the body need to be balanced. For the human body, the intellect was the instrument of regulation, while for the body politic of France it was the job of the government and the king. For the opponents of luxury, Catholic and Protestant alike, the damage caused by luxury spread from the individual luxury user to the society at large. One overeater became many overeaters. Entire segments of society became "infected" with luxury, and, as one part slipped out of balance, the entire body politic was endangered. Luxury spread like an infection endangering the health of the nation.[62]

For Catholic luxury opponents, the flow of wealth in the kingdom mirrored the flow of blood in the human body. During the Wars of Religion, wealth flowed upward to the king and nobility, starving the lesser members of the body politic. The royal court was now "corrupted and infected" with the disease of luxury.[63] As the luxury unbalanced the humors of the body of France, it created the disease of heresy. Protestantism now infected a significant portion of the French nobility, and war had resulted. The humors of the body politic were unbalanced, and the king was responsible. He must now act in the role of physician to heal the body politic of luxury and stamp out the disease of heresy. Leaguer Rolland admonished the king "to heal this body [France] so sick, it is necessary as a good and true doctor, that you have the will and desire to bring the healthful medicine."[64] Sumptuary laws were essential to halting this process. They served as preventative phlebotomy did, staving off a much larger bloodletting of civil war that was inevitable with the buildup of sanguineous humors in the body politic.

Protestants

Protestant writers during the French Wars of Religion agreed that luxury was more prevalent than ever and that luxury was both a cause and effect of France's current religious troubles. They also largely agreed with Catholic authors that the French nobility was the locus of the problem. Some Protestants too criticized excessive consumption of luxury food and banqueting.[65] However, Protestants did not rank the evils of excess at the table as highly as other types of overindulgence. Many Protestants argued that overspending on apparel was a much more pressing problem for France, especially vestments made from imported materials or that incorporated gold and silver accessories. The Protestant writer François de La Noue actually ranked several kinds of luxury items their order of damaging effects. "In first place would be superfluity in clothing" (115). He believed that architecture and housing had recently gotten out of hand, so he ranked luxury housing second, followed by furnishings third (195–197). Only fourth on his list were "expenses of the mouth," but combined with excessive attendants of the nobility. However, he went on to emphasize the number of horses and servants nobles kept rather than what the aristocracy spent on their tables (199.

Indeed, many Protestants argued that luxury meats, wines, and even banqueting were fine as long as done in moderation (see, for example, 587). When they did attack banqueting, they condemned lavish parties, particularly those that were accompanied by "masques, gambling and superfluous attendants" (119). On the other hand, Laffemas scoffed at past sumptuary laws that had been designed to "impede banquets and nocturnal debaucheries." These had not worked, he argued; instead they "provoke luxury rather than stop it."[66] Some Protestants even argued that the Catholic desire to restrict food, especially meat, is nothing more than a form of idolatry, a kind of "worship" of food.[67]

Most Protestants writers agreed that the worst form of luxury infecting France was the rage for apparel made from imported silks and velvets and the use of gold and silver to decorate clothing, furnishings, homes, and carriages. The purchase of foreign cloth and apparel decreased employment for the French people, and the use of specie in luxury items immobilized currency. These writers were increasingly influenced as the sixteenth century wore on by the economic "philosophy" of mercantilism. Mercantilists preached the importance of preserving gold and silver within the boundaries of France and advanced the domestic luxury industry to promote employment.[68]

This rhetoric reached its pinnacle in a series of economic treatises penned by the Protestant Barthelemy de Laffemas. He was arguably the Mercantilists' greatest opponent of foreign luxury items and items that incorporated gold and silver. He tirelessly campaigned for a government-sponsored domestic silk industry which he believed would create substantial employment. In a treatise written at the end of the Wars of Religion, Laffemas railed against "the abuse of gold and silver laces, and the evil brings pearls and precious stones . . . "[69] He called for sumptuary laws banning imported silks,[70] gold and silver laces, and gilded furniture. However, Laffemas hoped to legalize domestically produced silk for apparel.[71]

It was not the grotesque figure of a gluttonous Henry VIII that haunted French Protestants like Laffemas and de La Noue but the image of young French nobles elaborately decked out with hats "in the form of a crust of bread" and elaborate apparel bought from Venice. The irony was that while the Venetians and other Italian city-states became rich from these purchases, "the simplicity of their [Venetian] apparel make their coffers teem with riches, and their Senate shines with prudence and wisdom, and their [sumptuary] statutes are inviolably observed and to the contrary that we, with our short shoes and long doublets have thrown our [sumptuary] laws out of the window . . . and our coffers are almost always drained of gold" (La Noue 194–195). One of the greatest tragedies of the Wars of Religion, in Laffemas's opinion, was not the loss of life but the loss of French manufactures (5–6).

Protestants too employed a disease model to explain the dangers of luxury consumption. Luxury damaged the body politic leading to "most incurable sickness of the universal body" (33). Protestant authors also employed Galenic humor theory, arguing that "continuous superfluous expense" unbalanced the humors leading to fever and illness (191). However, Protestants used this model less often than Catholic authors who attacked luxury. Moreover, those Protestants who did employ the Galenic model used it in a different manner than their Catholic counterparts.

Protestants also drew parallels between the damage caused by luxury to the human body and the damage excess inflicted on the French nation. Rather than a disease metaphor, however, many Protestant authors saw luxury more as a "wound" to the body politic. For Protestants the danger of luxury was not only the buildup of humors *within* the body politic of France but the constant "bleeding out" of humor from the body politic in the form of cash to pay for imported luxuries. The flow of cash mimicked the flow of blood from a wound in the body. Most Protestants did not see luxury foodstuffs as the problem, indeed most saw food in moderation as healthy for the body. Even luxury apparel could be healthy for the body politic in moderation, if it was domestically produced and consumed. Such luxuries circulated the "blood" of the body politic creating employment and feeding the lower orders.[72] De La Noue made this distinction clear. He dismissed the need to individually discuss the damage done by each kind of luxury that was rampant in France in his time as being as pointless "as those who have invented auricular confession have divided mortal and venal sins into infinity of roots and branches." Rather, he argued, the damage done by luxury was in its "entire bulk" to the patrimonies of those who purchased luxuries and to the kingdom of France (116). For the Protestants, luxury did not pose an internal threat to the body and salvation of the individual. Rather, the use of luxury posed an external threat to the group, to the body politic of France.

THE REFORMATION AND SUMPTUARY LEGISLATION

Catholics, as we have seen, called for antiluxury regulations on food and banqueting, hoping to curb overeating and the damage done by gluttony to the body politic. Although some Protestants also wanted to restrict food and banqueting, more often French Protestants called for restrictions on clothing and foreign luxuries. These differing views of luxury during and after the French Wars of Religion not only give insight into the theological differences between these two branches of Christianity but also provides insight into the larger pattern of the sumptuary regulation of food in Europe in this period. Sumptuary restrictions were one means by which Catholics and Protestants enforced their theology in the post-Reformation era.

Although Catholicism is often correctly cast as the branch of Reformation Christianity that gave the individual the least control over their salvation, it was also true that the individual Catholic's path to salvation depended heavily on ascetic practices. The responsibility for following these practices fell on the individual believer. Sumptuary laws on food in Catholic areas reinforced this responsibility by emphasizing what foods should and should not be eaten and mirrored the central theological practice of fasting for the atonement of sin. Perhaps the historiographical cliché that it was only Protestantism which gave the individual believer control of his or her salvation needs to be qualified. The arithmetical piety of Catholicism ultimately placed the onus on the individual to atone for each sin. Moreover, sumptuary legislation tried to steer the Catholic believer away from the more serious sins that were associated with overeating, including gluttony, lust, anger, and pride.

Catholic theology meshed nicely with the revival of Galenism that swept through Europe in this period. Galenists preached that meat eating, overeating, and the imbalance in humors which accompanied these practices, led to behavioral changes, including an increased sex drive and increased aggression. These physical problems mirrored the spiritual problems that luxury caused, including fornication and violence. This is why so many authors blamed the French nobility for the luxury problem in France. Nobles were seen not only as more likely to bear the expense of overeating but also as more prone to violence.[73]

Galenism also meshed nicely with Catholicism because it was a very physical religion in which the control of the physical body figured prominently in the believer's path to salvation. Not surprisingly, by the seventeenth century, Protestants gravitated away from Galenism toward the chemical view of the body offered by Paracelsus.[74] Catholic sumptuary law embodied a Galenic view of the body where sin and disease were equated and therefore pushed regulations that advocated each person's control of his or her own body.

Protestant legislators, conversely, were not interested in the individual diner. Sumptuary legislation in Protestant areas ran the gamut from control of communal displays of eating, in places like Switzerland and Germany, to little or no concern with restrictions on luxury foods, as in England. For Protestants, it was the communal role of food and luxury use that was important. Hence the laws in Protestant areas targeted food in the context of weddings, baptisms, and even funerals. The English did not even bother to enact sumptuary restrictions on food after their break with Catholicism. The French Protestants who wrote on luxury glossed over the deleterious effects of meat eating, even proclaiming it to be healthful for the body while producing diatribes against the evils of imported luxury apparel. The use of Galenism in the French Reformed treatises suggests that Protestants too were concerned with a "body," but it was not the individual body of the believer that worried Protestant legislators. Sumptuary restrictions were designed to safeguard the mystical body of believers, or the "Elect" in the language of Calvinism. French Protestants used the Galenic model of the body to discuss the damage that luxury did to the body of believers in France, but ultimately to safeguard the economic welfare of all French subjects. The Calvinists of Switzerland used sumptuary legislation on food to protect those predestined for salvation from the dangerous eating practices of members of the community whose overeating suggested they might not be saved.

Ultimately, sumptuary regulations in the Reformation spoke to the Christian practice of fasting. Fasting served very different functions in Protestants and Catholic theology. Raymond Mentzer has suggested that Protestants "modified" the Catholic practice of fasting during the Reformation. The major reformers, including Luther, Calvin, and Zwingli, all rejected fasting as a path to salvation.[75] For Protestants, fasting was a "liturgical rite," part of the cycle of worship and a practice that served to "bind the community." Fasting was often a response to adversity, as during the French Wars of Religion. For Catholics, fasting was an individual act, just as sumptuary legislation in Catholic areas targeted individual diners. However, for Protestants, fasting was a communal act, "calling attention to the body of believers."[76] The symbolic nature of fasting, Mentzer argues, reflected Protestant rejection of transubstantiation. Catholics continued to believe that God was physically present in the host, but Protestants believed His was only a spiritual presence. When Catholics took Communion, they fasted to cleanse their own bodies so as to receive the real, physical body of Christ. Protestants, on the other hand, fasted as spiritual preparation because it was their spirits that connected with the spirit of Christ in the Eucharist.[77]

The public nature of fasting for Protestants was reinforced by the issuance of Lenten laws. A comparison of France with England and Scotland shows that the British enacted far more laws enforcing abstinence from red meat during Lent in the sixteenth century than Catholic France. The French issued only four royal laws ordering abstinence during Lent, generally prohibiting "the sale . . . of any type of meat during Lent."[78] By contrast, the English and Scottish enacted dozens of Lenten laws in the sixteenth and seventeenth centuries.[79] The first English law was enacted by the Calvinist-influenced Edward VI.[80]

This is not to suggest that the traditional interpretations of sumptuary laws as parts of other projects of governance are incorrect. French Protestants were clearly influenced by economic mercantilism, as were Protestants in other countries. Moreover, the authors of both religions who wrote against luxury in France targeted the nobility and wanted to use sumptuary legislation not only to curb aristocratic wealth but also to create a new role for the nobility in French society. This fact suggests that sumptuary legislation in this period was also motivated by a desire to stabilize the social hierarchy. This too can be seen in Italy where the sumptuary regulations on food contained laws that conform to both the "Catholic" pattern and the "Protestant" model. In Italy, however, where religion was debated but never really in doubt, social considerations probably outweighed religious motives.

At the bottom of all sumptuary impulses in the Reformation, however, was the notion of community. Sumptuary legislation was now being used as a form of religious policing, designed to force the members of the religious community to conform to the theological practices of the group. Just as Catholic governments destroyed books banned by the Church in the Index of Prohibited Books and Protestant governments enacted laws compelling Sabbath observance and banning adultery, sumptuary laws were used by both sides to enforce religious dogma. Both Catholics and Protestants in the sixteenth century incorporated into sumptuary legislation notions about the human body reintroduced by the medical humanism of the sixteenth century. These Galenic views of the body were transformed to express theological notions of sin, salvation, and membership in the Christian community.

Did these differing views of "community" impact the content of sumptuary laws during the Reformation? The answer must be both yes and no. There was a change in the content of laws from both Catholic and Protestant areas in the sense that there was an increased emphasis on the regulation of food. It is also clear that the content of Protestant and Catholic food laws was different. In Catholic areas, this meant sumptuary restrictions on food controlled the private acts of culinary excess, but in Protestant areas sumptuary laws controlled the public acts of food and banqueting.

This does not mean, however, that Reformation-era legislators enacted different sorts of regulations than those enacted by their medieval predecessors. It has been noted by several historians that there were food "patterns" associated with each religion. Northern European countries like England and Germany that converted to Protestantism also favored diets centered on beer, butter, and pork. This was true both before and after conversion. Southern European countries like France and Italy, however, favored wine, olive oil, and mutton, before and after the Reformation. They also remained Catholic.[81]

The content of sumptuary legislation also followed this pattern. Although the types of antiluxury statutes regulating food and banqueting differed by religion, the laws tended to be the same as those enacted in the same area before the Reformation. This begs the question, as Mack Holt has put it, what was the connection between food culture and religion in the Reformation? It seems likely that, as Holt found for drinking patterns, religion simply reinforced differences in eating patterns and the cultural hegemony of certain foods.[82] Clearly, food is always a central element in the affirmation of community. During the Reformation, food practices and the culture of food became one of many "tools at hand" that could be redeployed by the Reformation police to enforce new Reformation theologies and new definitions of community.

Notes

1. De L'Alouette, *Traité des nobles et des vertus*, 65.
2. Sumptuary programs stood at the crossroads of many legislative projects in the sixteenth century. Early modern restrictions on personal consumption regulated the social structure, instituted poor relief, promoted religious conformity, and managed the economy.
3. Isambert, *Recueil général des anciennes lois françaises,* 1:697–698, arts. 2 and 6.
4. Ibid., arts. 13 and 14.
5. The older historiography of sumptuary laws in France, for example, often presented early modern sumptuary laws as safeguards enacted, in the words of Vertot, to save the "great families from ruin." Godard de Donville and Freudenberger argued that sumptuary laws were intended to prevent a competition of display between the sword and robe nobilities. Other historians argued that sumptuary laws in this period were enacted to preserve distinctions in ranks after the rise of the robe nobility. Schalk saw sumptuary legislation in this period as an attempt to reinforce the old symbols of nobility, particularly clothing, because they were now available to wealthy non-nobles. See L'abbé de Vertot, "Dissertation sur l'Etablissement Des Lois Somptuaires," in C. Leber, ed., *Collection des Meilleurs Dissertations et Traités Particuliers relatifs à l'histoire de France* (G. A. Dentu: Paris, 1838), 10:467; Louise Godard de Donville, *Signification de la mode sous Louis XIII* (Edisud: Aix-en-Provence, 1976), 206, 211; Freudenberger, "Fashion, Sumptuary Law, and Business," 40; H. Baudrillart, *Histoire du luxe, privé et public depuis l'antiquité*, 4 vols. (Hachette: Paris, 1878), 3:441–442; and Davis Bitton, *The French Nobility in Crisis, 1560–1640* (Stanford: Stanford University Press, 1969), 67, 101–107. See Ellery Schalk, *From Valor to Pedigree, Ideas of Nobility in France in the Sixteenth and Seventeenth Centuries* (Princeton: Princeton University Press, 1986), 151–152. Legislators at times cited the desire to preserve fortunes as one justification for enactment. See, for example, the royal French edict of July 12, 1559. Isambert, *Recueil général des anciennes lois françaises*, 13:101.

6. See Greenfield, "Sumptuary Law in Nürnberg," 86; Frances Baldwin, "Sumptuary Legisla-tion and Personal Regulation in England," *Johns Hopkins University Studies in Historical and Political Science* 44 (1926): 270; Harte, "State Control of Dress," 151; Hooper, "The Tudor Sumptuary Laws," 96. See also Freudenberger, "Fashion, Sumptuary Law, and Business," 37; Hunt, *Governance of the Consuming Passions*, 183–189. Greenfield and Baldwin noted that sumptuary legislation in the Reformation was more "complex" and hierarchical. Greenfield, "Sumptuary Law in Nürnberg," 6; and Baldwin, "Sumptu-ary Legislation and Personal Regulation," 136.

  Early modern legislators we also more determined to enforce these new sumptu-ary restrictions. In the late fifteenth century, for example, the Venetian Senate created a new magistracy exclusively for enforcing sumptuary provisions, the Provveditori sopra le Pompe. This institution became permanent in 1514. See Chambers and Pullan, *Venice*, 177.

7. See for examples, Freudenberger, "Fashion, Sumptuary Law, and Business," 137; and Baldwin, "Sumptuary Legislation and Personal Regulation," 131. Greenfield tested the connection between the Protestant Reformation and sumptuary law in Nuremberg, but found no evidence to support this relationship. Sekora attributed the increased enactment of sumptuary law in this period to a "church/state rapprochement" and the takeover of sumptuary law enforcement from church courts in Protestant countries. See Sekora, *Luxury*, 60–61. Raeff attributed the changes in sixteenth-century sumptuary regulations to the newly shared "moral spiritual function" between church and state in Catholic areas and the relegating of luxury to the state in the Protestant areas of Germany. Raeff, *The Well Ordered Police State,* 82. However, some studies have disputed this connection. Alan Hunt noted that the connection with Protestantism was more convincing for "morals laws," such as those on gambling or Sabbath observance, not for sumptuary laws particu-larly. However, he also noted that these studies focused almost exclusively on Protestant areas and that very little work had been done on the sumptuary laws issued during the Catholic Reformation. Hunt found this surprising, as he contends that, anecdotally, there were more Catholic sumptuary laws than Protestant. Given the copious quantities issued by the Italian city-states, this is probably true. Hunt, *Governance of the Consuming Pas-sions*, xiii.

8. Isambert, *Recueil général des anciennes lois françaises*, 1:669 and 697–700.

9. January 1563, January 20, 1563, February 20, 1565, February 1566, and also January 12, 1573. There was also a 1629 law that regulated the table.

10. Shaw lists three enactments in the sixteenth century, 1550, 1551, and 1552, as well as one law in the seventeenth century in 1621. Shaw, "Sumptuary Legislation in Scotland," 90–96. There was also an additional sumptuary law on banqueting in 1581. Also see *Acts of the Parliament of Scotland*. For the texts of individual laws, see *Acts of the Parliament of Scotland*, 2:488, c. 22, 1551; A.P.S., 3:221, c. 19, 1581; A.P.S. 3:625, c. 17 and 18, 1621; A.P.S., 8:350, c. 80, 1681. Hunt lists a total of twelve laws for Scotland in the sixteenth century. Hunt, *Governance of the Consuming Passions*, 29, 32.

11. Fontanon, *Les édicts et ordonnances des rois*, 3:918–920, arts. 2 and 3.

12. Ibid., 2:918–919, arts. 2 and 3. Unfortunately the texts of several of these laws have been lost. See also January 12, 1573, ibid., 4:1240–1241.

13. Verga, "Le leggi suntuarie," 54.
14. Newett, "The Sumptuary Laws of Venice," 273.
15. October 8, 1562: reproduced in Chambers and Pullan, *Venice*, 179.
16. Verga, "Le leggi suntuarie," 54.
17. Chambers and Pullan, *Venice*, 179.
18. Isambert, *Recueil général des anciennes lois*, 16:264, art. 134.
19. May 31, 1517: Hughes and Larkin, *Tudor Royal Proclamations*, 1:128–129, no. 81.
20. See, for example, Elizabeth's proclamation of March 9, 1571: Hughes and Larkin, *Tudor Royal Proclamations*, 2:381–182, no. 601.
21. May 31, 1517: Hughes and Larkin, *Tudor Royal Proclamations*, 1:128–129.
22. Ibid., 128.
23. A.P.S., 1551, c. 22, 2:488; Shaw, "Sumptuary Legislation in Scotland," 90.
24. Reproduced in Vincent, *Costume and Conduct*, 33.
25. Greenfield, "Sumptuary Law in Nürnberg," 57.
26. Ibid.
27. Vincent, *Costume and Conduct*, 21.
28. Spices were often used in early modern medicine as drugs. It is very likely that legislators felt they needed to specify all possible uses of spices because diners often evaded sumptuary laws by "renaming" illegal items.
29. A.P.S., 1581, III, c. 19, 221.
30. A.P.S., 1627, c. 17 and 18, 625, act. 25.
31. A.P.S., 1681, c. 80, 8, 350.
32. 1485: Greenfield, "Sumptuary Law in Nürnberg," 58.
33. Vincent, *Costume and Conduct*, 32.
34. Ibid., 33.
35. Roper, "Going to Church and Street."
36. Vincent, *Costume and Conduct*, 35.
37. Greenfield, "Sumptuary Law in Nürnberg," 60.
38. Vincent, *Costume and Conduct*, 21.
39. Ibid., 27.
40. Rolland, *Remonstrances*, 27.
41. Ibid., 142.
42. Poncet, *Remonstrance à la noblesse de France,* 13.
43. Rolland, *Remonstrances,* 130.
44. Cromè, *Dialogue d'entre le malheustre*, 72.
45. Rolland, *Remonstrances,* 130.
46. See, for example, Albala, "To Your Health," for restrictions on wine.
47. Galen, "On the Cause of Diseases," in Grant, *Galen on Food and Diet*, 51.
48. Albala, *Eating Right in the Renaissance*, 25, 30.
49. Ibid., 104. Albala notes that the authors who wrote between 1530 and 1570 were particularly critical of gluttony; see 32–33.
50. Galen, "On the Cause of Diseases," 51.
51. Galen, "On the Powers of Foods," 154.
52. Albala, *Eating Right in the Renaissance,* 40; see also 64–79.

53. Ibid., 68, 81.

54. Galen, "On the Powers of Foods," 155. Galen suggested that his patients eat pork.

55. Albala, *Eating Right in the Renaissance,* 80–81.

56. Ibid.

57. Ibid., 144–147.

58. Ibid., 106.

59. Joannitius, *"Bloodletting": A Sourcebook in Medieval Science,* ed. E. Grant (Cambridge: Harvard University Press, 1974), 800.

60. Rolland, *Remonstrance,* 227.

61. The notion that the physical body reflected the state of the soul was fairly common in the Reformation, as was the use of an opponent's weight to criticize his spirituality. Lyndal Roper recently noted that Protestants regularly lampooned overweight popes and bishops. Images of Luther, on the other hand, depicted his large body as a sign of the rightness of his beliefs and "was central to his rejection of Catholic asceticism. See Lyndal Roper, "Martin Luther's Body: The 'Stout Doctor' and His Biographers," *American Historical Review* 115 (2010): 351–384.

62. For a discussion of the relationship between nutritional theory and the growth of the early modern state, see Albala, *Eating Right in the Renaissance,* 217–240.

63. Ibid., 241.

64. Ibid., 233.

65. See, for example, François de La Noue, *Discours politiques et militaires* (Genève: Droz, 1967 [1580]), 31.

66. Laffemas, *Advis sur l'usage.*

67. La Noue, *Discours politiques,* 785.

68. Laffemas was obsessed with the idea of developing a domestic luxury industry and ended the export of gold and silver to pay for foreign luxuries. See his *Les tresors et richesses.* For a discussion of mercantilist policies in this period, see the classic treatment by Cole, *French Mercantilist Doctrine.*

69. Laffemas, *Les tresors et richesses,* 18.

70. Ibid.

71. Laffemas, *Le Merite de travail et labeur,* 12.

72. See Laffemas, *Les tresors et richesses,* 18, 21, *Le Merite de travail et labeur,* 12; *Advis sur l'usage,* 71.

73. Several authors of the treatise against luxury of both religions blamed luxury on the nobility and noted that their pursuit of luxury and wealth led them to "abuse peasants" and become involved with the French Civil Wars. La Noue, *Discours politiques,* xxvi–xxvii.

74. See, for example, Lindemann, *Medicine and Society in Early Modern Europe.*

75. Mentzer, "Fasting, Piety, and Political Anxiety," 333–334.

76. Ibid., 340.

77. Ibid., 339–340.

78. February 20, 1565: Fontanon, *Les édicts et ordonnances,* 1:943.

79. Henry VIII issued three proclamations dispensing with Lenten fasts because he claimed there was a shortage of fish. See, for example, March 11, 1538: Hughes and Larkin, *Tudor Royal Proclamations,* 1:260–262, no. 177. Beginning with Edward VI, Lenten proc-

lamations enforced abstinence from meat. Edward issued three such proclamations. See, for example, March 9, 1551: Hughes and Larkin, *Tudor Royal Proclamations,* 1:510–512, no. 368. Elizabeth I issued seventeen proclamations enforcing Lenten fasts; see, for example, January 14, 1600, Hughes and Larkin, *Tudor Royal Proclamations,* 3:204–209, no. 800. This pattern continued under the Stuart monarchs in the seventeenth century.

80. January16, 1548: Hughes and Larkin, *Tudor Royal Proclamations,* 1:413, no. 297; and A. Luders, T. E. Tomlins, J. Raithby, eds., *Statutes of the Realm* (London, 1810–1828), vol. 4, pt. 1, 2° and 3° Edw. VI c. 19, 1548.

81. See, for example, Mack P. Holt, "Europe Divided. Wine, Beer, and the Reformation in Sixteenth-Century Europe," in Mack P. Holt, ed., *Alcohol: A Social and Cultural History* (Oxford: Berg, 2006), 25–40.

82. Ibid., 37.

CHAPTER 4

DIRTY THINGS

BREAD, MAIZE, WOMEN, AND CHRISTIAN IDENTITY IN SIXTEENTH-CENTURY AMERICA

Heather Martel

According to the sixteenth-century Milanese adventurer Girolamo Benzoni, the indigenous people of New Spain ate "dirty things."[1] In his recollection the women who prepared the bread did "not care if any hairs fall into it, or even some lice."[2] In order to make wine from maize, the women would "put it into their mouths and gradually chew it" and then "almost cough it out" into the pots where it would ferment.[3] While this practice of making maize wine was widely reported by other chroniclers of the region, and others expressed distaste at the use of saliva in the process, Benzoni's attention to the incorporation of women's hair and saliva in the indigenous bread and wine prompts explanation.

In the context of early modern European understandings of nutrition and Reformation disputes over the sacramental use of bread and wine, Benzoni's revulsion at American food expresses the complex dynamics of Christian identity amidst the dangers of both the Reformation and the conquest of America. There was great risk for those who sought to maintain the integrity of their Protestant or Catholic identity among those of a different faith as they moved between Protestant and Catholic regimes or their Christian homeland and the pagan New World. From Benzoni's perspective, his fellow Catholics, the Spanish, had not navigated the challenges of the New World successfully. The Spaniards Benzoni described seemed to have reverted to barbarism, surrendering their Christian values when they immersed themselves in gluttony for wealth and power akin to cannibalism.[4] Instead, Benzoni modeled a strategy for defining and maintaining an identity that could travel. Eschewing identification with either the Spanish or indigenous Americans, Benzoni expressed disgust at both the dirty deeds of the Spanish and the dirty foods consumed by Native Americans.

BENZONI AND HIS NARRATIVE

Girolamo Benzoni, the Milanese adventurer, "anxious to see the world and hearing of those countries of the Indians, recently found, called by everybody the New World . . . determined to go there."[5] He traveled through Spanish America from the Caribbean to parts of Peru for fourteen years (1541–1556). During these years of exploration, he participated in the Spanish colonial project, including the capture and enslavement of the natives. Though neither a missionary nor a demonstrative Catholic, he did align himself with Catholics, dedicating his book to Pope Pius IV and crediting "a noble French priest" with saving his life (12). He had enough status to be sought after by Spanish elites in the Americas, one of whom promised him wealth in exchange for his company on travels throughout the region (2). However, in explaining his motivations, Benzoni expressed a higher calling—not wealth alone, but a desire for knowledge, claiming to be "as desirous to see men and countries, as to become rich" (2–3). To his apparent disappointment, "already the Spaniards had almost destroyed this country; for out of the great multitudes of Indians that there used to be, there only remained a few petty chiefs" (3).

In an attempt to tell the story of that destruction and to record all he did see, Benzoni wrote his *History of the New World*, a lengthy narrative published in Venice in 1565, ten years after his return. In this account he recapitulated the entire history of Spanish America, exalting his fellow Italian Christopher Columbus and describing much of the brutality and tragedy of the conquest that preceded his journey throughout the region. His *History* was published seventeen times before 1600; translated into Latin, German, French, Dutch, and English; and included as part 4 and 5 of Theodor de Bry's fourteen-part collection of illustrated travel narratives, *Americae*, which was published at the turn of the seventeenth century.[6]

Benzoni's *History* was printed in the midst of the religious tensions and violence of the Reformation, in which reformers, attempting to address what they perceived as corruption in the Catholic Church, spawned a new Protestant Church. The result of these spiritual differences was a battle for souls between Catholics and Protestants that all too frequently turned to violence, including religious wars fought by armed branches of both churches, hangings, burnings, tortures, sieges, and the Inquisition. Theodor de Bry, a copper engraver and publisher of the German and Latin editions of Benzoni's narrative, had himself been a subject of the Inquisition when the Netherlands was a part of the Holy Roman Empire under Spain's Phillip II. Threatened by the intimidations and violent reprisals of the Inquisition's Council of Blood, De Bry fled to Strasbourg, Germany where he illustrated and published travel narratives that favored a Protestant interpretation of Spanish imperialism, including Benzoni's *History of the New World*.[7]

BENZONI IN EARLY MODERN FOOD HISTORY

A "pivotal issue" dividing Catholics from Protestant reformists was their conflicting interpretations of the sacramental meaning of bread and wine in the Eucharist.[8] Since the thirteenth century the official doctrine of Catholics was that transubstantiation turned the bread and wine into the body and blood of Christ during the ritual of communion. Medieval Catholics believed "Christ's true body and blood 'are physically taken up and broken in the hands of the priest and crushed by the teeth of the faithful, not only sacramentally but in truth.'"[9] According to historian Christopher Elwood, there was also a "popular fascination with seeing and worshiping the sacred host," which fed the late fifteenth-century reformist critique that this "extraliturgical viewing" was tantamount to idolatry.[10] They called the belief in transubstantiation "superstition" and objected to the "practice of showing the elements to the congregation 'lifting them up, and causing them to be worshiped by all, as idols.'"[11] Protestant reformists believed that Christ's body was "nowhere else but in heaven" and that the "substance of bread and wine [rather than the body and blood of Christ] remain on the altar after consecration."[12] This difference between Catholics and Protestants proved to be incommensurable and saturated all of their experiences, including their encounters with indigenous Americans.

Though Catholics and Protestants disagreed about whether the consecrated bread and wine was a sign of Christ's body or his actual flesh and blood, the process by which indigenous American bread and wine became "dirty" also reflected fears of strange food in the Galenic model of the body and drew on ideas about nutrition and identity shared by all early modern Christians. As historian Trudy Eden has shown, caution and sometimes disgust toward the consumption of indigenous foods was a common response among early modern Europeans who looked to their bodies for explanations of identity, bodies that they believed to be fluid, temperamental, and transitory and that could signify an exchange of one identity for another depending on proximity, behavior, and diet.[13]

To guard against such transformations, early moderns practiced what Eden calls a "philosophy of food security" in which the "quality" as well as the quantity of food consumed mattered because "early modern Europeans believed their identity depended on what they ate." For example, it was believed that consumption of English food or anglicized food would maintain English identity.[14] In the process of food assimilation, the body most easily incorporated similar foods, foods that most resembled the flesh they replaced, including bread and wine. According to Ken Albala, in this Galenic model of nutrition foods that were not similar and thus assimilable were "poisons" or "venomous foods, which alter our body, are slowly converted into us, and with accumulation come to destroy us."[15] As a result, travelers to the Americas feared indigenous food might transform them, altering their physiology and thus their spiritual identities in a real or cultural death. Christians who consumed native foods might become native, physiologically, culturally, and spiritually. As Eden puts it, food assimilation "resembled a negotiated and potentially hostile takeover in which the body altered and assimilated food, and the food in turn produced change within the body, mind, and soul."[16]

Benzoni's disgust at the "dirty things" that fell into indigenous bread and wine was a part of this alimentary system and worked to stabilize his Christian identity. Though the Reformation set Catholics and Protestants against each other and informed their representations of indigenous Americans, Europeans in the Americas identified themselves as "Christians" in opposition to pagan Native Americans. Confronted by the differences between his Christian world and the Americas, Benzoni's focus was to preserve his Christian identity from the corruption of pagan influences. As this chapter will argue, his aversion to native foods worked as a conditioned response to new cultural influences and served the goal of maintaining Christian cultural and spiritual identity.

Indigenous Bread and Wine-Making

In his narrative, Benzoni recorded the process by which indigenous American women made various breads. They made the "common people's bread" from maize. The women *molandaie* "wet a quantity of this grain the previous evening with cold water." In the morning they grind it "between two stones" until they have "made a mass." Then "by sprinkling in water with the hand, they shape it into little loaves, either long or round." These loaves are then placed "into some leaves of reeds" and "with as little water as possible, they cook them." This bread, Benzoni related, "lasts two days and then mildews." The "chief's bread" was also made from ground maize. However, after grinding it, the women "wash it with hot water and pick out the husk, leaving only the flour, which they grind as much as they can." This flour was then shaped into "small cakes," which were cooked in "a round pipkin," an earthenware pot used for cooking directly over a fire. Benzoni also explained that the natives make a more lasting bread from cazabi roots, which they peel and cut with "sharp stones that they find on the beach." They then "squeeze out the juice, which would be poison to anyone drinking it." This is then formed into cakes of paste, "some thick and some thin" and cooked over the fire "leaving them as long as they will hold together" and then put into the sun to dry. In Benzoni's assessment, this cazabi bread was "a wretched article of food, but if put into a dry place it would continue good for three or four years" (84–86).

Also made from maize, indigenous wine, required saliva to turn starch to sugar that would ferment and become alcohol. According to Benzoni, the ground maize was soaked in water "in some large jars" and cooked in a pipkin until they have "rendered it somewhat tender." The softened maize flour was then "handed over to some other women, whose office it is to put it in their mouths and gradually chew it." This masticated paste was spit out "upon a leaf or platter" and transferred "into a vase with the other mixture." Unaware of the chemical process by which saliva creates sugar, Benzoni was under the impression that this mixture was what was required to create alcohol, claiming that "otherwise this wine, or rather this beverage, would have no strength." This mix, Benzoni wrote, was "then boiled for three or four hours," cooled, and then "poured through a cloth." It was "esteemed good in proportion as it intoxicates," Benzoni explained, "in the same way as if people drank real wine." While he acknowledged the production of "wines of other kinds, of honey, of fruits, and of roots," Benzoni's description focused on maize wine because "these do not intoxicate as the first does" (86–87).

Contemporary European observers agreed with Benzoni that the task of bread and wine making fell to women. As Jean de Lery recalled, "I have seen no distinction made between the young girls and the married women in this respect, the men nevertheless hold the firm opinion that if they were to chew the roots or the millet to make this beverage, it would be no good."[17] There was some discrepancy regarding which indigenous women participated. Protestant Staden of Germany and French Catholic Thevet emphasized the presence of "young girls," "certain virgins or maidens," and that "if a woman be called thereto, she must first abstain certain days from her husband."[18] Catholic José de Acosta, on the other hand, claimed that "it must be chewed by decrepit old women, which is disgusting even to hear about, and yet they show no repugnance toward drinking that wine."[19]

Whether differences in age or sexual development of the women who made the wine and bread were regional or due to the observer's degree of openness to consuming indigenous foods, Christian descriptions dwelled on the part played by female bodies in making bread and wine. Benzoni's description of bread making emphasized the presence of women's bodies as they worked the dough, observing that, "some stand up to it, others kneel on the ground; nor do they care if any hairs fall into it, or even some lice."[20] In a graphic description of wine making, Benzoni observed that the women chewing the maize for the wine, "with an effort . . . almost cough it out" onto the leaf or platter. Other Christians reiterated the physical presence of women who "sit down to it," "stand up to it," "kneel on the ground," and "crouched around" as they processed the grain. Clearly struck by the chewing in particular, observers described how they "chew it in their mouths," "twist them around in their mouths," and "chaw or champ it in their mouths."[21]

In such descriptions, maize wine, with its association with saliva and maize bread, prepared by "decrepit old women" or polluted with hair and lice (which had been parasitically devouring the woman's blood on her scalp) implicated the bodies of the women who had prepared it.[22] For Christians, drinking such wine and eating such bread was akin to taking in that pollution. Their disgust suggests that in consuming indigenous bread and wine their bodies also assimilated the bodies of the women who had prepared it, polluting and thus transforming those who drank it.[23] In the Galenic nutritional system of identity, Europeans would assimilate that food, and it could "poison" or "alter" those who drank it as it was "converted into" them.[24] If they consumed bread and wine polluted by native women's bodies, the cultural and spiritual implications could run deep, even as far as converting Christians into pagan Americans.

According to the Galenic model of nutrition, wine was the substance considered closest to blood, while bread was esteemed as "readily assimilated" (Albala 67). Thus both held strong nutritional value because they so easily replaced qualities lost to the body. Bread was valued for its glutinous, "stick to your ribs" quality and because it was "tempered," or "having no dominant humour or qualitative effect on the body" (67, 84). Visually, bread that was coarse and brown was deemed appropriate for less refined people, whereas elites imagined refined, white bread had qualities appropriate and better assimilable to their physiology and cultural status (165, 196). The identification between wine and blood went further than appearances. Early modern Christians also noted that wine and blood went through a similar process of "crushing, fermenting, separating from various by-products, and ultimately refining for use" (74). This nutritional system did allow that processing food could transform it into something more "palatable" while also "counteracting food's adverse qualities by balancing them with corrective condiments" (7).[25]

Benzoni and other Christians may have been anxious because the Native American process of making maize wine and bread differed significantly from that of the Christians. In observing indigenous cooking, Benzoni saw women adding to, rather than counteracting, the adverse qualities of the maize they used to make bread and wine. As he says, "maize is not good either hot or cold" (84). Beyond the "dirty things" that fell into the bread, Benzoni also distinguished between the "common people's bread" which "lasts two days and then mildews" and the more refined, de-husked "chief's bread," which he also cast aspersions on, describing it as "not good but when fresh, and not very good then nor when cold." Benzoni described the "wretched" cazabi bread as "harsh and difficult to swallow"; it seemed "like earth in the mouth," requiring accompanying moisture, like meat broth (85). Though he had identified the equivalent to bread in indigenous cuisine, Benzoni's description of all indigenous breads' appearance and flavor as coarse and unpalatable suggests he was suspicious of the effect it could have on his body.

While Benzoni's caution toward indigenous bread suggests resistance to incorporating the bodies of the native women who made it, Protestant Jean de Lery attempted to assuage such fears of indigenous wine making. Aware that his readers would be repulsed by the wine (or *caouin*) making practices of the Tupinamba he encountered in Brazil, Lery acknowledged, "I have no doubt that some of those who have heard what I have said concerning the chewing and twisting around of the roots and millet in the mouths of the savage women when they concoct their *caouin*, will have been nauseated, and will have to spit." In an attempt "to allay this disgust," he aligned the processes of Tupinamba caouin making and European wine making. Lery reminded his readers of the European tradition of crushing grapes with their feet and even shoes, which was "hardly more pleasing than this custom of chewing among the American women." Lery then suggested a comforting commonality and challenged his readers to overcome their revulsion. "If thereupon someone says, 'Yes, but as [wine] ferments in the vats the wine expels all that filth,' I reply that our *caouin* is purged the same way, and that therefore on this point the one custom is as good as the other."[26]

Indigenous Bread and Wine in the Eucharist

If the process of fermentation "expels all that filth" of indigenous women's bodies, the sacramental rite of communion offered another place where Christians could process native American bread and wine, making them safe to eat. In addition to practices of food security used to maintain the health of the Christian traveler to the Americas, the emphasis in early modern travel narratives on indigenous breads and wines had a "sacramental" significance for Christians through the Eucharist. Although both Protestants and Catholics identified as Christians with respect to indigenous Americans, their doctrinal differences over the transformation of the bread and wine at communion divided their responses to indigenous bread and wine.[27]

Indeed, when their supply of European wine began to run low, Protestants and Catholics at Fort Coligny, Brazil had a hot debate over practicing the Eucharist with the "bread and wine in the land where they were."[28] Protestants held that "when Christ instituted the Lord's Supper, being in the land of Judea, he had spoken of the ordinary drink of that region" and "there would be no obstacle to celebrating the Lord's Supper with the commonist things for human nourishment that took the place of bread and wine in the land where they were."[29] As a result, some Protestants did not conceal the fact that they partook of bread and wine and chose to "progress from disgust to acceptance" in what Janet Whatley calls an "alimentary 'going native.'"[30] Protestants Lery and Staden both indicated a firsthand knowledge of the indigenous wine. According to Staden, who spent ten months living with the Tupinamba, "it is thick, but of agreeable flavour."[31] Though he admitted he had experimented with making maize wine himself in hopes that they "could avoid the spitting that . . . the savage women use," Lery described how "little by little, we accustomed ourselves to drinking the other as it was."[32]

While Protestants were open to indigenous foods, the identification of the local equivalent to bread and wine was important to their sacrament. As Andrea Fisch argues, "the fact that the bread [and wine] never undergoes an ontological conversion into the body of Christ does not mean that just anything could occupy the place of bread [and wine] in the sacrament." She explains that the value of indigenous bread and wine was directly linked to the "idea of nourishment."[33] According to Calvin, "as bread nourishes . . . so the body of Christ is the food and nourishment of the spiritual life . . . such use as the wine serves the body, the same is spiritually bestowed by the blood and Christ."[34] For Protestants, it was important that the spiritual nourishment of Christ's body and blood was signified by the bread and wine. Indigenous food could stand in for that sign.

In contrast, Benzoni's revulsion at the preparation of polluted bread and wine by native women demonstrated a Catholic sensibility toward its sacramental use in the Eucharist.[35] Spanish missionaries in Peru felt they had to intervene when one converted native "said that the [maize wine] was the blood of Jesus Christ" and used it in an indigenized holy communion.[36] As Frisch has shown, Catholics would have objected to this substitution because they saw "an essential connection between bread and Christ's body, and between wine and His blood."[37] Through the performance of the consecration rite by an ordained Catholic priest, the bread and wine literally became the body of Christ. As one Catholic hymn explained, "into Flesh the true bread turneth / By His word, the Word made Flesh; / Wine to Blood; While sense discerneth / Nought beyond the sense's mesh."[38] This transformation was not visible to the senses, but had to be taken on faith. Thus it was "not possible to change anything of the sacraments' essence or nature."[39]

Using indigenous bread and wine would most certainly have meant a significant change in the essence of the sacrament, down to the grain used and the process of preparation. However, although the qualities of the bread used by sixteenth-century European Christians was substantially different from the bread of the Middle East used by Jesus in the first communion, resistance to indigenous bread and wine probably had more to do with its preparation by native women. Because the flesh and blood of Christ replaced that bread and wine on the altar, signifying the "one body" of the Holy Roman Catholic Church, this "symbol of unity in Christ" could not be polluted by the bodies of the unconverted indigenous women who had cooked it.[40] In a near anthropophagic act, Catholics might literally consume and then assimilate the bodies of indigenous women through using their bread and wine in the Eucharist.

As Benzoni and other Catholics in New Spain would have been aware, Protestant propagandists did see a connection between cannibalism and the Catholic doctrine of transubstantiation in which the bread and wine became Christ's flesh and blood and were eaten by the people. Critical of his Catholic fellow colonists at Fort Coligny, Protestant Lery compared the belief and practice of transubstantiation and Catholic Reformation violence to cannibalism, saying, "if it comes to the brutal action of really (as one says) chewing and devouring human flesh, have we not found people in these regions over here, even among those who bear the name of Christian, both in Italy and elsewhere, who, not content with having cruelly put to death their enemies, have been unable to slake their bloodthirst" for the flesh of Christ.[41] In Montaigne's "Of Cannibals," he imagined indigenous Brazilians observing the Eucharist, "expressing their astonishment that the French should eat their god" and struck by the irony of "Europeans condemning cannibalism yet practicing theophagy."[42] The consumption of Christ's body was widely understood as an incorporation of his spiritual qualities through nutritional assimilation. As one Protestant pamphlet put it, "theophagites . . . you eat God to strengthen yourselves."[43]

For his part, Benzoni's disgust at indigenous foods included their practice of eating "human flesh" as well as "lice, as monkeys do, spiders, worms, and other dirty things" (10). Benzoni also projected this belief in nutritional assimilation onto the natives he observed, claiming that though "they are accustomed to eat human flesh," some "were afraid to eat the flesh of Spaniards, thinking that even in their bodies it might do them harm" (73). The association with anthropophagy here is no accident. Theoretically, in this nutritional system, the most easily assimilable foods would be human flesh and blood (Albala 69). However, these early modern Galenic nutritionists did not have in mind the consumption of Native American flesh and blood. As Jean de Lery recalled, he and his group of stranded Huguenots came to depend on the Tupinamba for food to survive banishment in Brazil from Fort Coligny. But, unlike other Christians lost in the Americas, they would not practice cannibalism. As he noted, "when they presented us with the human flesh of their prisoners to eat, we refused it" and acknowledged that this meant the French were not "showing proper loyalty" to their hosts.[44] Though Lery depended on native hospitality, he stopped at this ultimate sign of assimilation.

INDIGENOUS USES OF BREAD AND WINE

Beyond the implication of indigenous American bodies in the bread and wine that became the blood of Christ in the Catholic Eucharist, the sacramental uses of maize bread by indigenous Americans to connect with their own gods added to Benzoni's negative impression of it. "Touching on their religion," he described the use of bread in their worship of idols and the devil. In one ceremony, "when the cacique of *La Española* wished to celebrate a feast in honour of his principle false deity," the natives were invited to a temple wherein "the ministers were dressing the idol." The cacique played on a drum, while ceremonially dressed men "painted black, red, and yellow, with plumes of parrots' and other feathers, with ornaments of sea-shells round their necks, their legs, and their arms" entered to dance. The men were followed by the women, who were "not painted at all." In fact, Benzoni claims, "the girls were quite naked" (79). Once in the temple, he observed them "dancing and singing certain of their songs in praise of their idol, while their chief saluted them with his drum."

Having described their cultural fashions and ceremonial dancing, Benzoni then turned to the use of indigenous food in that rite. First, in what he described as "foolish ceremonies," they attested to their empty stomachs: "by putting a stick down their throat, they vomited, so that the idol might see they had nothing bad either in their stomach or their breast" (79). Then, "baskets adorned with roses and various flowers, and filled with bread," was introduced into the rite by "some other women." Benzoni did not discern a distinct ceremonial role for these women, though he noted that "they went round to all those who were singing, and repeated a little prayer to them," which the "singers jumped up on their feet to answer." They then "presented the bread to the idol." Finally, in priestlike fashion, "the ministers now took and blessed it, and shared it with all the people, as if it was a holy thing or good relic." Here again, Benzoni showed the significant role of women in the ceremony and of their bodies in his comment on the nakedness of the singing women. Just as in making their bread and wine, indigenous women were overly present, Benzoni saw them as central to a ceremony that ended up as a rite much like the Eucharist. The ministers blessed the bread and "shared it with all the people" who mirrored the popular respect shown the bread in Catholic ceremonies, treating it as "a holy thing" (79).[45]

While Benzoni does not describe any rites involving wine, other observers of indigenous American ceremonies were struck by rituals involving excessive drinking and vomiting. In describing a similar ceremony among the Tupinamba, Hans Staden noted that "on the spot where they drink, they also void off their wine."[46] According to Lery, drinking ceremonies were a physiological preparation for battle in which "as long as this caouinage lasts, our American rakehells and carousers heat their brains hotter and hotter, singing, whistling, egging each other on, and exhorting each other to behave valiantly, and to take many prisoners when they go to war." He also associated their drunkenness with cannibalism, explaining that "in this costume they kill and eat a prisoner of war." Lery likened the drinking of the natives to a bacchanalia, which was a pagan rite associated with sexual and drunken excess, and to the Catholic interpretation of the Eucharist, writing that "drunk as priests, they are enacting the Bacchanales of the ancient pagans, and it is a sight to see them roll their eyes."[47] Lery interpreted excessive drinking and vomiting not only as ceremonial but as an expression of masculinity in which "to abandon the game would have been to be reputed womanish."[48]

Historian Thomas Abercrombie notes that Spanish colonization did increase the use of maize wine by commodifying it and making it more broadly available for recreational use by indigenous Americans and Spanish colonists. As a result, Christian observers expressed concern and moralized over the abuse of alcohol by sixteenth-century Native Americans.[49] Jean de Lery recalled a story in which the Tupinamba found "casks full of some good Spanish wines" and reported that "after we had drunk our fill, we were so stunned and stupefied that for three days, it was not in our power to wake up." Lery speculated that, after "a truly bacchanalian celebration . . . it is not a wonder if, after such a blow on the head, they found themselves also, in their turn, suddenly helpless."[50]

Though Benzoni wrote about the intoxicating qualities of indigenous American wines, he focused more critically on their abuse of tobacco. He described how it was grown and dried. Then "they take a leaf of their grain (maize) and putting one of the [tobacco leaves] into it, they roll them round tight together." In lighting up this cigarette, he was amazed to see them put it to their mouths, then "draw their breath up through it, wherefore the smoke goes into the mouth, the throat, the head, and they retain it as long as they can." Benzoni echoed Lery's description of the Tupinamba's immoderate drinking practices, explaining the natives smoked, "for they find pleasure in it, and so much do they fill themselves on this cruel smoke, that they lose their reason." As the accompanying woodcut illustrated, "there are some who take so much of it, that they fall down as if they were dead, and remain the greater part of the day or night stupefied." Smoking habits varied, Benzoni explained, and "some men are found who are content with imbibing only enough of this smoke to make them giddy, and no more." However, he found this habit disturbingly compelling to the natives, ranting, "see what a pestiferous and wicked poison from the devil this must be" (80–81).

GLUTTONY, HEALTH, AND IDENTITY

This lack of moderation spoke of self-destruction and physical weakening through excess according to the Galenic model of the body. Certainly, these accounts demonstrate a culturally sanctioned lack of control that appeared immoderate by Christian standards. In terms not only of the

Galenic model of nutrition but of the seven deadly sins, among them gluttony, all Christians interpreted excessive eating and drinking as unhealthy and admired moderation instead. As a result of the Protestant Reformation's "intolerance toward indulgence," gluttony came to reflect the lack of integrity of both body and soul during the period of Benzoni's travels and writing (Albala 8). Gluttony was a distraction from God, and it threw the body out of balance, putting the soul under the influence of the foods assimilated by the body that was its vessel. Christians were wary not only of eating native food and of incorporating the cultural values of the people who prepared that food. They were also concerned with observing practices of moderation meant to preserve the health of their bodies and their Christian identities.

Other Christian travelers to the Americas expressed this concern in travel narratives in which they encountered indigenous people whose moderation they admired. In Protestant sympathizer Thomas Harriot's *Brief and True Report of the New Found Land Virginia*, he complimented the Powhatan for their "sober" habits of "eating and drinking," explaining that they were "consequently very long lived because they do not oppress nature."[51] So too did Jacques Le Moyne, a Protestant explorer in the failed attempt to colonize Florida. Of the Timucuans Le Moyne observed that "although they give big feasts, they never overeat, and therefore usually live to a great age." He then told the story of one of the chiefs who "swore that he was three hundred years old and that his father, who he pointed out to me, was fifty years older than himself—and indeed he looked to be nothing but skin and bones."[52] Le Moyne and Harriot's observations indicated the health, virtue, and integrity of Powhatan and Timucuan cultural identity in early encounters.[53] As Harriot observed, "they make good cheer together, yet are they moderate in their eating whereby they avoid sickness."[54]

In contrast to indigenous American moderation and health, both Harriot and Le Moyne noted Christian excess. Le Moyne made a point of comparison for his Christian audience, arguing that "such facts might well make us Christians ashamed, for we are so immoderate in both our eating and our drinking habits that we shorten our lives thereby. We might easily learn sobriety and wisdom from these men whom we consider only as savages and wild beasts."[55] While these Christians still intended to "civilize" the natives, this was an area where Christians might learn from them. Wrote Harriot, "I would to God we would follow their example, for we should be free from many kinds of diseases which we fall into by sumptuous and unseasonable banquets, continually devising new sauces, and provocation of gluttony to satisfy our insatiable appetite."[56]

When Harriot blamed the Christians' desire "for new sauces" and "gluttony to satisfy our insatiable appetite," he made a connection between gluttony and disease, which reflected broader concerns about health and Christian identity. While he and Le Moyne claimed to have encountered three-hundred-year-old indigenous Americans, Christians' excessive thirst and hunger was shortening their lives. Comparisons between native American and Christian health in early travel narratives revealed uncertainty over which culture would dominate. That indigenous Americans in Virginia and Florida were so moderate and long-lived suggested that they might be difficult to overwhelm.

Unlike Harriot and Le Moyne, Christians in New Spain observed excessive use of intoxicants by indigenous people who also consumed "dirty things." As Benzoni had explained, of the "great multitudes of Indians that there used to be" in New Spain "there only remained a few petty chiefs" (3). He described the hopeless resistance of these multitudes to Spanish colonialism, including withholding food and violent insurrection. In the end, Benzoni recounted, "finding themselves intolerably oppressed and worked on every side, with no chance of regaining their liberty," the natives, "with sighs and tears longed for death." He described a mass suicide in which women "with the juice of a certain herb, dissipated their pregnancy" and then the people "hung themselves, after having killed their children." Others jumped off cliffs, drowned themselves, starved to death, and "killed themselves with their flint knives," while "others pierced their bosoms or their sides with pointed stakes." In the end, Benzoni concluded that "finally, out of the two millions of original inhabitants, through the number of suicides and other deaths, occasioned by the oppressive labour and cruelties imposed by the Spaniards, there are not a hundred and fifty now to be found: and this has been their way of making Christians of them" (77–78).

Benzoni's tone was sympathetic toward the natives when he described this tragedy. However, he was also making a larger point about failure of the Spaniards in "making Christians of them." In the text of his *History* this story is followed by his eye-witness description of their worship of idols and the devil, including the ceremony involving bread. After describing their religion, Benzoni then turned to his critique of their use of tobacco, their use of tobacco as medicine, their practice of polygamy, their thieving, their nakedness, and then to the "dirty things" they ate and the preparation of their polluted and unseemly bread and wine. Because early modern travel narratives are typically structured in this stream-of-consciousness style, it is unclear whether Benzoni's organization made a conscious or unconscious link between Spanish "cruelties," the mass suicide, and indigenous Americans' cultural practices and eating habits. Benzoni may have imagined a great culture reduced to eating such food by Spanish imperialism.

SPANISH EXCESS AND THE PROTESTANT RECEPTION OF BENZONI

What was apparent to contemporary Protestant readers of Benzoni, was that he was critical of Spanish colonialism, perhaps explaining why his *History* was illustrated and published by Protestant propagandist Theodor de Bry and never translated into Spanish.[57] Benzoni's representation of the excess of Spanish conquest of the Americas provided more of a cautionary tale than a celebration of Catholic colonialism. According to Benzoni, Spanish gluttony quickly alienated and exhausted indigenous Americans. Even Columbus found that "the natives would in no way furnish him with provisions, neither for barter, nor entreaties, nor for goodwill, and that he could not get them by force" (42). This resistance included withholding the very food that repulsed Benzoni. He recounted an incident in which "the greater part of the islanders not only had refused to sow their lands with any grain for making bread, but had destroyed all that was left of the harvest; thinking that if the strange people did not find anything to eat, they would be forced to leave the island." They did this without hopes for their own survival, "for like desperate people, on account of the cruel servitude to which they were reduced, they were content to die of hunger themselves" (26).

Benzoni represented the Spanish as excessively greedy and thirsty more than once. In one story he described "some [Spaniards] who went so far inland, thirsting for gold, that they got into desert places, where, not knowing the constellations . . . they were unable to advance or retreat, and died there together with all their followers" (76). In this tale of Spaniards lost in "desert places" under strange "constellations," Benzoni gave the impression that the Spaniards had lost their way, their Christian identities compromised by their thirst for gold. Benzoni identified this "thirsting for gold" as a self-destructive Spanish passion of which indigenous Americans were aware as well. In the most famous act of indigenous resistance, Native Americans retaliated directly against Spanish greed when they murdered Spaniards with molten gold. As Benzoni recalled, "of those whom they caught alive, especially the captains, they used to tie the hands and feet, throw them down on the ground, and pour gold into their mouth, saying : 'Eat, eat gold, Christian.'" Once the Christians were thus slain, they were dismembered and eaten. According to Benzoni, "the more to ill-treat and disgrace them, with knives made of flint, some cut off an arm, some a shoulder, others a leg, and then roasting it on the embers, eat it, dancing and singing, suspending the bones in their temples, or in the houses of their chiefs, as trophies of victory" (73).

In Benzoni's narrative, the Spaniards' loss of Christian civility was signified not only by their greed for gold and dismemberment by cannibals but by their exploitation of the indigenous people they enslaved. He had participated in that exploitation, recalling that "we used often to wait all day expecting to make prisoners, and on the Indians arriving, we jumped out like wolves attacking so many lambs, and made them slaves" (6). Among the crimes of the Spanish against enslaved indigenous people, Benzoni claimed that women were used for sex and then sold away, even pregnant, "without any conscience" (11–12). As with their other excesses, he portrayed the Spanish as indiscriminate rapists who compromised their health in the process. According to Benzoni, "nor was there a girl but had been violated by the depredators; wherefore, from much indulgence, many Spaniards entirely lost their health" (8).

Spanish abuse of enslaved natives and rape of indigenous women signified a barbarism caused by their unchecked greed. The association between venery and gluttony in other Christian travel narratives was due to the fact that Christians associated cannibals' desire for human flesh with sexual desire, which in some cases led to assimilation and incorporation into American cultures. Jean de Lery reported that some Frenchmen who had spent years in the Americas had taken to "accommodating themselves to the natives and leading the lives of atheists." In so doing, he claimed, they not only gave up Christian identity and "polluted themselves by all sorts of lewd and base behavior among the women and girls . . . but some of them, surpassing the savages in inhumanity, even boasted in my hearing of having killed and eaten prisoners."[58] These Frenchmen had willingly slipped their Christian identities and gone native. Andre Thevet, a Catholic member of the same French community at Fort Coligny in Brazil, observed that there was a direct connection between being devoured by cannibals and taking an indigenous wife. Thevet claimed that prisoners "shall be very well treated, a few days after shall be given him a wife . . . he is served with the best meats that can be found, minding to fatten him like a crammed Capon against he shall die."[59] Christians feared that acceptance of food and women prepared them for assimilation into the host culture through an initiation rite that was either literally or symbolically cannibalistic.[60] To resist this, the Christians at Fort Coligny were forbidden "upon pain of death" to accept the gift of "a maid to minister unto [their] necessaries."[61]

To Benzoni, women were either victims of brutality and rape or ominous warnings against such lapses. During a visit to Cumana, Venezuela, "there came an Indian woman, a wife of one of the principal chiefs of the province with a basket-full of fruit, such a woman as I have never before nor since seen the like of; so that my eyes could not be satisfied by looking at her for wonder" (4). Benzoni's wonder, like his disgust, was a visceral response to this woman's body, which had been transformed by her indigenous fashion. He described her "as old, painted black, with long hair down to her waist." This body had been deformed, "her earrings so weighted her ears down, as to make them reach her shoulders, a thing wonderful to see; she had them split down the middle and filled with rings of a certain carved wood." In addition to this, "her nails were immoderately long, her teeth were black, her mouth large, and she had a ring in her nostrils called by them Caricori; so that she appeared like a monster to us, rather than a human being." Ever conscious of indigenous female embodiment, Benzoni added that "she was quite naked, except where modesty forbids, such being the custom throughout the country" (4).

In the accompanying woodcut, the Cumana woman's body and the basket of fruit were cut with the same basket weave, indicating her darker skin and visually associating the basket of food with her body. Just as "gluttony paved the way to lust," the narrative and illustration implicitly linked the Cumana woman's nakedness, indigenous fashion, and the strange fruit she offered, as a woman and as a hostess, to the risk of transformation for the body.[62] Christians viewed indigenous women with ambivalence. As cultural intermediaries who might feed and seduce them, native women were a gateway for either colonization or assimilation into native cultures. The invitation to those open to partaking of Cumana culture was represented by the Edenic reference of the basket of fruit. However, like the "dirty things" indigenous people served, the "monster" Benzoni made of the Cumana woman also warned against the physiological and spiritual consequences of succumbing to this new fall.

In Benzoni's view, the Spanish had not only decimated that region environmentally and culturally, they had shamelessly crossed religious and sexual lines. He was critical of the Spaniards he traveled with because they were gluttonous—for the products of their conquest, including slaves, gold, and women. In his view, they were transformed by devouring America because in assimilating the land, its people, and their commodities they had lost their way and acted barbarically. In Benzoni's view, the Spaniards he observed had been corrupted, transformed, and even endangered by the fruits of their conquest. This association between food indigenous women prepared, which was polluted with their hair and saliva and thus their bodies, was part of Benzoni's criticism of Spaniards' exploitation of women's bodies. His horror at those transgressions was in part expressed through his rejection of indigenous foods and the implication of women's bodies in that food and wine during their preparation.

The assimilation of Native American food bore more than an allegorical relation to the dynamics of conquest and colonialism: though Spain had devoured this region and its people, the Spanish had been changed by what they took in, including American gold, slaves, women, bread, and wine. In this predator/prey relationship between Spanish and indigenous Americans, Benzoni saw the consequences of colonialism. By taking a critical view of Spanish and indigenous excess, Benzoni distanced himself from both the Spanish and Native Americans. His narrative was in part about the ruin of Spaniards who had indulged themselves, intoxicated by wealth, power, and the bloodlust of wolves among sheep. This warning would have been integral to his book's attraction among Protestants. It was about going wild and men who had abandoned themselves to barbarism. Thus it foretold the fall of the Spanish Empire.

More than that, Benzoni's disgust at indigenous American foods was an expression of his Christian affinity and the internalization of European norms of diet and sociability.[63] In the early modern European nutritional system, overconsumption, eating native food or drinking native wine, put Christian bodies at the risk of going native.[64] Benzoni's disgust toward native food was part of a larger refusal of mixing with indigenous people in order to preserve Christian identity, which he saw compromised by the Spanish practices of slavery, rape, and brutality. Benzoni found a third way to travel in America with his Christian identity unscathed. He neither went native nor succumbed to unchecked colonialist greed. As he had written, in the first pages of his *History of the New World*, he was "as desirous to see men and countries, as to become rich" (2–3). He avoided indigenous bread, wine, and women and kept a critical distance, observing rather than immersing himself in all he saw.

Notes

1. Benzoni, *History of the New World*, 10.
2. Ibid., 83–84.
3. Ibid., 86–87. Benzoni also thought American chocolate seemed "more suited for pigs than for men" (150).
4. Whatley, "Food and the Limits of Civility"; Martel, "Hans Staden's Captive Soul" and "Ferocious Appetites."
5. Benzoni, *History of the New World*, 1.
6. W. H. Smith, "Translators Introduction," in ibid., i.
7. Among the other Catholic narratives De Bry published was a richly illustrated edition of Bartholomé de las Casas's *Brevísima relación de la destrucción de las Indias*, later translated into English as *A Brief Account of the Destruction of the Indies* and subtitled *Or, a faithful NARRATIVE OF THE Horrid and Unexampled Massacres, Butcheries, and all manner of Cruelties, that Hell and Malice could invent, committed by the Popish Spanish Party on the inhabitants of West-India* (Cornhil, near the Stocks-Market, 1689).
8. Elwood, *The Body Broken,* 119.
9. Quoted in Elwood, *The Body Broken,* 13, who cites "the passage from the so-called Confession of Berenger of 1059, which was prepared for him by Humbert Cardinal of Silva Candida," n. 4.
10. Elwood, *The Body Broken,* 15.
11. Ibid., 12.
12. Ibid., 103, 130.
13. Eden, *The Early American Table.*
14. Ibid., 10, 23.
15. Albala, *Eating Right in the Renaissance,* 65–66, 73.
16. Eden, *The Early American Table,* 20.

17. Lery, *History of a Voyage,* 75.

18. Staden, *The True History,* 36; Andre Thevet, *The New Found Worlde, or Antarctike* (London: Benrie Byneeman, for Thomas Hackett, 1568), 32.

19. Acosta, *Natural and Moral History,* 199.

20. Benzoni, *History,* 84.

21. Acosta, *Natural and Moral History,* 199; Thevet, *New Found Worlde,* 32; Lery, *History of a Voyage,* 74–75; Staden, *The True History,* 36; and Benzoni, *History,* 84.

22. Eden, *The Early American Table,* 9–22.

23. Rozin and Fallon, "A Perspective on Disgust," 23; Rozin et al., "Disgust," 66, 69, 73; Albala, *Eating Right in the Renaissance,* 4; and Eden, *The Early American Table,* 60.

24. Albala, *Eating Right in the Renaissance,* 65–66, 73.

25. Whatley, "Food and the Limits of Civility," 392–393.

26. Lery, *History of a Voyage,* 77.

27. Janet Whatley distinguishes between "ordinary" and "sacramental" uses of food in the preservation of Christian identity in the New World. Whatley, "Food and the Limits of Civility," 391.

28. Lery, *History of a Voyage,* 49.

29. Ibid., 49.

30. Whatley, "Food and the Limits of Civility," 390–391.

31. Staden, *The True History,* 135–136.

32. Lery, *History of a Voyage,* 77.

33. Frisch, "In a Sacramental Mode," 85.

34. Quoted ibid.

35. Ibid., 84.

36. Pedro Ramirez de Aguila, translated by and quoted in Abercrombie, *Pathways of Memory and Power,* 270.

37. Frisch, "In a Sacramental Mode," 84.

38. Quoted in Elwood, *The Body Broken,* 16.

39. Florimund de Raemond, quoted in Frisch, "In a Sacramental Mode," 84.

40. Elwood, *The Body Broken,* 18–19.

41. Lery, *History of a Voyage,* 133. Translator (Janet Whatley), n. 15, p. 246: "Probably a sardonic reference to the Catholic doctrine of the Real Presence, that of Christ in the bread and wine of the Eucharist, by transubstantiation."

42. Hoffmann, "Anatomy of the Mass," 209.

43. Quoted ibid., 210.

44. Lery, *History of a Voyage,* 128; Whatley, "Food and the Limits of Civility," 391. The question of whether indigenous Americans actually practiced cannibalism is up for debate. For further discussion, see Martel, "Hans Staden's Captive Soul."

45. Elwood, *The Body Broken,* 15.

46. Staden, *True History,* 135–36.

47. Lery, *History of a Voyage,* 75.

48. Ibid.

49. Abercrombie, *Pathways of Memory,* 107; Martin, "Old People, Alcohol and Identity in Europe" ; "During the period of Christianization of Peru, etc., exhortations as to the

abuse of chicha formed a large part of the sermons of the missionaries." Louis, *Phantastica*, 142; Fussell, *The Story of Corn*, 249.

50. Lery, *History of a Voyage,* 76.

51. Thomas Harriot, *A Briefe and True Report of the New Found Land of Virginia* (New York: Dover, 1972), 61.

52. Le Moyne, in Lorant, *The New World,* text to image 27.

53. Eden, *The Early American Table.*

54. Harriot, *A Briefe and True Report,* 61.

55. Le Moyne, *The New World,* text to image 27.

56. Harriot, *A Briefe and True Report,* 61.

57. Henry William Smyth, "Translator's Introduction," in Benzoni, *History of the New World,* i–ii. At least it hadn't been translated into Spanish by 1857, when Smyth wrote this introduction. For more on the reception of Benzoni's text, see Benjamin Schmidt, *Innocence Abroad*, 46–47. "The concomitant Hapsburg plundering of the treasure houses of Italy and America during the sixteenth century make it only natural that the Italian-born Benzoni might have adopted a somewhat skeptical, if not cynical, view of Spain's 'mission' overseas" (52).

58. Lery, *History of a Voyage,* 128. Whatley, "Food and the Limits of Civility," 391–392.

59. Thevet, *New Found Worlde,* 61.

60. Martel, "Hans Staden's Captive Soul."

61. Thevet, *New Found Worlde,* 65.

62. Miller, "Gluttony," 95.

63. Rozin et al., "Disgust," 77.

64. Eden, *The Early American Table,* 58.

Enlightened Fasting

Religious Conviction, Scientific Inquiry, and Medical Knowledge in Early Modern France

Sydney Watts

In 1698 the archbishop of Rouen received news of highly irregular activity at the Benedictine abbey in Le Tréport on the channel coast of northern France. Members of the monastic order had offered "the forbidden flesh" during Lent with the claim that it was a proper food for the holy fast. According to the parish priest who exposed the sinful behavior, the animal in question (a puffin) was in keeping with the dietary laws of the Catholic Church. Not only was this species truly fatty, but its natural habitat was as much terrestrial as aquatic, its feathery features more avicular than pisciform. The puffin's morphology posed a problem of taxonomy for the monks who identified the animal as a source of protein akin to fish but not of the family of warm-blooded birds. The archbishop did not delve into the semantics of their observations, but ruled its consumption to be highly unorthodox: Such a proposal would be abusive to the spiritual discipline of the monks, as it breeched the rules of religious fasting that set the Lenten season apart from the meat-laden meals prepared for Carnival and feast days. His written response—to be read from the pulpits of all the local parishes—was swift and unequivocal, putting an end to what seemed to be a minor dispute. The investigation that ensued with the intent to appeal the ruling must have taken the parish priest by surprise: not only did it involve the Benedictine brothers who, familiar with puffins that nested along their rocky coast, cried fish not fowl, but also the doctors from the medical college in Rouen who convened to study the biological and nutritional properties of puffins over the course of several weeks of culinary experiments. These findings, presented at the clerical assembly at Saint-Ouen in April, convinced the archbishop to overturn his decision.[1]

The multifarious efforts of both scientific and holy circles to categorize the esoteric as not only edible but sacrosanct bring into focus one of the central problems in early modern religious life: how acts of piety changed during the Enlightenment with the focus on rational, scientific understandings of the world. The abbey's investigation of puffins reveals how a reformulated taxonomy of taboo foods confronted the rules of the Lenten fast. During this forty-day period of abstinence, the Church dictated what Catholics (and among the reformed communities what many Protestants) could not eat,[2] what dishes cooks should prepare in place of meat, poultry, and dairy products as well as when butcher stalls would be closed to the public. In this instance, eating such an unusual bird challenged the communal tradition of Lent as a time of penance and fasting that prepared Christians for the Easter season. Yet, as Caroline Walker Bynum has shown through her study of the medieval cult of the Eucharistic host, the religious meanings of food and hunger are historical notions contingent upon intellectual understandings of piety. For the patristic poets and theologians of the early Church, "hunger meant human vulnerability, which God comforted with food, or it meant human self-control, adopted in an effort to keep God's commandments," while in the high Middle Ages "hunger was unquenchable desire; it was suffering."[3] In seventeenth- and early eighteenth-century France, Lenten food habits were under attack because they revealed as much about a believer's commitment to divine inspiration as his rational understandings of dietary nutrition. This chapter examines the collaboration of both holy and scientific circles to highlight the complex interplay of religious and secular thought. More often than not, those who upheld traditional notions of the Lenten fast were also well versed in the latest theories of digestion. Their commitment to religious dietary law varied according to different beliefs about its influence over the body and the soul. The doctors and theologians who debated over which dietary regime best maintained good health also came into conflict over the proper penitential response to Lent as preparation for Holy Week and Easter Sunday.[4]

Viewed within a broader scope, the problem of maintaining the Lenten fast, especially in urban areas, became increasingly visible to contemporaries as individuals blatantly ignored, abused, or transgressed the Church's commands. And, as the eighteenth century progressed, critics of the Church (led by its premiere spokesman, Voltaire) contributed to the desacralization of Lent as they voiced opinions about the hypocrisy and injustice of its dietary rules. In his *Philosophical Dictionary*, under the entry "Lent," Voltaire poses the question directly: "Why, on days of abstinence, does the Roman Church consider it a sin to eat terrestrial animals, and a good work to be served with sole and salmon? The rich Papist who has five hundred francs' worth of fish on his table shall be saved, and the poor wretch dying with hunger who has eaten four *sous'* worth of salt pork, shall be damned."[5] The eighteenth-century philosophe aimed his critique of the "absurd law" at the blind followers of Christian legalism. His acerbic wit, which decried "the aversion of bishops to omelets," breeched the respectful boundaries kept by earlier thinkers of the French Enlightenment such as Descartes, who avoided any attack on the dominant religion's obligatory credence and obedience.

Looking to Voltaire and other French philosophes, historians have argued that by the mid eighteenth century there emerged a new public sphere led by an educated elite whose exercise of skepticism and critical judgment tipped the scales toward an irreversible process of secularization in France. This chapter follows recent scholarship that challenges secularization construed as a determinate historical process, triumphed by the Age of Reason.[6] It aims to reveal an earlier phase of the Enlightenment where men collaborated fruitfully in the reasoned pursuit to better the human condition, where scientists and clerics sought divine purpose in the study of human health and physiological function, and where dietary choices held moral bearing upon those who willingly and knowingly made them. Rather than seeing the Lenten fast as an autocratic prescription based on Church dogma, these men examined dietary choices in light of biological evidence and sought ways to unite Christian precepts of fasting with medical knowledge of nutrition and physiology. Their search for a viable food choice points to the common insistence of clergy in this period of Catholic Enlightenment claiming that Christianity and reason complemented each other as part of the divine plan to be followed.

FRENCH CATHOLIC REFORM

While many studies have focused on France as the center of the Enlightenment, a place where religious skepticism took the most radical turn, most historians agree that France remained a stronghold of Catholic orthodoxy during the Reformation. Evidence of religious piety existed throughout France under Louis XIV and continued, according to John McManners, well into the eighteenth century.[7] Likewise, Church reform, which brought a revitalization of Catholicism in France, began with the Council of Trent (1545–63) and continued to be implemented by Crown and Church throughout this period. These reforms aimed primarily at the Protestant challenge to Christian orthodoxy, in particular the meaning and execution of the sacraments and the question of faith versus works in gaining salvation. Intending to reinvigorate faith among believers and uphold Catholic orthodoxy, Church leaders sought ways to reeducate the clergy and laity in basic Christian tenets, as well as renew liturgical and penitential practices to which the Catholic Church held fast. While not central to their teachings, Tridentine decrees underscored Lent as a sacred time of penitence which required believers to follow specific forms of religious observance in order to reconcile themselves with God.[8] Yet, even as the Roman Church defended Christian tradition, they followed the Protestants' shift from the legalistic understanding of penitential acts to win salvation to more spiritually driven expressions of personal piety, fasting among them, by decreasing the number of official fasting days throughout the year under the Tridentine decrees.

Further relaxation of Lenten rules could be seen as eggs, butter, and cheese, which had been forbidden during Lent, were now approved for popular consumption by ecclesiastical authorities on a handful of occasions. Historians have pointed to the Church's moderate attitude toward dietary law, particularly in regard to collective dispensations as evidence of the waning of the Lenten fast. Yet the evidence is not convincing. During a period of eighty-four years, from 1670 to 1754, the Church granted permission for the laity to eat eggs during Lent only eighteen times. These dispensations were not granted willingly. They were accorded once the lieutenant of police had addressed the Parliament of Paris with a case for the dearth of fish and vegetables. If the magistrates agreed, and the Parliament endorsed the proposal, then it went to the archbishop of Paris to pray for a dispensation for Parisians. The prelate responded with a *mandement,* which had to be executed by the Parliament under a legal decree (*arrêt*). Such lengthy procedures made blanket dispensations difficult to obtain.[9]

French Catholicism was renewed during the decades of reform that followed Trent, most directly through the hundreds of newly established seminaries and religious communities devoted to clerical education as well as the primary education of young men and women. Chief among these orders were the Jesuits (founded in 1540) and the Ursulines (founded in 1535, established as a convent in 1612 in Paris), who sought official sanction from their "most Christian King." Jesuits pursued scholarship in humanistic studies and scientific inquiry as well as theology and played a large role in the care of souls as private confessors to kings and queens as well as numerous religious chapters and parishes. The confessional impact of teaching orders was felt broadly among the laity as the priests, monks, and nuns who served them focused on the moral status and interior life of individuals. Sexual sins and gluttony now seemed more dangerous than economic sins like avarice or usury. Even penance was understood as less a "restitution" that would reintegrate one into the Christian community than a process of coming to feel a true sense of contrition for sins. Historians such as John Bossy have argued that the Reformation ended communal Christianity, creating in its place a more introspective, self-disciplined religious practice that saw greater emphasis on meditation and prayer.[10]

The Congregation of Saint Maur (established in 1621) followed the wave of reformed clergy who sought new rules in the wake of Catholic revival.[11] Their reinvigorated monasticism swept through a number of religious houses in northern France, including the puffin-eating monks of Le Tréport mentioned at the opening of this chapter. By the end of the century, the congregation had become the largest branch of the Benedictine order in France, the greatest concentration of which dominated upper Normandy. Benedictine Maurists, as they were commonly known, valued scientific study and classical scholarship as well as strict forms of piety. Over nearly two centuries they produced monumental tomes on history, theology, philosophy, and diplomacy, which earned these scholarly monks a reputation for their arduous, intellectual work, *travailler à la benedictine*. The Maurist movement of the seventeenth century also sought greater emphasis on liturgical practices, which regulated their lives throughout the day and the calendar year. The congregation focused on self-discipline, encouraging monks to practice acts of mortification, denying themselves not only meat but even fish. Its zeal for reform hearkened back to the original intentions of Saint Benedict's Rule, which focused on fasting and abstinence as a way of gaining spiritual acuity through the depletion of bodily pleasure.

Even as fasting implies total abstinence from food and drink, the stomachs of most well-provisioned religious men and women, however, were never empty for more than a day. Even the mendicant orders were permitted to sustain themselves with *parvitas materiae* (literally, the "slightness of matter"), which was a small quantity of nourishment such as bread and vegetables not to exceed eight ounces, a quantity of sustenance that by definition did not break the fast. Other relaxations of the fast included an evening drink, known as the *collation,* which could mean a light meal with water or, in many monasteries, beer, wine, or fortified wine. Many parishes that lacked the funds to pay orators to preach during Lent attracted them with food. Even behind the cloistered walls of monasteries *la collation du prédicateur* was an excuse for monks to entertain numerous guests and sample various wines. Convents enticed guest preachers with detailed descriptions of their accommodations to encourage competition for the residential position: "for 40 days he will enjoy . . . the compliments of vicars and minor clergy, will sit down at well furnished tables where they will offer him the choicest morsels. . . . He may very well never fast at all, and Lent will end all too quickly for him." [12]

CHANGING TASTES AND HEALTH CONCERNS

While some may have seen Lent as a season to indulge in a whole other variety of foods, many more Christians felt the strains of a Lenten fast that focused on the meagerness and monotony of eating root vegetables, legumes, and salted fish for six weeks, especially the much loathed red herring of northern Europe. With the development of trade routes and commercial life throughout the interior of France, green vegetables and fresh fish became more prevalent in the market stalls of major cities. Yet, even with the rise of more innovative cookery after 1650, a vegetarian or fish-based diet was most often associated with self-denial and penitence.

Public rituals, such as the "au revoirs" of Saint-Rémy, where clerics on their way to church paraded (and tried to squash) salt herring tied on a string, aimed to ease the affliction with humor.[13] Indeed, the association of Lent with austerity and deprivation, a time that was entered into with some sinking of the heart, is evident in the common seventeenth-century expression *face de carême,* meaning pale, dower, or glum.[14]

Even as both vegetable and fish recipes gained prominence in the new culinary fashion forwarded by cookbook authors La Varenne and Nicolas de Bonnefons, the royal court at Versailles continued to regard them as penitential foods, serving them almost exclusively during Lent and especially on Good Friday. By the end of the seventeenth century, we see a clear division between the court's traditionalism and the innovation of Parisian cooks whose "nouvelle cuisine" became the trend for urbane men and women of taste who sought the natural flavors of foods, lighter preparations, and fewer courses served in more intimate settings.[15] Their search for refinement extended beyond royal banquets to Parisian salons where they could cultivate what was "convivial, genteel, well-bred and morally decent all at once."[16]

As much as elites tempered their diet with fish, poultry, and vegetables, the vast majority of the working population, especially in the Parisian metropolis, sought meat as part of their daily diet. Most French in the early modern period considered some form of red meat to be vital in maintaining good health. Bouillon had long been the prescription for the infirm and the mainstay of hospitals. Meat broth's restorative powers made it the most popular treatment for a number of conditions including malnourishment. Nearly every major city in France supported a Lenten butchery at the central hospital where the sick, the aged (over seventy), and the young (under twenty-one) as well as pregnant and nursing mothers could purchase freshly butchered meat.[17] Most statutes dictated that parish priests grant personal dispensations to allow access to the Lenten butcheries, but in 1657 the Parliament of Paris gave physicians the authority to prescribe meat during Lent. These allowances meant that any person seeking the restorative powers of bouillon no longer needed to submit to an examination of one's conscience in front of a priest, but could, instead, present one's bodily complaints to a doctor. Historians have made much of this change in procedure as evidence of the relaxation of dietary law, which not only fueled business for the city hospitals in Paris and Lyon but also spurred the growth of an even larger black market among experienced butchers and itinerant meat sellers.[18] This widespread fraud became an embarrassment to Church leaders who saw their authority over dispensations vanish, citing more vice than virtue in religious practice. Likewise, it was a frustration for the urban police who could not contain the steady flow of rogue butchers entering the city to sell meat out of courtyards. As enforcement waxed and waned over the eighteenth century, the French were deeply conflicted over dietary law. Yet, even under the "debauched" reigns of the Duke d'Orléans and Louis XV, policing and arrests continued.[19]

Finally, in 1774, the government responded to the abuses by granting any licensed merchant the right to sell meat during Lent and allowing all food merchants to keep their shops open throughout the year. The royal declaration ended the monopoly that the city hospital, l'Hotel Dieu, held over the Lenten meat trade, while it emphasized the pragmatic necessity of liberalizing commerce. The reasons given are for the public good (especially for the poor) and to end exclusive privilege, "having become more onerous than profitable" and "being only prejudicial to the Public by its abuses when resulted necessarily from them, by numerous [instances of] fraud, etc." The decree also required all Parisians to conform to the "Laws of the Church," which permitted the consumption of meat "according to the conditions prescribed by them."[20] Whereas authorities could be accused of accommodating the sacrilegious behavior of business-minded merchants, the royal declaration saw fit to hold to the religious tenets of dietary law, giving Parisians the choice of eating or fasting according to their own physical and spiritual needs.

The transfer of authority from the parish priest to the physician granted by the Paris Parliament in 1657 was by no means automatic nor clear-cut. Doctors now held the responsibility of determining whether or not a person was "fit" to fast. This very choice, by law, rested primarily on the physical needs and temperament of a particular patient and secondarily on his or her religious obligation. Nearly seventy years later, the dean of the medical faculty published a stern reminder of doctors' rights over Lenten prescriptions, reminding each *curé* that he could not give a dispensation to a parishioner without an official medical certificate from a doctor.[21]

Reading a patient for his or her illness meant taking into consideration the major organs and bodily humors in conjunction with the environment and lifestyle that either maintained or offset a patient's temperament. This practice of medicine followed the Galenic tradition, which

considered the human physical condition as a careful balancing act between health and illness. Good health meant practicing moderation in
the use of the non-naturals: air temperature and quality, sleep habits, the
passions and emotions, and, most especially, a dietary regime. As much
as doctors understood the importance of dietetics to prevent illness and
maintain good health, their focus remained on the categories of foods
that could pollute or corrupt a given constitution. This Galenic paradigm
directed their thinking toward an individualist view of health and its con-
servation, away from any universal definitions based upon human physiology and nutrition. Even as new understandings about the digestive
process gained ground among the scientific community, many physicians
either ignored them or adapted them to the Galenic theory. Historian of
science Mary Lindemann argues that this tendency to revert to Galen's
humoral terms drew on "a broad substratum of common beliefs about
health, illness, and therapeutics that most members of society shared."[22]

However rudimentary their knowledge of actual biological functions,
most doctors believed that certain foods enriched the blood better than
others and commonly used food therapy to cure a variety of conditions.
Eating fresh, red meat was commonly considered the best way to nourish
the body, as the doctors considered its essences particularly rich. The sanguine qualities of meat had a powerful effect on the bodily humors. But
eating too much of it was potentially dangerous because it corrupted the
body's delicate balance. If it remained too long in the stomach, red meat
could overpower the liver, the organ thought responsible for making good
blood that nourishes all parts of the body. According to one of the early
treatises on dietetics, *Le Thresor de santé* (1607), beef was high in caustic
properties; it "engendered a very crude blood, from which those who are
of natural melancholy derive different maladies," and "the frequent usage
of this meat engenders cankers, tumors, itching, leprosy, quatrain fever,
or turgidity of the spleen accompanied by dropsy." [23] Eating too many
vegetables was likewise seen as a potential health threat, for its choleric
qualities brought on flatulence, colic, fluxes, and dysentery.

Most doctors who followed the theory of non-naturals, and the growing number of readers who subscribed to the literature that abounded
on the topic, focused on maintaining a proper regimen appropriate to
one's humoral temperament, age, and activity. So the heat generated by
eating meat was appropriate for laborers, who expended great amounts
of energy, and lactating and pregnant women, who depleted more than
their normal amount of vital fluids. Galen spoke of the curative pow-

ers derived from the essence (*le suc*) of red meat, prescribed to pregnant women as its sanguine characteristics were thought to be an essential component of reproduction. For the aged, meat was necessary to maintain thick blood that restores health and prolongs life. Popular medical treatises also pointed out the dangers of beef, as the vulgar quality of this particular meat made it unworthy for the more sedentary members of the social elite. These medical prescriptions continued well into the eighteenth century, found in popular dietary regimes that cited beef as "very healthy (*saine*) and with a very good taste. It contains the coarse juices that, once condensed in the fibers, do not easily separate; it is why those who eat lots of beef are strong, vigorous, and robust." In the same way, meat gives energy to an active person, for a sedentary person, meat contracts (*resserre*) the body, leading to "harmful blockages" whose cure required diuretics and other forms of purgation. [24]

Even as popular medicine clung to Galenic theory, increasingly in the seventeenth and early eighteenth centuries, doctors understood digestion as central to bodily health. Often diagnoses were focused on poor digestion as the trigger of illness that corrupted the blood and generated bad and foul humors. Scientific investigation into digestive health was well underway by the mid seventeenth century, most notably in the laboratory work published by René Descartes, Francis Glisson, Giovanni Borelli, and Franciscus Sylvius de Le Boë.[25] Their findings about this biological function would subvert the conventional wisdom about diet and therapeutics that had reigned for nearly two millennia. Most significantly, they demonstrated the chemical properties of food and the physical ways in which food was broken down in the digestive system. Their pioneering work in laboratory science and their critical reading of natural philosophy led them to adapt their observations to theories about humors and physiology in various ways, arriving at different therapies for the same condition. Doctors now had to consider competing theories about the chemical and mechanical processes of digestion and the absorption of food. By the early eighteenth century, the point of contention was as much theological and medical, as the debates over digestion turned to the doctor's role in prescribing or dispensing with a Lenten diet.

DOCTORS DEBATE THE LENTEN DIET

By the end of the seventeenth century, there was little dispute among doctors over the anatomical structure of the digestive organs or the fact that food transformed into chyle in the stomach and then passed via the lacteal ducts to the bloodstream. At issue was the actual process by which food was broken down and metabolized in the bloodstream. The older, more established school of iatrochemists, led by Jan van Helmont and Franciscus Sylvius de la Boë, explained digestion as a result of acid-alkali fermentation—a "dangerous fermentation"—that took place in the stomach. The process of digestion continued as nutrients were absorbed through a metaphysical process of assimilation of matter-and-spirit, whereby material changes were governed by a spiritual agency Helmont called *Blas*. While iatrochemists held to the older physiology of assimilation, drawn from Aristotlian models of the nutritive or vegetal soul where food was converted into humors and spirits, they also recognized the importance of saliva and pancreatic secretions in the digestive process.

The opposing school of iatromechanics, or iatrophysics, led by Giovanni Borelli followed the laws of physics and precise mathematical rules. Digestion was explained not as a chemical change effected by fermentation but as a physical change effected by grinding. These mechanical interpretations were often characterized as purely functional and less metaphysically driven, which may have exposed some iatrophysicists to unmerited criticism by old-school iatrochemists. The points at issue between these two systems of thought proved to be much more than academic, as opponents sought religious and moral reasons to discredit each side in various publications.

In the early 1700s these two scientific schools became the center of a public debate in the *Mémoires de Trévoux*, a journal that reviewed physiology books, particularly those that offered chemical explanations of digestion. The newspaper's name came from its place of publication, which also happened to be the French base of the Jesuit religious order. Discussions often turned to the relative importance of a meat-based diet for well-read, polite society, especially for those valetudinary creatures who claimed dispensations for health reasons. In 1700, the Paris physician, Barthélemy Linand, attacked the equivocations of lapsed believers, arguing that corporeal delicacy was no adequate reason to grant dispensations. Linand contended that Catholics should exert more self-discipline and fast more regularly without the Church's imposition of dietary rules. The reviewer of Linand's book concurred, while engaging in playful casuistry, "nowadays when the laxity of Christians is so great, one is obliged to Mr. Linand for removing the vain pretexts which they use to avoid the painful duties that Religion imposes on them."[26]

Such discussions took a more heated turn in 1709 when Philippe Hecquet, doctor at the Paris medical faculty, published his treatise on Lenten dispensations (*Traité des dispenses du Carême*) to proclaim the moral bankruptcy of the Church and to radically change the food habits of the French. His argument was rebutted the following year in an anonymous work actually written by a fellow faculty member and rival, Nicolas Andry de Boisregard. Andry was three years Hecquet's senior. Both had attended the College des Grassins in Paris, perhaps as classmates. Both obtained their first medical degrees from Reims and then entered the medical faculty within a few years of one another. Hecquet served as dean of faculty in 1712 and Andry became dean in 1724. Even though the two shared career paths, they followed opposing sets of religious convictions and scientific leanings. Andry, an iatrochemist, whose opinions echoed many of the Jesuit editors of the *Memoires de Trevoux,* held more Molinist leanings characterized by Jesuit teachings that minimized the fallen nature of man and emphasized his residual goodness. Hecquet, an iatrophysicist, was a Jansenist who served at Port-Royal-des-Champs, a well-known center of Jansenism, before coming to the Paris faculty. Jansenism stressed the depravity of man as a result of his fall from grace. God only bestowed efficacious grace to those elect who engaged in unremitting labor of good works and self-denial.[27] For a Jansenist, fasting was an authentic expression of religious devotion that followed Cartesian dualism: in order to elevate the soul one needed to quell the needs of the body. For a Jesuit, fasting was maintained as a traditional practice, but not by embracing physical pain and bodily deprivation in ways that bordered on religious fanaticism. Hecquet would hold to his own ascetic principles throughout his lifetime in ways that informed his scientific understandings of the body and his medical prescriptions for dietary health.[28]

For Hecquet and Andry, their opposing religious beliefs informed their opposing views of physiology. While Hecquet may have imbued scientific causation with divine providence later in his career, his early publication of the 1709 *Traité* took a less godly focus; rather, it stressed the mechanical explanation of digestion and the qualities of food that promoted good health. Aside from his social critique of Lenten practices, and his theological defense of them, the treatise promoted a new digestive theory of "trituration" that emphasized the grinding action of mastication and peristalsis of the muscle walls of the stomach. Hecquet regarded trituration as the primary biological function of contraction and dilation, as the force that regulates the body—food had no regulatory affect. Hecquet, like other physicians, had been influenced by the works of early modern physiologists Giovanni Borelli and Archibald Pitcairn who abandoned iatrochemical explanations and replaced them with physical explanations of digestion.[29] Mechanical trituration of food, in particular, posed a direct challenge to the Galenic suppositions of many doctors of the age who explained nutrition and dietary health in terms of humoral effect. Nonetheless, Hecquet paid attention to diet insofar as one food could be more easily digested than another. Yet, unlike popular medical opinion, he regarded vegetables and fish to be superior foods because of their material composition, which was easily broken down through trituration. According to Hecquet's medical opinion, the bodily effect of a Lenten diet was not simply benign; it was healthful and prolonged life better than a meat-based diet. Later in his career, Hecquet would credit the origins of this biological process to the Creator; the all-encompassing, life force of trituration that alternated between contraction and dilation was due to God's personal intervention.[30]

In his *Traité des alimens de caresme*, Andry challenged Hecquet's findings on all fronts. Trained as an apothecary in the provinces, then later as a chemist, he forwarded his iatrochemical view of digestion that emphasized the textures and chemical properties of foods while keeping many Galenic understandings of dietetics. More important for Andry than Hecquet's misinterpretation of the digestive process was his promotion of the meatless diet as superior to all others. If fish and vegetables were as healthful and pure as Hecquet claimed, what purpose was there for the tradition of Lent? Andry asked. The Church's prohibition of meat resided on the widely accepted view that meat nourished the body better than any other food and that fish and vegetables were watery, "cold" foods that hampered digestion. Andry contended that meat's energizing effect—the fact that it is "too good a food" and too much of it "fortified the passions"—was precisely the reason the Church demanded a fast that included "lean foods that nourished less well, and, without being harmful in themselves, satisfied the needs of the body a little less."[31]

Claims and counterclaims over the benefits and the reasons for fasting filled their publications over the next six years. While the debaters aimed to limit their discussion to scientific fact, the rifts between their two camps revealed the theological differences upon which they viewed their role as leading physicians of dietary science.[32] Both Hecquet's religious heterodoxy and his newfound medical authority mediated his dietetic reforms for an overindulged clientele, many of whom stigmatized fava beans and root vegetables as not only unhealthy but also socially degrading. Conversely, Andry, who sided with more traditional medical opinion, sought ways for hungry but obedient Catholics to maintain their increasingly refined lifestyle, if not their notion of good health. Seen another way, the high moral tone that characterized this public debate pointed directly to schism in the medical profession, undermined by the intrusion of lay practitioners and barber-surgeons who perpetuated popular misconceptions of the Galenic dietary system for their own gain, while it underscored the Jesuit/Jansenist divide that widened into a partisan conflict between the crown and the judges of Parliament in the mid eighteenth century.

While Andry may have sided with the losing party (the Jesuits were expelled from France in 1764), Hecquet's theologically inspired iatromechanics would soon be discredited by the secular impulse of scientists who led the field of physiology into the nineteenth century. Yet, at this moment when physicians and scientists worked together to address the problem of how best to fast, Andry claimed to have the more reasoned, enlightened view. His moderate stance that, on the one hand, sided with Church orthodoxy in keeping the Lenten fast a liminal experience to separate oneself from the temptations of the world, on the other hand promoted his own "wise discernment" whereby his recommendations neither extolled the virtues of bodily deprivation nor condemned gustatory desires for exotic preparations. Rather, by pursuing the *juste mileu*, Andry explored questions of taxonomy in dietary law on scientific grounds, seeking a broader, more ecologically informed understanding of animal classification and the "correct" interpretation of a given food's role in digestive function. In so doing, Andry applauded those who sought ways to accommodate the special dietary needs of Lenten practitioners (like the Benedictine Maurist of Le Tréport, allergic to salted fish) by finding alternatives to the traditional fast. Andry agreed that the zeal which characterized those who justified fasting as a way of life was not only unenlightened, but prejudicial, as it blinded their ability to make accurate observations about the nature of animal life. Citing Hecquet's objections to the Church's allowance for amphibious creatures such as mackerel, tortoise, and otter, Andry attacked his opponent's flagrant disregard of biological fact as well as his lack of scientific method. Andry then cited the "clearly developed reason" and careful observations upon which the celebrated monks of Le Tréport drew in making their successful case for the dispensation of puffins, along with the laboratory work of medical professionals, all of which, according to Andry, convinced ecclesiastical authorities to reconsider the aquatic bird for Lenten fast "in its infinite wisdom and generosity."

This accommodationist position, one that welcomed scientific pursuit of knowledge as a way to greater wisdom and allegiance for all Catholics, happened to represent the Church's view as well, a point made plain by the royal censors of Andry's treatise. In his forward to Andry's 1713 edition, rector and theologian Berthé of the University of Paris applauded the revised work that "shed light on every corner" of this subject, "giving a double blow to trituration [in ways that] ended up pulverizing the system." Berthé also enticed readers by identifying the two conditions that prevent many from keeping the fast: on the one hand, there is "the blind sensuality, [of the] less enlightened Christian [who] is attached to eating meat [and sees any other food] as a source of corruption and death." On the other hand, Berthé characterized men like Hecquet, "the more spiritual Christian [whose] zealous enthusiasm transforms meat into poison and conveys an excellence and deliciousness to vile vegetables, which claims to infinitely surpass the most exquisite fat and must captivate the refinement of kings."[33]

Andry aimed to discredit Hecquet's findings by emphasizing the role of science and reason. He hoped to convince the reading public that little-known foods could be reclassified through *règles plus sûres*. His exaltation of these "sure" methods did not, however, preclude the role of taste, which determined how to select an appropriate diet. Andry allowed that everyone's tastes differ—at the very least, taste determines what is good or bad for us. By proclaiming taste, on the one hand, relative to an individual's palate and, on the other hand, a mechanism that allows all humans to discern the edible from the inedible, Andry demonstrated a more modern view than the holistic theories of medicine that had directed food therapy for centuries. Such an intellectual departure may reflect Andry's familiarity with Lemery's *Traité des aliments* (1705), a standard food reference in the eighteenth century that systematically categorized foods by their physical properties and sensory qualities, especially taste. Each food entry suggested proper preparation in order to gain the greatest gustatory results. Lemery's work is credited as a turning point in the liberation of dietary science from the culinary preferences of what determined good taste.[34] This liberation did not mean that doctors had abandoned food therapy or that their attention to diet in diagnosing and caring for the body had waned. To be sure, doctors, laymen, and even clergymen remained attuned to the healthful effects of foods. But, increasingly, they saw the importance of the "noblest of senses" and the skills necessary to prepare foods that taste good, like the monks at Le Tréport, whose various preparations of the puffin were done to overcome a fellow brother's disgust for (and vomiting of) salted fish. Their culinary experiments looked to balance flavor and cooking techniques that revealed the fleshy quality of the aquatic fowl as much as it appealed to the more refined palates of the fasting gourmet. According to Jean-Louis Flandrin, taste came to mean "the idea that the quality of a dish is an intrinsic property of the dish itself, independent of the temperament of the person who eats it. Good taste was an objective fact and cooking, as in literature and the other aristocratic arts such as hunting, fencing and dance, had become an object of study for those whose sensibility and acumen excelled in these classical forms as *hommes de gout*."[35]

This "objective fact" did not escape the world of the Jesuits, and the humanist concept of good taste was as familiar to them as the culinary notion of what tasted good. Most famous among these priestly gastronomes being Guillaume-Hyacinthe Bougeant and Pierre Brumoy, who met as fellow contributors to the *Memoires de Trévoux* and, in 1739, contributed their thoughts on the development of haute cuisine through the refinement of the French palate in the preface to the 1742 edition of *Les Dons de Comus* by François Marin, the text that proclaimed the shift from classic to modern through its new definition of taste.[36]

> Cooking, like any other art invented for need or for pleasure, was perfected along with the national genius of each nation and became more delicate as the nations became more polite. . . . Among the civilized nations, progress in cooking followed progress in all the other arts. . . . The Italians civilized all of Europe, and without a doubt it was they who taught us how to eat. . . . Although good cooking has been known in France for more than two centuries, it is fair to say that it has never been as delicate as it is now, or done so properly or with a taste so refined.[37]

Like his Jesuit brothers Bougeant and Brumoy, Andry's willingness to appeal to the validity of one's taste, and his embrace of the widening selection of food preparations and ingredients, demonstrates what was perhaps a more cosmopolitan, if not more "enlightened," interpretation of what diet had become to many discerning French elites. By the end of the eighteenth century, the more individualized notion of what was palatable would eventually win out, as elites sought new tastes and preparations in a burgeoning marketplace. To be sure, consumer-driven tastes in a world of ever increasing choices shaped how individuals moderated their desires for particular foods as Lenten rules became more relaxed after 1774, when the Crown removed barriers to the meat trade that had existed during the forty-day fast. In questioning their blind duty to the Church's teachings, and in searching for more authentic means of atoning for sin, believers encountered a new set of possibilities for keeping the fast, inasmuch as the pursuit of a more refined and discerning sense of taste had contributed to the ways in which the French were learning how to eat.

The Lenten diet was of as much interest to theologians and men of letters as it was to physicians and chemists, with all seeking to better the condition of their clientele, whether for spiritual or bodily needs or both. Their inquiry into the science and tradition of Lent targeted an elite audience often seen as self-indulgent and in need of discipline. While men and women of taste advocated lighter, more refined food habits, the social expectations of this privileged lifestyle too often led its followers to overeating and digestive maladies. Even as the individual made his or her own choice about dietary regimen, these choices carried cultural stigmas and moral consequences that reflected the proclaimed virtues and vices of a society in the midst of dramatic transformation of needs and wants. To be sure, these debates over the meaning and significance of Lenten observances reveal the diversity in religious convictions in early modern France, yet, as we have seen, these differences do not neatly fall into secular versus religious camps. Rather, the understandings of science and theology fed into the intellectual pursuits of physicians and clergy in novel ways, as they sought reasoned justifications for dietary regimes during Lent. The Lenten diet proved to be the centerpiece of a convergence of concerns about health, taste, piety, and penance that were being tested and challenged by competing medical theories and an increasingly vocal world of religious heterodoxy.

Notes

1. For a detailed discussion of the Benedictine study of puffins, see "Dissertation sur le Pilet" published as a separate essay in Andry, *Traité des alimens de caresme*, 475–495.

2. See Mentzer, "Fasting, Piety, and Political Anxiety."

3. Bynum, *Holy Feast and Holy Fast*, 54.

4. See entries "Fast" and "Lent" in *The Catholic Encyclopedia* (New York, 1907–12). For further discussion on medieval practices, see Henisch, *Fast and Feast*, 30–49.

5. *The Portable Voltaire,* ed. Ben Ray Redman (New York: Penguin, 1977), 147.

6. McCleod and Ustorf, *The Decline of Christendom in Western Europe*, 7.

7. McManners, *Church and Society*, 2:96–98, 106–118.

8. Jaroslav Pelikan and Valerie Hotchkiss, eds., *Creeds and Confessions of Faith in the Christian Tradition: Reformation Era*, 4 vols. (New Haven: Yale University Press, 2003), 2:853.

9. Luynes, *Mémoires du duc de Luynes*, 11:59 and 13:183.

10. Bossy, *Christianity in the West*.

11. Robinson, *Regulars and the Secular Realm*, 2.

12. McManners, *Church and Society*, 2:60.

13. Helen Waddell, *The Wandering Scholars* (London: Folio Society, 1970), 150.

14. See Littré, "Carême."

15. Pinkard, *A Revolution in Taste*.

16. Daniel Gordon, *Citizens Without Sovereignty: Equality and Sociability in French Thought, 1670–1789* (Princeton: Princeton University Press, 1994), 74. See also Benadetta Craveri, *The Age of Conversation*, trans. Teresa Waugh (New York: New York Review of Books, 2005), 219–221, 228–230.

17. Documentation in the municipal archives of Lyon, Caen, Marseille, Rouen, as well as Paris, detail the provisioning of Lenten butcheries and the regulation of the urban meat trade during Lent throughout the seventeenth and eighteenth centuries. Most often, city officials contacted with private butchers to supply fresh meat to city hospitals for the infirm as well as those whose physical condition made meat a necessity.

18. Abad, "Une indice de déchristianization?"; Montenach, "Esquisse d'une économie illicite."

19. See police arrests in Paris from 1722 to 1732 in Archives de la Bastille, ms. 10973, 10752, 10980, 10985, 10999, 11069, 11116, 11150, 11151, 11174, 11193, and 11406. Ordinances from 1769, 1775, and 1776 prescribe a fine of three hundred livres for violations Lenten regulations. Bibliothèque nationale de la France, MS français 11355: "Table chronologique des édits, déclarations, arrêts et sentences contenus dans le traité de la Police."

20. Archives de Paris 2AZ2.

21. Letter dated March 5, 1726, in A. Franklin, *La vie privée d'autrefois*, 184.

22. Lindemann, *Medicine and Society in Early Modern Europe*, 11–12.

23. *Le Thresor de santé* (Paris, 1607) as quoted in Flandrin, "From Dietetics to Gastronomy," 421.

24. *The Best and Easiest Method of Preserving Uninterrupted Health to Extreme Old Age: Established upon the justest laws of animal oeconomy and confirmed by the suffrages of the most celebrated practitioners among the ancients and moderns* (London, 1748); translated to the French by L. Preville as *Méthode aisée pour conserver la santé jusqu'à une extreme vieillesse, Fondée sur les Loix de l'oeconomie animale, & les Observations pratiques des meilleurs Médecins, tant anciens que modernes* (Paris, 1752), 78–79.

25. Leake, *Some Founders of Physiology*.

26. *Mémoires pour l'Histoire des sciences*, 32–33.

27. Doyle, *Jansenism*, 21–22.

28. Brockliss, "The Medico-Religious Universe," 191–221.

29. Merton, "Old and New Physiology"; Rothschuh, *History of Physiology*.

30. See Hecquet, *La médecine théologique*.

31. Andry, *Traité des alimens de caresme*, 6.

32. Brockliss claimed that "Hecquet did not only strengthen his medical prejudices through his religious opinions, but also used his science to confirm his theology." See "The Medico-Religious Universe," 215; I would contend that Andry's orthodox views about Lenten practices informed his own writings, which sought religious sources for scientific observation and discovery.

33. Preface to Andry, *Traité des alimens de caresme*.

34. See Flandrin, "From Dietetics to Gastronomy."

35. Ibid., 430–31.

36. Pinkard, *A Revolution in Taste*, 158.

37. See "Avertissement" in Marin, *Suite des Dons de Comus* (Paris, 1742), cited in Flandrin, "From Dietetics to Gastronomy," 430.

CHAPTER 6

THE SANCTITY OF BREAD

MISSIONARIES AND THE PROMOTION OF WHEAT GROWING AMONG THE NEW ZEALAND MAORI

Hazel Petrie

At the beginning of the world, says the book of Genesis, God told man to "be fruitful, and multiply, and replenish the earth," adding that He had given "every herb yielding seed, which is upon the face of all the earth, and every tree in which is every fruit of a tree yielding seed" to be "meat" for humankind.[1] But, for Christians, one seed, not known in all parts of the earth, would assume much greater importance than others. That seed was wheat, and its introduction into New Zealand's indigenous Maori society—largely for secular reasons—would be accompanied by many of its spiritual symbolisms. As bread, however, it did not merely retain its significance for Christian ritual but supplanted an indigenous food staple in certain ceremonies.

When the British navigator Captain James Cook first landed on New Zealand shores in 1769, the Maori inhabitants had no seed crops. Their staple food, the kumara or sweet potato, raised from seeds in their more tropical ancestral homelands in Polynesia, could only be grown from tubers in New Zealand's temperate climate. But, from the time of Cook, European voyagers left behind a number of previously unknown crops—just as they had done elsewhere in the Pacific. They did so in hopes that familiar foodstuffs would be available to them and other Western mariners when they passed that way again. While those early explorers and the occasional whaler were merely fleeting visitors, members of two early French expeditions to New Zealand, those of Jean-François Marie de Surville and Marion du Fresne, reported that the Maori they encountered took an immediate liking to bread and ship's biscuit. As well as white potatoes and other vegetables, British and French explorers left wheat seed behind, but apparently with little instruction as to how to grow or use it. Although the French did attempt the introduction of wheat cultivation into New Zealand, their reports of Maori responses are ambiguous.[2] De Surville felt they had "cast their seed on barren ground," and du Fresne's lieutenant, Julien Marie Crozet, thought Maori "had no more mind for [grain cultivation] than brutes." Yet, Crozet's shipmate, Jean Roux, reported that they were pleased with the French wheat plantings and promised to take great care of them.[3]

Whatever the initial response to wheat at that time, potatoes were a more immediate success. Maori were able to cultivate this root crop using techniques similar to those used to grow the kumara and were soon aware of the economic advantages of growing a product much in demand by visiting European and American ships that called at their ports to reprovision. Potatoes had other advantages as well. Yields were much higher than kumara, which were also vulnerable to frost, prone to rot, and had a limited storage life. Another important factor, however, was the lack of embedded spiritual restraints associated with new cultivars like the potato. The word *taboo,* used in English to mean something forbidden, derives from the Polynesian and Melanesian languages. The New Zealand Maori version is *tapu*, indicating spiritual restriction.

Maori applied a variety of spiritual sanctions to food production and consumption, but especially to the cultivation of kumara, their prized carbohydrate. The men who prepared the ground for planting kumara ornamented their hair and their spades with feathers before planting the tubers in perfectly straight lines on hillocks in holes facing east toward the rising sun. The workers moved along in rows chanting songs to propitiate Rongo, the god of cultivated food. Having finished their work for the day, they washed their hands and then held them over a protective fire before taking their first meal of the day. Carved wooden images, painted with red ochre to signify the state of tapu, were stuck into the ground to warn passers-by not to enter or interfere with the growing plants. No women or slaves were permitted to enter, and only men could take part in the harvesting, which was also attended with important rituals and could not begin before the sun was well up. The introduced white potato, on the other hand, was free of such restrictions.

There are many oral traditions concerning the kumara, but one recounts a fierce argument between two sons of Rangi and Papa (Heaven and Earth, the primeval parents) over a kumara plantation. The upshot was a battle in which Rongomaraeroa (who represented the kumara) was killed, cooked, and eaten by Tumatauenga (who represented man and warfare).[4] Consequently, because food holds the *noa* element, the ability to remove or abrogate tapu, cooked food is an important medium in *whakanoa* (tapu lifting) ceremonies. For example, newly completed meeting houses or other buildings could be rendered safe for use through various rituals including the *tohunga,* or spiritual expert, and an older woman of rank carrying a cooked kumara into the building.

In Maori society, leadership is underpinned by *mana*, a psychic force giving power and prestige, and tapu is the source of that *mana*. The more prestigious the person, the greater their tapu. Despite their status, chiefs still worked alongside their people—making fishing nets, fishing, felling trees, building canoes, planting, and harvesting—but they could not engage in food preparation. Cooked food being so destructive of tapu and chiefs far more vulnerable to those forces, they could not go near ovens or places where it was being prepared or cooked.

However, as the most important crops of both Maori and Europeans were employed in their religious rituals, so, too, were the connections between peace and agriculture common to both cultures. Because kumara was usually eaten on festive occasions and required a state of peace for its cultivation, it was symbolically associated with peace, whereas fern root, a wild plant, was more often connected with warfare. As will be seen, these spiritual aspects of the staple carbohydrate and its associations with peace would eventually allow wheat to take on some of the same connotations in Maori society as it had in the Western world.

In the meantime, however, the early explorers were followed by trading and whaling ships, which began to call at the Bay of Islands in northern New Zealand from about the late 1790s or early 1800s. Although limited, this interaction increased the familiarization of Maori in that area with flour-based products such as ships' biscuit, of which they became very fond. These ship visits aroused Maori curiosity about the wider world, too, and a number of young men took passage to foreign parts. Many signed on as crew on whaling ships, visiting Australia, Europe, and the Americas long before any Europeans had taken up residence in their country. Because it was the most often visited port, a large proportion of those leaving New Zealand shores were from the Bay of Islands area.

One of those who signed on to a whaling ship in 1805 was a young man of chiefly rank called Ruatara. His plan was to reach England and meet with King George III. Although he reached his destination, he was prohibited from disembarking his ship and failed to meet the king. Perhaps worse than that, he was seriously maltreated and abandoned by ships' masters on several occasions. In 1809 he was rescued by Samuel Marsden, the chaplain of New South Wales, who was returning from a visit to England aboard a convict ship called the *Ann*. Finding Ruatara ill and vomiting blood as a consequence of beatings by previous shipmates, Marsden arranged for him to be taken care of and invited him to his home in Sydney. The chief spent eight months there, during which time he realized that introducing wheat cultivation to New Zealand would not only provide his people with a valuable new food source but also an export opportunity. Despite being the staple food of the British population, little wheat was grown in Australia at that time. Once again, Ruatara's first attempt to return to New Zealand—some twelve hundred miles across the treacherous Tasman Sea—was stymied when he was defrauded and abandoned yet again; this time on Norfolk Island. However, around 1812, he did reach his home again—armed with a supply of seed wheat.

Ruatara quickly began distributing the seeds to members of his tribal group, but, because Maori had not previously known any grain crops, his people were incredulous of his claims that it could be used to produce the bread and biscuits they were already familiar with. Their ridicule only increased when, without a mill, he was unable to grind the first wheat that he harvested in 1813. However, things began to change when, in 1814, Marsden sent an advance guard of missionaries to New Zealand to consult with Ruatara about the possibility of establishing a Church Missionary Society (CMS) mission station under his patronage and protection. Marsden had taken this opportunity to send a number of gifts, including a hand-operated flour mill. That mill allowed Ruatara to demonstrate the process of turning wheat into flour, which he is said to have cooked into a cake in a frying pan. This was the breakthrough that allowed him to convince his fellow northern chiefs that his claims were not mere fancy, and he began distributing fresh seed wheat, which Marsden had sent along with the mill, among other chiefs of high rank.

So it was that Maori began growing wheat before the first missionaries set up residence in New Zealand, but Ruatara was still keen to enhance his knowledge and accompanied the missionary delegation when it returned to Sydney. There he spent some five months more studying European agricultural techniques and other skills. Moreover, because the governor of New South Wales and others were keen to establish friendly relations with Maori and ensure that the planned mission was securely founded, they gave him additional gifts including a mare, a cow, and other livestock. These were supplemented by poultry and other useful plants which were brought by the missionaries Thomas Kendall, William Hall, and John King, who arrived with their families in December 1814 to establish the first mission at Ruatara's settlement of Rangihoua in the Bay of Islands.

Sadly, Ruatara died prematurely the following year. Although his successor, Hongi Hika, also grew wheat, he put more effort into extending his production of potatoes, which were in great demand by visiting whalers and trading ships. Mission stations were a very real economic and political asset for the local tribe as their presence encouraged shipping to call most often at those locations. Hongi's control of the missions and the key northern ports allowed him to monopolize trade and accumulate an extensive arsenal of muskets, which gave him significant advantages over his rivals within and well beyond the Northland region. Indeed, his military and political power was such that Hongi was able to contain the early mission stations within the areas under his authority.

Very much under the Maori thumb, the early missionaries could not avoid involvement in trade but did not lose sight of their evangelical purpose. Seeking not only to convert the indigenous population to Christianity but also to "civilize" them, their approaches to these always intertwined tasks drew on the theological, political, scientific, and philosophical understandings of their society and their time. Biblical injunctions, contemporary "scientific" and philosophical ideas, and entirely pragmatic motivations underlay missionary eagerness to convert Maori to Western ways of living, dressing, and eating. The introduction of wheat, as a crop and a dietary staple, was an important consideration in these contexts. Bread, particularly wheaten bread, was a staple food of the

Bible. As the very "staff of life," it has featured prominently in religious rituals, especially the Eucharist in which Christ's body is transubstantiated into or represented by bread.

Four years after establishing a New Zealand mission, Samuel Marsden wrote that he "should feel a joy inexpressible to see the New Zealander [Maori] returning home from his cultivated field with his sheaf with him." He anticipated "the day when he will plough with his yoke of oxen like the ancient prophets and rejoice with the joy of harvest when his crops are gathered in."[5] Maori had long celebrated the "joy" of their own harvests with *hakari,* or feasts that were often referred to by Europeans as a "harvest-home," but the desire for them to emulate the crops and agricultural methods of the Holy Land was always evident. Indeed, when the Wesleyans, who arrived in 1823, brought in their first wheat harvest at Whangaroa, they were so pleased to see Maori chiefs approaching their home, carrying sheaves, their "delightful anticipations" were awakened "of that period when the prophetic vision of Micah shall be realized by these noble tribes of barbarians: 'They shall beat their swords into ploughshares, and their spears into pruning-hooks.'"[6]

However, Hongi's military dominance had given him such a stranglehold that it was not until the mid 1830s, some six or seven years after his death and in the wake of a resulting power vacuum, that Christian teachings could expand south of the Bay of Islands. And, as missionaries and Maori catechists or lay teachers moved south, so did their exhortations for Maori to grow wheat. They needed local food supplies and encouraged settled habitations to allow for regular Christian instruction, but they were still heavily influenced by biblical injunctions and ingrained ideas of morality and civilization.

Biblical metaphors such as those equating certain societies with "fertile soil," which "sifted the wheat from the chaff," or "harvested" souls, pepper the writings of early nineteenth-century missionaries in New Zealand. The Reverend John Butler, who was glad to be able to feed his Maori workers with a "good wheaten loaf" in March 1822, wrote a year later that the "sixteen natives" then under the care of his mission were "regularly fed with the bread of this life and, as far as we are able to communicate it to them, with the bread 'which cometh down from heaven and giveth life unto the world.'"[7] Maori were encouraged not only to eat the bread of this life but also to produce it, and early converts, referred to as "leaven" among their people, worked similarly to propagate the "bread from heaven." Metaphors of conversion, such as John Morgan's report from the Waikato that "the missionary already looks forward to the glorious harvest he hopes to reap and rejoices in the prospect of entering the heavenly garner with his arms filled with the golden sheaves," appear to have had real substance in their minds.[8]

As the missionaries were able to venture beyond the far northern part of the country, so did foreign ships begin to call at other ports too. A number of accounts are recorded of the first experiences of diverse tribal groups with a triad of new products: flour, sugar, and soap. One account refers to a northern chief believing that biscuit was pumice stone.[9] Another tells of some Taranaki people who helped themselves to stores aboard a wrecked ship in 1834 but threw the flour away thinking it was a type of sand.[10] Yet another story from an island in the far south of New Zealand referred to a group of Maori who did the same when they raided the stores of some sealers, thinking it was ashes.[11] Whatever the initial reaction, the introduction of flour-based products was remembered, a liking for them quickly cultivated. Such a preference was reflected in the term *utu pihikete,* or "paid for in biscuits," one of several derogatory terms for half-caste Maori children. Among the many services Maori offered at the ports favored by foreign shipping was that of sexual favors in exchange for material goods: the phrase implies they were the product of a commercial transaction with visiting sailors.[12]

Like Ruatara, tribal leaders in other areas were only too happy to adopt items of Western diet, but, as with other aspects of Christian teachings, they did so for their own reasons and tended to incorporate them into their existing systems and worldview. In this process the inherent symbolisms became closely associated not only with their spiritual connotations but also with the Maori-British alliance, which strengthened with the arrival of the first British government official in 1833.

James Busby was appointed British resident in response to pleas from both Maori leaders and the small community of British traders now established in Northland who were concerned about matters of law and order—concerns that were exacerbated by the different legal and value systems held by Maori and Europeans. Even though Busby had limited powers and no military support, his arrival signaled the beginning of "on the ground" support for missionary endeavors.

On landing at the Bay of Islands, Busby addressed an assembly of tribal leaders, explaining that he was a representative of King William charged with investigating any complaints they might have concerning His Majesty's subjects. He told them how Britain had once been an un-civilized country, but that, after God had sent his son into the world, its people learned to cultivate their land so that they "had abundance of bread." Now, he said, God had sent his servants, the missionaries, to dwell amongst them so that their land, too, would flourish: "Instead of the roots of the fern, you shall eat bread, because the land shall be tilled without fear, and its fruits shall be eaten in peace. When there is abun-dance of bread, men shall labour to preserve flax, and timber, and pro-visions for the ships which come to trade, shall bring clothing, and all other things which you desire. Thus shall you become rich."[13] Timber and prepared flax were big income earners for many northern communi-ties during the 1830s, but his message was that bread was the key to both peace and wealth.

In February 1840, after much consideration by the British government and negotiation with a number of Maori leaders—mostly from the north-ern regions where the missionaries lived and had greatest influence—New Zealand was annexed to Britain under the Treaty of Waitangi. Protestant missionaries played a prominent part in fostering support for the agree-ment, and, from this point on, the missions, which now included Angli-cans, Wesleyans, and Roman Catholics, gained considerable political and economic backing as well as support for their evangelical mission.

The emphasis on the desirability of wheat cultivation and bread con-sumption served the overlapping aims of complying with Christian im-peratives to make the land fruitful, improving the moral and spiritual good of Maori, civilizing them, and assisting the process of coloniza-tion. Among the more pragmatic reasons was the ever present need for missions to be self-sufficient and to feed the students who attended their schools. Moreover, given the widespread acceptance of philosopher John Locke's theory that those who used the land most productively had the greatest moral right to its ownership, it was sometimes evident that mis-sionary encouragement was intended to head off settler attempts to de-prive Maori of their land on the basis that they were not meeting this requirement.

The seemingly insatiable settler demand for freehold land heightened tensions between Maori and the government, but the relationship be-tween the government and the Church Missionary Society in particular was one of mutual support. Government officials expected that converting the indigenous population to more intensive farming methods would free up more land for settler occupation, while missionaries wanted a settled congregation to preach to. The Reverend John Morgan, based at Otawhao in the Upper Waikato from 1841 to 1863, was an especially zealous promoter of wheat farming, flour milling, and bread baking. He explained his rationale to his superiors in London by saying, "Prone to wander and scatter themselves they will by the growing of wheat and building of mills be drawn together to certain favourable localities within 25 miles round the mission station, by which the visiting of each tribe will become more regular and easy."[14]

As the practical, spiritual, and "scientific" motivations behind missionary endeavors to convert Maori to wheat growing and a flour-based diet were always intertwined, so, too, were those driving government policies aimed at the same ends. However, the connections between Christianity, wheat growing, and "improvement" were often evident, as in November 1842 when the assistant protector of Aborigines, Edward Shortland, was pleased to report an increase in the number of Christians among the people living at Te Tapiri, near Matamata. A "remarkably elegant chapel" had been built there by the local chief Wiremu Tamihana, he said. "Improvements seem[ed] to be going on with spirit, & [he] was much pleased to observe several acres of flourishing wheat" in the neighborhood as well.

During his first governorship of New Zealand, from 1845 to 1853, George Grey supported missionary efforts to promote wheat cultivation with gifts of seed, farming implements, loans to purchase hand-operated or water-powered flour mills, and he sometimes supplied agricultural instructors at government expense. Put in place immediately following a rebellion by a number of tribal groups in Northland, this policy saw an enormous growth in Maori wheat and flour production. Popularly called his "flour and sugar" policy, the strategy was intended to reduce the chance of further rebellion as well as make the new colony self-supporting.

John Morgan was particularly adept at drawing government support for his mission. His correspondence with Grey was businesslike, hitting all the political and financial buttons the governor would have been looking for, while biblical metaphors were restricted to his journal and letters to fellow missionaries. One such letter, written to the secretary of the CMS in London, exemplifies the direct connections between Christianity, civilization, and a Western diet that were frequently evident. It asked whether "so many of the rising generation" should be allowed to die for want of improper food, or whether efforts should be made "to save the race by the blessings of christianity and civilization"?[15]

An article in a government-sponsored newspaper contained all the common messages including the religious significance of wheat. It began by reminding Maori readers that Providence had placed among them "a civilized, energetic, and industrious race—the English," that former forests and swamps (where they had long caught birds and eels) were now "corn fields and meadows," and that their duty was to progress, not retrograde for to retrograde was to perish. The writer, who called himself "a friend in Auckland," told them not to merely grow potatoes for their own consumption but to "become agriculturists in the true sense of the word,—GROW WHEAT." Wheat, it continued, had been the "staff of life" from the earliest ages, the "most distinguished nations of the earth" had always cultivated wheat as their principal article of food, and Christians regarded it "as a blessing only second to Revelation." Potatoes, he continued, had a much more recent provenance, the market was a small one, and "experience" had taught "that from its exclusive use as food an infinite variety of social evils will always spring." So, even the potatoes beloved by mariners as a convenient, storable food that warded off scurvy, were not fit for civilized people.

This article went on to explain that wheat cultivation would force a number of the arts of civilization upon their attention with opportunities for acquiring knowledge and rising in humanity. Wheat was "gold" and, having been blessed by Nature, "ever proved the fruitful source of prosperity" and a means to preserve the Maori race.[16] This advice was published in 1851 when the Irish potato famine of the 1840s would still have been fresh in the minds of the settlers. But the idea that wheat was superior to potatoes was in place well before that. The *Gentleman's Magazine* of 1836, for example, proclaimed that "the potato, useful as it is, will always be pauper-food; while wheat is the staff of independent life."[17] Thomas Chapman reflected these ideas when he expressed the hope that the building of flour mills would induce Maori to increase their wheat cultivation so that "the blessing of God [would] introduce a better system than their present one of potatoes only."[18]

Potatoes may have been denigrated before the Irish famine highlighted the dangers of relying totally on that crop, but the sacred nature of bread was very clear in an article entitled "The Arabs' Respect for Bread" that appeared in a later Maori-language newspaper. Indicative of the writer's perception as much as the lessons it sought to impart, the item explained that when an Arab drops a crumb of bread he takes it in his right hand, kisses it, and presses it to his forehead before placing it on a fence or branch for a bird to eat. Everyone, it claimed, whether Arab or Christian, has respect for bread.[19]

The establishment of the British government had seen a number of officials add their support to missionary concerns about Maori diet. For example, in 1844, John Fitzgerald, medical officer to the Maori of Wellington, gave advice concerning the care of mothers and newborns in the government-sponsored newspaper *Ko te Karere o Nui Tireni*. He not only recommended a diet of fresh pork, poultry, fish, and flour mixed with sugar as the most suitable for babies but also stressed the importance of mothers abstaining from fermented foods in order to improve the quality of breast milk and avoid the many illnesses said to result from a bad maternal diet.[20]

The settler government even sought to legislate against the consumption of fermented or, as they preferred to call it, "rotten" food. In 1860, the country's first chief justice, Sir William Martin, proposed to outlaw "eating rotton [sic] food, rotton corn [maize] or potatoes &c.; causing another person to eat such food; making, pits for sleeping [perhaps "steeping?"] and preparing such food." The penalties for involvement in such activities were to be stiff: "not less than five shillings, or more than twenty shillings. And upon conviction of the offence the Kai-whakawa [Magistrate] shall certify to the runanga [Maori district council], and the runanga shall cause such food or the pits for making the same to be destroyed."[21]

The missionary brethren had an equally strong aversion to the various fermented foods that Maori enjoyed. A particular favorite was *kanga pirau,* or fermented maize, which many early European visitors referred to as "putrid maize," "rotten corn," or "stinking corn." Although bread, wine, and cheese depend on fermentation processes for their production, these were clearly recognized as "civilized" food. Fermented maize, cooked and eaten as a sort of porridge, was condemned explicitly but also implicitly by classifying it as putrid, rotten, stinking, or decayed.

The connection between fermented maize and a lack of both civilization and Christian sensitivity was evident when Reverend Benjamin Ashwell expressed his disappointment in a young Maori man who had been "brought up in the best society," educated by an officer of the East India Company, and taken to Calcutta, Sydney, and elsewhere but who was, by 1851, living with the Ngati Pou tribe. Ashwell clearly considered the young man to have retrograded. He told the Church Missionary Society in London that this man had returned to New Zealand in his late teens and been tattooed (a sign that he had rejected Christianity and "civilization"). Now "a complete Native, wearing a Blanket and eating decayed corn," Ashwell attributed "his ingratitude and return to Barbarism" to "a *want of Christian principle.*"[22]

Although, on the one hand, missionaries condemned the eating of fermented foods, on the other, they and other Europeans often complained of a lack of variety in their diet. Thomas Chapman was deeply grateful when a Maori teacher from the East Coast gave him some flour as a gift because, he said, his health soon suffered if he ate "more than a very small quantity of vegetable food."[23]

Flour and bread, frequently recommended as the ideal infant foods, were also closely connected with the concept of wholesomeness, which embodied ideas of both physical and spiritual health. During 1851, Jane Woon, wife of the Wesleyan William Woon, advised a Maori woman whose child persisted in eating fermented maize to take him inland where there was a flour mill in order to "get him some wholesome bread."[24] Government newspapers agreed with her prescription, advising that flour was the "first thing necessary for children,"[25] although it was sometimes mentioned that baked flour was actually better for infants than bread: "There are only two kinds of food really necessary for children, flour, baked, or made into bread, and milk. Arrowroot, rice, sago, are all good, specially for babies, who like change of food, but most children thrive on bread and milk. Flour baked in a pot till dry is better for babies than bread."[26]

Government and Christian-sponsored newspapers in the Maori language extolled the virtues and wholesomeness of wheat farming and a flour-based diet, and instances of Maori growing wheat, milling flour, and eating bread (of which there were many) were applauded.

Neither fermented food nor potatoes were considered "wholesome," but bread was especially so, as the Reverend Alfred Brown noted in January 1849 when Maori in his area had begun to bake in the European style. His journal recorded a twenty-five-mile walk after morning service when, "instead of being laden as usual with potatoes as food for our journey," the Maori who accompanied him "had a large supply of wholesome home-baked bread, for they have become of late on a very extensive scale, practical farmers, millers and bakers." "The Natives have named their pa [fort] Samaria," he added.[27]

Charles Hursthouse appealed to potential immigrants' desire for wholesomeness when he told how the "cultivation of a new country materially improves its climate" and how land once "fertile only in miasma" was converted into "wholesome plains of fruit and grass and grain" by the plow.[28] A sense of purity and wholesomeness was even perceived in the machinery used to process wheat. Thomas Chapman recorded a visit to a Maori village in the Bay of Plenty where, having turned a corner, he found "a new patent Flour Mill, just purchased, having a pack of dirty, very common playing cards, lying carelessly on its top."[29] His reaction invokes a sense that the purity and virtue of the mill had been violated by unwholesome playing cards.

High Maori mortality rates in the early decades of European contact related in large part to their lack of immunity to newly introduced diseases, but medical science had not yet recognized this. Instead, Western ways of living, together with a Western diet—both considered more wholesome—were recommended to counter poor health statistics.

Because poor health and high death rates among Maori children were frequently associated with a lack of flour in the diet, the government's Maori newspaper explained that "the greatest wealth a man can have is his children, 'a gift and heritage which cometh from the Lord.'" The article exhorted Maori leaders to stop the evil. "In areas near the East Cape, the people have cows, and milk them, and the women make large loaves of bread," it said. "They bake them in iron pots [and] in those parts the children have began to multiply again." At Otawhao, it reported: "the children in Mr. Morgan's [mission] school have milk and bread all the year and only one dies in a year for 84 who live. In the Maori villages, where the children eat potatoes only and rotten corn, one dies every year out of 34."[30] In order to encourage English-style baking and cooking and increase consumption of flour-based foods, instructions for making leaven, bread, and plum pudding often appeared in Maori newspapers from the late 1840s on.[31]

The ownership of a flour mill would surely bolster production and consumption. At Otamarora in the Bay of Plenty region, both Christian and non-Christian groups wanted a water-powered flour mill, but the latter lacked the wherewithal to complete such a project on their own. So, after some negotiation, the "heathens" agreed to help the Christians build a new chapel before a jointly owned and operated mill was constructed.[32]

Practical support in acquiring flour mills was often dependent on sponsorship from an influential missionary. For some missionaries, it was also the key to gaining converts albeit, perhaps, on a superficial level, but the ability to influence government in granting loans or other assistance could be a two-edged sword. The Anglican Reverend Taylor must have felt this when he was locked into a "souls for flourmills" battle with the Catholic Father Lampila along the Whanganui River.

Lampila had a material advantage in the form of a lay brother who was also a millwright. This vexed Taylor, who feared that his previous and potential converts were being tempted by the "Papists'" offers of subsidized flour mills. He protested that these were "a snare of Satan to entrap their souls."[33] Having learned that two of his Maori teachers had allowed the Catholics to construct mills for their people, he expressed disappointment that they connected mill building with religion.[34]

Because subscribing to Christian tenets was so often the key to gaining support, Maori did perceive close connections between religion and flour mills and sought to better their chances of receiving this material support by emphasizing their piety. So, when a group of chiefs from Manawatu wrote to Governor Grey asking for a plow and "small hand mill," they explained that these would assist them to grow and grind wheat while they were "engaged in greater pursuits."[35] Europeans certainly interpreted the appearance of flour mills, churches, Western implements, and farm animals as confirmation of their success in converting and civilizing their charges.

John Morgan had introduced wheat to Otawhao, and his relationship with Grey had allowed him to introduce agricultural machinery and water-powered flour mills to the area as well. As a result, Otawhao and the nearby settlement of Rangiaowhia came to be considered "model villages," providing the young capital of Auckland with essential food supplies.[36] But Morgan's zeal was not appreciated by his superiors, who accused him of neglecting his religious duties. Thomas Chapman was one who chastised him for overemphasizing civilization through agriculture: "we must never forget that civilization itself cannot illuminate the darkness of the heart . . . and that large barns and stacks of corn, cannot give your people, the peace of God which passes all understanding."[37]

Morgan responded that his congregation's "wandering habits pre-vented their advancement in civilization and Christianity" and that his agricultural instruction kept "each little party continually under the sound of the Gospel," as well as providing them with better food and other benefits. "Civilisation," he added, was necessary for Maori to build churches and to support their ministers and mission schools.[38]

The plow and plowing, which the Bible refers to as representing virtu-ous labor and peaceful productivity rather than idleness, were as sym-bolically important in the New Zealand context as they were elsewhere. From around 1840, when Sir Thomas Fowell Buxton published *The Afri-can Slave Trade and Its Remedy,* biblical metaphors relating to the plow acquired "scientific" substance. The idea that the introduction of the plow into a society represented the advent of civilization was promoted and accepted even into the latter half of the twentieth century.

Maori may not have understood the Western concept of "civiliza-tion," but metaphorical links between agriculture and peace were cross-cultural and, in this context, wheat growing became the supreme exam-ple. An English language newspaper found it "positively delightful . . . to hear how the tea and fern scrubs are giving place to the wheat and barley closes; how the wilderness is becoming rich with the fruits of agriculture,—how lone, and but recently savage streams are being dot-ted with busy mills, and how, in reality and *practical* truth, the plough is superseding the musket."[39] So, through European eyes, "savage" streams could be pacified by "busy" flour mills, but Maori were also adamant that agriculture and the adoption of Western farming practices signified their peaceful intent.

In 1857, one month before hostilities broke out over who had the right to sell lands in the Hawke's Bay for European settlement, a group of local chiefs wrote to the regional newspaper. They confirmed that they wel-comed settlers in their area and that they intended to follow "those pur-suits that will tend to advance and improve our condition; such as the erection of flour-mills, the production of food, the breeding of sheep, and so forth."[40] Six years later, when their new flour mill was commissioned, they publicly welcomed other tribes as well as European settlers to the opening celebrations. The event conformed to the customary practice of holding a feast to strengthen bonds of friendship and good relations be-tween communities. The mill owners sought to reassure the settlers of their safety while battles were now raging elsewhere.[41]

In 1860, when war had broken out in Taranaki, the government was anxious to shore up support from tribes not then involved, and their attestations of loyalty often made explicit reference to wheat and flour production. Hakopa Te Waharoa, for example, referred to Romans 6:23 when he deplored murder and confirmed his people's commitment to "ploughing the land for wheat, potatoes and corn for us to sell."[42]

At a subsequent conference between government representatives and noncombatant leaders, William Nero Te Awaitaia gave his understanding of the missionary message and the material benefits they claimed would accompany Christian belief: "There is a fountain above in Heaven and from this fountain the Earth is supplied. The Missionaries came bringing what they had received from Heaven for the salvation of the soul, and they made their errand clear."[43]

Peace is closely associated with loyalty, and both require reciprocity. So when the wheat and flour market collapsed in the mid-1850s, and Maori were effectively disenfranchised by the establishment of a settler government at much the same time, John Morgan was very disappointed by the consequences. In 1858, the Waikato tribes among whom he had been working with so much apparent success established their own king. Te Wherowhero was to be a protector for Maori interests in partnership with Queen Victoria, but the settler government interpreted his appointment as a threat to British sovereignty, and, after the outbreak of war, the king's followers did eventually join the "rebel" side. Maori were divided politically into pro- and antigovernment factions, with the psychological and ideological associations, in this milieu, between the British queen and flour often evident. The inherent symbolisms had become closely associated with the Maori-British alliance, and, consequently, those who remained loyal to the government were associated with the foods they had introduced. Richard Taylor recorded one example of this, a derisory chant which linked "sugar, flour, biscuit, and tea consumers" with worthless people who should be banished to Europe.[44] On the other hand, those tribal groups that chose not to fight with the "rebels" understood that by engaging in activities associated with peace they were also demonstrating their loyalty.

Further to the east, on the Mahia Peninsula, is the site of an old *pa* named Kaiuku (clay eating). The name derives from an incident that occurred around 1830 when the people were besieged by other tribes from the Waikato region. After two months their food supplies ran out and they were forced to survive on a diet of blue clay, found in the cliffs, which they mixed with water and boiled in much the same way as missionaries prepared flour. That incident was recalled some thirty years later when wars again raged in the area—this time between the British and their supporters, on one hand, and "rebel" tribes known as "Hauhau," on the other. The Hauhau were supporters of a millennial religious movement which combined Jewish and Christian elements with Maori beliefs. During this period, those loyal to the British are said to have remarked, "The Waikatos gave them clay, but the Queen gave them flour."[45] This was a direct allusion to the metaphorical connections between flour and the alliance with the British.

Still later, in 1878, a Maori newspaper reported that a Taranaki leader named Te Kahui was encouraging his people to plant wheat at Te Waimate because planting crops was preferable to fighting.[46] This was significant because Taranaki was where war had broken out in 1860, and Te Kahui had more recently worked with the prophets Te Whiti o Rongomai III and Tohu Kakahi who adopted strategies of peaceful resistance. A modern township had developed under their leadership at a place called Parihaka, which their people refused to vacate after the government confiscated it as retribution for alleged rebellion. Tensions were mounting, but, rather than offer armed resistance, the people of Parihaka responded by disrupting the work of surveyors and asserting their ownership rights by plowing land that was being occupied by European settlers. Despite the symbolisms, this considered policy of peaceful protest was not appreciated by the government, which sent more than fifteen hundred soldiers to Parihaka to remove the community by force.

As they approached the village on November 5, 1881, the troops were met in a traditional Taranaki way by women who bade them welcome with *poi* (balls attached to a cord and used to accentuate a dance). After them came a line of two hundred small boys and then about sixty girls with skipping ropes. The children offered the soldiers some of the five hundred loaves of freshly baked bread that had been prepared to share with the "visitors." But their intimations of peace were ignored, and, as the people huddled together, the troops closed in, destroying their gardens, demolishing their houses, raping the women, and arresting the men who were held without trial for several years.

As this incident indicates, semiotic connections between agriculture and peace readily crossed cultural boundaries. The Maori word *rongo* and the god of the same name embrace both meanings. So the symbolisms that linked agriculture, and especially wheat growing, with peace were not difficult for Maori to understand, and they often made this understanding explicit, especially when addressing missionaries or government officials or soliciting assistance: "Europeans and Maori will work together in peaceful activities like this [flour] mill"[47] and "I will only fight with a mill. My head shall be down and my heels up in working at a mill. Give a mill, a mill."[48]

The association between wheat growing and peace appears to have been adopted readily, but the fear engendered by the destructive effects of food on tapu took much longer to overcome. For example, some young chiefs who accompanied missionary Richard Davis on a journey in 1833 had been "very particular as to what burden they carried"[49] They could not carry bags containing flour. This was because, after the head, the back is the most tapu part of the body, so contact between food and a chief's back could have deadly consequences. As this and other similar reports reveal, the rules of tapu applied equally to "foreign" food as to items of customary diet—although there was sometimes confusion as Maori began to respond to Christian teachings. One man asked Richard Taylor whether he could still eat his produce because someone had "dropped down dead in his cultivation," which, in Maori terms, would previously have rendered it tapu and therefore unsafe.[50]

Samuel Marsden was distressed when Ruatara, the chief who first introduced wheat cultivation into New Zealand, became ill soon after the first mission was established and was forbidden by his *tohunga* to eat or drink for five days for reasons of tapu. He wrote that his friend had been accustomed to eating bread, rice, and sugar and to drinking tea and wine, and he feared that this prohibition had made his death inevitable.[51] Nine years later, when the Reverend Samuel Leigh sought to administer medicine to another Northland chief, he had to wait while protective rituals were undertaken by a *tohunga* with a prepared basket of kumara. Some two weeks later they called on another man who was laid up with a bad leg. After dressing the leg, Leigh took a piece of bread from his pocket and gave it to the man in the hope of inducing him to violate the tapu, which, he hoped, would help to lessen its force and open the way for Christian conversion. Initially agitated, the man eventually overcame his fear and took the bread, placing it by his side. The missionary felt that his anxiety was heightened by the presence of an aged chief, but the patient turned to the old man explaining that the Europeans claim "our tapu is of the devil." Another chief who was present responded by permitting the missionary to dress his brother's leg, but prohibiting him from visiting any other sick people.[52] Interactions such as this gradually chipped away at long-held beliefs, but Maori were also using bread in their own ways, too.

One of the key reasons for Maori agreeing to sign the Treaty of Waitangi was to protect their lands, which had often been subject to unscrupulous claims of purchase by Britons and other foreigners. So, when the New Zealand Company laid claim to land that the local Ngati Toa people denied having sold and dispatched surveyors to those lands in early 1843, the Ngati Toa chiefs evicted the surveyors and burned the temporary shelters they had erected. Police magistrate Henry Thompson and company representative Captain Arthur Wakefield responded by arming some of the settlers and attempting to arrest the chiefs for arson. The ensuing hostilities resulted in the death of twenty-two Europeans, including Wakefield, and at least four Maori. Giving evidence subsequently, Reverend Samuel Ironside recounted that when Wakefield's body was found a piece of bread or damper had been placed under his head. Asked whether he was "aware of any native custom which would account for this being done," he replied: "The head of a chief is held sacred, and nothing common should come near it; and therefore bread, being common, and being placed there, it was intended as an insult."[53]

In the days before Christian influence, when a person died inside a house, it was burned down to remove the spiritual potency of the deceased person, but, because modern homes are a more permanent and expensive asset, the practice has been replaced by a ritual called *takahi whare*. This ceremonial walking through the deceased person's home after burial is accompanied by a prayer or incantation to lift the tapu and render it safe for the living to reoccupy. For some Northland Maori, this involves touching the walls of the house with bread, a practice that seems to follow the earlier pattern in which a cooked kumara might be used to lift the tapu from a newly built meeting house.[54] Also in Northland, at Te Karetu, Ngati Manu mourners are cleansed of tapu following a funeral by the application of water and the sprinkling of small pieces of bread over the body.[55] It involves the sprinkling of water in other communities, too, but among the Tuhoe people it may also require the *tohunga* to consume the bread used in the ritual. This is so the evil influences may be absorbed into the bread and removed through the digestive process.[56]

So Maori did not merely grow and eat the new crop but absorbed bread into their own spiritual practices. By turning to Christianity, they had adopted many of the understandings, rituals, and festivals associated with the faith, too. For example, the Reverend Thomas Samuel Grace was very pleased when, in March 1852, he was invited to an English-style "Harvest Home" put on by East Coast Maori who had been entertained in the same way at the mission school a short time before. Roast pork, potatoes, and apple pudding were followed "by a plentiful supply of well-sweetened tea, and good bread and butter."[57] In the twenty-first century, bread and steamed pudding still feature strongly on the menu at Maori communal gatherings.

As missionaries and government had multiple motives for promoting wheat production and flour consumption among Maori, Maori, too, had multiple motives for growing it and producing flour. In practical terms, it offered a more reliable food supply than their previous crops and was a profitable trade item. On another level, though, the implications of loyalty and peaceful intent served to bolster good relationships with the Crown, which, in turn, brought material advantages such as schools, employment contracts, loans to purchase trading ships, flour mills, and other benefits. However, these innovations were also infused with their own spiritual restraints. So, for reasons of tapu, laundry and swimming were prohibited in waterways that powered flour mills and thus produced food. In fact, during the mid nineteenth century, the name of one stream on the Whanganui River was renamed Kaukore, meaning "no swimming" as an ever present reminder.

In 1861 one chief expressed the opinion, unthinkable today, that his language ought to die with his generation: "as the taste of the fern-root and the mamaku will be lost with the old men who are now passing away. Let the tongues which have tasted of English food only utter the language of the great nation." Clearly, this man had adopted the missionaries' linking of "English" food with other aspects of the "Christianity-civilization" package, as had others apparently, because the magistrate who reported his speech claimed that his view was "warmly supported."[58]

In the twentieth century, when giving evidence to the Waitangi Tribunal in support of a claim asserting that the Maori language was a *taonga*, or treasure, that the government was obliged to protect under the treaty, the prominent Maori leader Sir James Henare recalled a visit by a school inspector during his childhood. The inspector told him and his fellow pupils that "English is the bread-and-butter language, and if you want to earn your bread and butter you must speak English."[59] Given the religious connotations of bread instilled by Christian missionaries, its application as a metaphor for something mundane or commonplace is somewhat ironic. Those missionaries of a hundred years earlier could not have known that, in the Christian Maori era, the significance of bread did not diminish but instead expanded to fulfill additional spiritual functions.

Notes

1. Genesis 1:28–30.
2. Salmond, *Two Worlds*, 356; and Crozet, *Crozet's Voyage to Tasmania*, 27, 75.
3. Crozet, *Crozet's Voyage to Tasmania*, 27, 75; and Salmond, *Two Worlds*, 406.
4. Colenso, "Contributions Towards a Better Knowledge," 35. Some tribal groups consider Rongo to be a son of Tane, god of the forest, and grandson of Rangi and Papa.
5. The Revd. Samuel Marsden to Messrs. Kendall, Hall, King, Carlisle, and Gordon, February 24, 1819, in Elder, *The Letters and Journals of Samuel Marsden*, 233.
6. Strachan, *The Life of the Rev. Samuel Leigh*, 155.
7. John Butler, *Earliest New Zealand*, 217 and 263.
8. Morgan, "Letters and Journals," September 1, 1846, MS 213.
9. White, *The Ancient History of the Maori*, 10:125, http://www.nzetc.org.ezproxy.auckland.ac.nz/tm/scholarly/tei-corpus-WhiAnci.html (June 10, 2009).
10. "History and Traditions of the Taranaki Coast: The Wreck of the 'Harriett' 1834," *Journal of the Polynesian Society* 19, no. 13 (1910): 109.
11. Beattie, "Traditions and Legends," 129.
12. Meredith, "A Half-Caste on the Half-Caste."
13. James Busby to the chiefs and people of New Zealand, May 17, 1833, cited in Marshall, *Personal Narrative of Two Visits to New Zealand*, 337.
14. John Morgan, Report of the Otawhao Station for the year 1852, transcript, Morgan, "Letters and Journals," vol. 3, MS 213.
15. Morgan to Venn, July 1, 1852, Morgan, "Letters and Journals," vol. 3, MS 213.
16. *Maori Messenger: Ko te Karere Maori*, August 14, 1851, 2.
17. *Gentleman's Magazine*, April 1836, 390.
18. Chapman, "Journal," February 12, 1855, typescript, MS 56.
19. *Te Korimako*, February 22, 1887, 5.
20. *Te Karere o Nui Tireni*, August 1, 1844, 40.
21. *Maori Messenger: Ko te Karere Maori*, July 31, 1860, 5.
22. Ashwell to CMS, July 28, 1851, Letters and Journals.
23. Andrews, *No Fear of Rusting*, 198.
24. Woon, "Extract from His Journal," June 30, 1851.
25. *Maori Messenger: Ko te Karere Maori*, November 15, 1859, 3.
26. Ibid.

27. Brown, "Journal, 1835–1859," January 15, 1849, MSS and Archives A-179. Spelled *Hamaria* in Maori, this settlement was on the shore of Lake Taupo. The place is now called Hallett's Bay.

28. Hursthouse, *New Zealand*, 110–111.

29. Chapman, "Journal," June 21, 1848, vol. 1, MS 56.

30. *Maori Messenger: Ko te Karere Maori*, August 15, 1859, 4.

31. For example, *Maori Messenger: Ko Te Karere Maori*, November 22, 1849; *Ko Aotearoa*, January 1, 1862, 30; and *Manuhiri Tuarangi*, May 15, 1861, 16.

32. Chapman, "Journal," July 28, 1856, MS 56.

33. Taylor, "Journal," October 29, 1852, typescript, MS 302.

34. Ibid., October 31, 1853.

35. Hori Takerei, Maka Te Papa, Ngawena Tamarua, and Ngawaka to Grey, July 20, 1853, Letter 411, GNZMA.

36. Howe, "Morgan."

37. Chapman to Morgan, January 1852, Morgan, "Letters and Journals," vol. 3, MS 213.

38. Morgan to Chapman, March 4, 1852, Morgan, "Letters and Journals," vol. 3, MS 213.

39. *Daily Southern Cross*, February 25, 1851, 2.

40. *Hawkes Bay Herald*, October 10, 1857, 3; *Supplement* to the *New Zealander*, November 4, 1857, 2.

41. *Te Waka Maori o Ahuriri*, July 11, 1863, 3, July 25, 1863, 1–2.

42. *Maori Messenger: Te Karere Maori*, May 31, 1860, 11.

43. *Maori Messenger: Ko Te Karere Maori*, June 30, 1860, 2–13.

44. Taylor, *The Past and Present of New Zealand*, 133–134 (translation mine, but based on Taylor's).

45. White, *The Ancient History of the Maori*, 21:166.

46. *Te Wananga*, March 23, 1878, 127.

47. *Te Waka Maori o Ahuriri*, August 8, 1863, 2 (my translation).

48. Enclosure 1 in Wynyard to Grey, February 22, 1855, British Parliamentary Papers, 10:86–90.

49. Church Missionary Society, Missionary Register, December 1835, 555.

50. Taylor, "Journal," June 22, 1850, vol. 7, typescript, MS 302.

51. Elder, *The Letters and Journals of Samuel Marsden*, 212.

52. Strachan, *The Life of the Rev. Samuel Leigh*, 187.

53. Wakefield, *Adventure in New Zealand*, 395.

54. Sadler, "A Clash of Cultures."

55. Munn, "Ngati Manu," 86.

56. McNeill, "Te Hau Ora," 179.

57. Brittan et al., *Pioneer Missionary*, 31–32.

58. William B. Baker, resident magistrate to the native secretary, January 3, 1862, no. 2, E no. 9, sec. v, Appendices to the Journals of the House of Representatives, 5.

59. Report of the Te Reo Maori Claim, 3.2.6, www.waitangi-tribunal.govt.nz/ . . . /2580F91B-5D6F-46F4-ADE0-BC27CA535C01.pdf (September 13, 2009). The Waitangi Tribunal was established to consider claims by Maori against the Crown regarding breaches of principles of the Treaty of Waitangi.

CHAPTER 7

COMMENSALITY AND LOVE FEAST

THE AGAPE MEAL IN THE
LATE NINETEENTH- AND EARLY
TWENTIETH-CENTURY BRETHREN IN CHRIST CHURCH

Heidi Oberholtzer Lee

From its salted pickles to its red beets and snitz pie, the love feast, or agape, of the late nineteenth- and early twentieth-century Brethren in Christ Church represented for this religious community a central moment and site of pious practice, sacred eating, theological wrangling, and evangelization by gastronomy. The love feast had been a characteristic and distinctive practice of the church from its emergence in 1780 among the rural German-speaking population of Lancaster County, Pennsylvania.[1] It continued in popularity and practice through the nineteenth century and still exists in many Brethren in Christ congregations today. Other now extinct denominations, such as the German Seventh Day Baptist Church, which reached its height in the mid eighteenth century, as well as the eighteenth- and nineteenth-century Glasites or Sandemanians, also practiced the love feast. The historic and contemporary congregations of the Moravians, Primitive Methodists and United Methodists, Old Order River Brethren, Church of the Brethren, Catholic Neocatechumenal Way, Mennonites, and some Masonic traditions, likewise, in many cases, maintain a tradition of some form of love feast. For the Brethren in Christ in particular, the love feast, with its tradition of congregational feet washing, fellowship meal, and communion meal, once required of each of its host churches many months of planning, food enough for two days of feasting by hundreds of (or even one thousand) church members and visitors, and overnight housing. The typical event included a time of personal testimonies for most of a Saturday; Saturday evening with a feet washing ceremony, fellowship dinner, and subsequent sharing of a communion (Eucharistic) meal; Sunday morning with a church service and afternoon with sharing, preaching, and religious instruction.[2] The order of service varied, though, from one congregation to the next or from one region to the next.[3] Congregations sometimes held the services and meals in barns, church buildings, and homes, and occasionally even outdoors. In the late 1800s and early 1900s it was not unusual for a congregation to hold at least two love feasts per year, one in the spring and one in the fall, sometimes intentionally planned to coincide with the full moon so that congregants would have sufficient light by which to travel home on Sunday.[4] Today most Brethren in Christ and Brethren love feasts consist primarily of feet washing and one potluck meal for local congregants and generally include a time of sharing, church services, and sometimes baptisms as well.[5]

This chapter focuses particularly on late nineteenth- and early twentieth-century lay and clerical narratives and remembrances of the significance of the love feast. In the church's history, at the turn of the century, the love feast served as a notably pivotal ceremony by which church members could assert their sect's distinctiveness even while gesturing toward an ecumenical welcome and gentle embrace of those not a part of the church.[6] The Brethren in Christ traditionally thought themselves called to be "a peculiar people," to be "separate from the world," literally separatist, but they also showed interest in demonstrating hospitality to their neighbors for the purposes of evangelization, charity, and simply reaching out toward others with the love of Christ. Because religious meals can help a church articulate its own standards for holy living in contradistinction to the "worldly" values held by the surrounding culture,[7] the Brethren in Christ love feasts both drew together the community and set them apart from others. Furthermore, lay members celebrated the spiritual refreshment and renewal they received at and from the love feast as well as the excitement and socialization it provided, especially for young people. They remarked on the physical expressions of faith the feast prompted, evidence of "somatic piety."[8] Like early American Baptists, the Brethren in Christ experienced through their love feasts an "embodied faith . . . as belief was experienced through the body."[9] The Brethren in Christ looked for spiritual development to bloom from their bodily fellowship and ritual feasting.[10]

While the seemingly separatist "Brethren" distinguished themselves from many other churches and religious groups by their plain dress, untrimmed beards, pacifism, forswearing of oaths, practice of the "holy kiss," and baptism by trine immersion, their language and descriptions of their love feasts reveal their connection to larger religious trends and controversies of the nineteenth and early twentieth centuries. During that time, American separation of church and state, as from the early days of the nation, continued to allow for and promote the proliferation of many new Protestant denominations, sects, and religious groups. The authority of these groups did not go unchallenged, however, as many of them struggled to preserve moral and social control of their communities during the late nineteenth-century rapid urbanization of America. Propelled by a dramatic increase both in international immigration and in emigration of rural populations to urban centers that offered economic opportunity, cities hosted large populations of people unacquainted with and sometimes uninterested in the beliefs and behaviors of the churches in their midst. These churches subsequently often initiated programs of social reform to try to help educate the urban poor, with the goal that the poor adopt as much as possible the manners and beliefs of these social workers, reflected, for example, in their habits of hygiene.[11] In this period, most American Protestants strongly emphasized a relationship between sanitation and faith. A purity or cleanliness of body, they believed, could demonstrate or even develop a purity of heart, a spiritual conversion, or a spiritual wellness.[12]

The Brethren in Christ remained largely and intentionally separate from much of mainline American Protestantism during the nineteenth and early twentieth centuries because of their linguistic, ethnic, and theological particularities and emphases as well as their situatedness in still predominantly rural and agricultural communities, but they did reflect their connection to the larger American Protestant world in a few significant ways. The letters and opinion pieces they sent to their church publications, and particularly to the church newsletter the *Evangelical Visitor*, called for congregants to improve their love feast, for example, with both greater hygiene and better conduct, as well as to eschew wine. Thus, like their contemporaries, the Brethren in Christ linked sanitation and etiquette with spirituality. Abstention from alcohol similarly associated foodways with spiritual health and was a hallmark of nineteenth-century American religious controversy and alimentary reform at large, especially as related to Eucharistic debates.[13] This suggests that there was some continuity between or even influence of the larger Protestant world on this small denomination. Like many other Protestant churches at the time, the Brethren in Christ also engaged in missions, revivalism, and evangelism.[14] Whereas their denomination was not characterized by the extensive urban social work movements of other contemporaneous denominations, their church documents about overseas missions and some urban missions reflect that they, too, were grappling with how to respond to the differing practices of hygiene and behaviors that they encountered in the peoples that they had attempted to convert and who, in many cases, had then become a part of their own church.

While Brethren in Christ archival material about the love feast shows the denomination to be rooted in many of the same cultural issues and debates that concerned other denominations of their day, these documents, at the same time, contain some material clearly unique to their own denomination's internal debates. Brethren in Christ pastors, for instance, wrote treatises on the love feast that insisted that congregants not conflate the love feast as a whole with the communion meal in particular. They argued that, while the love feast had been practiced in the New Testament, Christ had only instituted the communion meal, not the love feast. Clearly, nineteenth-century members of the Brethren in Christ community had elevated the love feast to such importance, and articulated its "gustatory theology" through a language of feasting and commensality, that pastors felt it imperative to offer a corrective to what had effectively become for some church members a sacrament regularly celebrated by this decidedly nonsacramental church.

LOVE FEAST AS ORDINANCE

Because the historical Brethren in Christ Church generally rejected the language of "sacraments," associating sacraments with Roman Catholicism and "works-based salvation," the clergy tended to emphasize the love feast as falling under "the means of grace," as opposed to "the doctrine of the sacraments." The love feast, explained Bethany Biblical Seminary professor William M. Beahm (1896–?), "is regarded as one of

God's means of grace," and the "character and intention of the minister, and especially of the communicant, are important for the validity" of the ordinance, as opposed to a Catholic sacrament that would not depend upon the purity or intention of the priest or communicant.[15] According to most clerical descriptions of the love feast, the feast should entail three or sometimes four parts: a time of preparation, feet washing, fellowship meal, and communion meal (or Eucharist, though the Brethren in Christ seldom, if ever, labeled it as such). The time of preparation and of feet washing are often folded into one broadly conceived time of preparation. Rarely do lay accounts of the love feast preserve so clearly the distinction between these four parts.

In Jesse Engle's 1889 *Evangelical Visitor* article titled "The Lord's Supper," which was later compiled with his other articles into a short treatise "approved by a Committee of the Church and published by order of the General Council," Engle explains to readers that love feasts, also called "feasts of charity" or "agapæ" in Greek, "were in practice among the early Christians as seen in Jude, verse 12, and incorporated but were clearly not the same as the communion meal. The author insists that charity was "the main characteristic" of the love feast and that all who were able to contribute food or funds were expected to do so. He further cites the writings of church historians to underscore his point that while love feasts in the early church were "frequently celebrated in connection with the communion . . . not one of these writers makes any reference to these feasts as a command, given either by the Savior or his Apostles; should these feasts have been considered indispensable, by our Savior, we would have much reason to regret the imperfection of the Gospel, since they are nowhere commanded therein." By contrast, the author points out, Jesus clearly commanded and instituted the practice of the communion meal, as recorded in Matthew 26:26, 27, Mark 14.:22, 23, and Luke 22:19, 20, and confirmed in 1 Cor. 11:24, 25.[16] His insistence on separating out the communion meal from the love feast as a whole suggests that at least some laity had conflated the two or did not clearly understand that the church practiced the former in response to Christ's direct command while it considered the latter to be an ordinance, or holy practice, but one instituted by humans, not by God himself. This distinction was especially pressing as the church sought to distinguish its own stance on the love feast from that of the Dunkers, who had elevated the love feast to the status of a sacred meal that could perhaps be placed on the same table as the fellowship meal.[17] Thus church teaching on this matter served both to reiterate the Brethren in Christ's own position on the love feast and to distinguish its position from that of other churches that might influence its congregants.

LAY REFLECTIONS ON THE IMPORTANCE AND REMEMBRANCE OF THE LOVE FEAST

The *Evangelical Visitor*, an official Brethren in Christ church publication self-described in many of its issues as "a semi-monthly religious journal for the exposition of true, practical piety and devoted to the spread of Evangelical truths and the Unity of the church," yields a wealth of lay response to the love feast, their memories of how their home congregations had recently practiced the ordinance of the love feast, and what this ordinance meant to them. These lay accounts typically take the form of letters written to the church paper, first published in 1887 and continuing its publication and circulation until 2004. These writers generally communicate their sentiments through simple and unadorned language that concisely relates their deeply felt religious experiences and describes their reenactments of the rituals that their church traced back to the interactions of Christ and the apostles. As contemporary Brethren pastor Frank Ramirez writes in *The Love Feast*, "Jesus says we should wash feet. We wash feet. The text says we should share a meal. So we eat something."[18] This self-aware literalism and terse explanatory style characterizes many of these accounts. Perhaps this style at least partially reflects the fact that, as late as the second half of the nineteenth century, many Brethren in Christ church members spoke only German until they went to elementary school, so their prose could display some linguistic discomfort with English or qualities of bilingual language processing. Furthermore, the Brethren in Christ emphasis on humility and the church's religiocultural resistance to or distrust of education in general fostered both a habitual and cultivated plain style of expression.[19]

These lay reports of love feasts tend to follow a certain form—first an account of the location and date of the feast, followed by a short remark on the weather, numbers of people in attendance, and from where they came—their towns, their counties, their states, or even their countries of origin. Clearly, the further the congregants had traveled to attend the feast, the more the local congregants felt the honor of their presence and emphasized how these distant church relations were now bound to them more effectively after having communed with them. As S. G. Engle notes in a report about a love feast held at Philadelphia Mission in 1900, "What helped to make it a blessed feast, must be largely attributed to the visiting brethren and sisters, who came spirit-filled, and we believe that they were the better for their having been with us. . . . We invite the brotherhood to pay us repeated visits as a mingling with each other is for improvement."[20] The age of the attendees also occasionally bore mention, as in the case of an anonymous 1907 account, which explains that the "participants ranged in age from ten and twelve years to upwards of eighty. A fair proportion were young in years. Thus, time after time do we observe these memorial services."[21] The awkwardly inserted "thus" suggests here that at least this author found the age of the participants a marker of the important continuity of this ritual from one generation to the next, not an unusual phenomenon in cookbooks and recipes, as these means of transmission importantly function to preserve memories from one generation to the next, create continuity, and transcend time to bind together different generations.[22] Henry Davidson, at one point editor of the *Evangelical Visitor*, anticipates this historical insight, remarking on the importance of passing ministerial responsibility from one generation to the next, which the planning of the love feast and its attendant testimonies highlight. He writes, "To those who are younger but upon whom devolves much of the responsibility of the work now feel that the responsibility is very great [*sic*]."[23] More often, though, letter writers comment on the youth in attendance as a celebration that their congregations clearly have a future and that beliefs are effectively being transmitted across the generational divide. George Detwiler remarks that "some yet young in years, were present, and their readiness in testimony gave added interest to the service."[24] S. G. Engle further notes of the Philadelphia love feast, "Such fathers [visiting lay members from nearby counties] in Israel are a real help to the younger ones here."[25] Mentoring of youth through the love feasts clearly was a valued function of this ritual.

Often a summary of the content of the love feast testimonies and sermons followed the record of attendance, with a short remark on who delivered these addresses and, at times, an account of the attendee's personal spiritual response to the event, but more often an assessment of how the event was experienced communally. Record of community response may have given these writers what they thought to be an appropriate venue for or veiled expression of their individual response, for, had they focused exclusively upon their personal response, they might have run the risk of displaying pride, egotism, or self-importance. In 1891 *Evangelical Visitor* editor Henry Davidson pleaded with congregants to provide the newsletter with accounts of the "result of these meetings," recommending that congregants "not think these accounts should be in that stereotyped style that so often is the case, but meetings and the interests in meetings should be given as though we felt the interest." He charges, "If there is any special circumstance connected with it that is especially interesting let us make a note of that, if the attendance is large, if the experiences are especially warm, if the behaviour is good, if the preaching is with more than ordinary power, if sinners are awakened or converted, if any unite with the church, give all these incidents." He reassures his congregants that while "some think these accounts and the church news look like bragging . . . we don't. . . . An honest faithful account of God's work . . . will be to his glory." He reiterates that "it is not boasting, it is only telling what God has done even though he has made you or some other brother or sister the instrument by which the work was accomplished."[26] Subsequent reading of issues of the *Evangelical Visitor* suggest that few congregants took up his charge to break away from the stereotypical form of report that Davidson discouraged, perhaps because the appearance of pride or braggadocio was indeed so frowned upon by and a particular concern of the Brethren in Christ church. However, the very "stereotyped style" of the report, as Davidson calls it, may indicate more than simply a resistance to boastfulness but likely also a fond adherence to the standardization of form of what essentially functions like a recipe or cookbook, the predictable formatting of important gustatory memory for easily referenced communication to other congregations and younger church members.

LOVE FEAST PREPARATIONS

As with any feast, the love feast required extensive individual and communal preparation. Prior to partaking of the meals, church leaders charged congregants to engage in a period of self-examination and to consider whether they were in need of "making themselves right" with God or with others, both inside and outside the church. Sister L., of Martinsburg, Pennsylvania, for instance, remembers in her account of the

October love feast at Woodbery that congregants "heard much what it is to eat unworthy of the embldms [*sic*] of the Christ's body."[27] If a member found himself to be unworthy, he was encouraged to repent, confess, and mend the broken relationship. Leah Steckley, of Bethesda, Ontario, remembers, "Then came the love feast and communion, and I was tempted to stay back, fearing that I might eat and drink unworthy, but I went with the rest and felt better until the next love feast."[28] Spiritual preparation and physical preparation for eating went hand in hand, or even foot in foot, as both clergy and laity considered the feet washing ceremony to be part of the preparatory process for the subsequent feasting. During the feet washing ceremony, same-gender congregants removed their shoes, socks, or stockings and washed each other's feet in a basin, modeling their behavior after Christ's washing of his disciples' feet in the New Testament as explained in John 13 and commanded in verse 14 of that same chapter. Feet washing symbolized the humbling of oneself in love to another, and it was intended to foster fellowship and open the means of grace as well as symbolically to purify and cleanse the self, both for the subsequent events of the love feast and through the general spiritual process of sanctification.[29] According to Noah and Mary Zook, in a 1900 report, "On Our Mission," "The consequence [of feet washing at this love feast] was love and unity prevailed which is essential to holding a real love feast."[30] Presumably, then, a false love feast, or an inauthentic or ineffective love feast, would produce divisiveness rather than the sense of community that this portion of the feast promoted.

Feet washing prepared participants for the meals and church services that followed by requiring a physical demonstration of humility that could prompt additional spiritual humility and devotion. Church members sought to follow "their blessed Lord in this humble command" and "earnestly prayed that their hearts might be washed in Jesus's blood as they had washed each other's feet."[31] After participating in his first feet washing ordinance, Charles Cocklin of Gormley, Ontario, remarks, "I think this communion is a very important matter. The apostle Paul tells us the bread is the body of Christ and the cup is his blood. When we look at these things dear brethren and sisters, are they not binding? Yes, they bind us together as one."[32] His use of the word *communion* here seems to point both to the feet washing itself and to the meals that follow, the line between them seemingly unimportant to him as he elides his experience of the former ordinance with the commemorative body and blood of the latter sacrament, each serving a similar function of unifying the community.

THE FELLOWSHIP MEAL

In the *Evangelical Visitor* few church members comment specifically on what foods they ate or what foodways were practiced during their fellowship meals, but archived diary accounts and later twentieth-century interviews with elderly congregants who remember the love feasts of their youth provide ample material on what congregants actually ingested during their fellowship meals and the arrangements by which they did so. Church communities served their congregants and visitors "family style," with appointed servers filling and refilling dishes, and, when one group finished eating, they would clean their plates with a piece of bread so that the next group could take their places at the same table to use the same utensils and the top or bottom sides of these same unwashed dishes. Standard meals included bread, fruit, coffee, soft-boiled eggs, and beefsteak for breakfast, and then afternoon and evening meals of the breakfast leftover meat, served cold, or beef noodle soup, as well as pickles, red beets, cheese, rolls, apple butter, snitz (dried apple) pies, coffee, cheese, and stewed prunes and dried peaches.[33] Some Brethren in Christ churches, such as the Ringgold congregation in Franklin County, Pennsylvania, could seat up to two hundred people at one sitting for their typical meal of beef, applesauce, stew, prunes, red beets, cheese, apple butter, and coffee.[34] Other congregations savored meals of bread, beef, potatoes boiled in the beef broth, rice soup, salted pickles, red beets, snitz pie, coffee, and crumb cakes.[35] While these foods were not restricted to the menus of love feasts, their sheer abundance at the feast or their status as holiday foods or foods suitable for hosting company set this menu apart as something special.

This menu reflected not only the celebratory nature of the meal but also its representativeness of late nineteenth- and early twentieth-century special occasion food culture, and particularly German American food culture during this time. The love feast chefs significantly featured sugar in their meals, for example, because by the late nineteenth century sugar was fully democratized and continued to be increasingly more sought out throughout America as a desirable ingredient, one capable of marking the importance and sentiment of an occasion.[36] Sugar also enabled these love feast cooks to honor easily the principle of "seven sweets and seven sours" that characterized their Pennsylvania Dutch (a corruption of Pennsylvania *Deutsch*, or Pennsylvania German) cooking heritage. They served their sweets, such as their dried fruits and hallmark apple butter, not as desserts but instead as side dishes presented simultaneous with the main meal and with their sours, like the pickles or distinctive pickled red beets. Even in their unique use for the love feast, their noodle dishes, snitz creations, crumb cakes, and pies likewise historically and even today distinguished their meals as rooted in mid-Atlantic Pennsylvania Dutch cooking, even as their church growth and missions sometimes transported these cooking habits to new regions.[37]

This mid-Atlantic regionalism persisted even as American home menus from 1820 through 1920 became more homogeneous as a result of the growing urbanization of America and as a diverse nationalized cuisine gradually and typically displaced much of the cooking of smaller ethnic communities like that of the Brethren in Christ.[38] While soups had gained popularity in America during this time, especially with the opportunities afforded by mechanized food processing techniques, particularly canning, this had little impact on the Brethren in Christ love feast soups, which were homemade.[39] However, industrialization and mechanization likely affected the Brethren in Christ's patterns of meat consumption. In the early part of the nineteenth century, the increasing role of beef in most Americans' diets, promoted by the development of the beef industry in the American West, as well as railroads and new refrigeration methods, did not directly contribute to love feast cooks' use of beef instead of the pork that the Pennsylvania Dutch had historically preferred, since these cooks still largely came from agricultural communities that raised their own beef. Indirectly, though, industrialization affected them, as they had to consume more of their own home-raised beef when their English neighbors, who had previously purchased this beef, began purchasing it from other sources made available by the railroads. Eventually, though, even cooks from rural Pennsylvanian communities began importing their beef from the West and thereafter reduced pork in their diets. Poultry, especially chicken, was also central to the Pennsylvania Dutch diet and to most American diets during this era, as was an expanding palette of vegetables and fruits that met the demand for more diverse dietary options, sometimes even vegetarian options as related to spiritual and health concerns.[40] The love feast menus, reported in archival documents in the form of extensive lists, showcase this diversity of foods as well as the treasured traditional foods of this church community. Their inclusion of new trends and old favorites signals the special nature of the feast, designed to welcome new guests as well as familiar faces from the congregation.

In addition to requiring planning for special foods, love feasts also called for special seating arrangements and physical accommodations. Depending on the church venue, congregants enjoyed their meals at special pews that had "adjustable backs hinged at the ends . . . [that] converted into a table . . . [or that] reversed so that persons seated on it faced the table."[41] Without pews like these, Samuel Baker, of Gormley, Ontario, remembers that at the love feasts he attended usually "there was a table on each side of the barn floor and part way across the end, leaving an open space of three or four feet between the tables. At the centre of the end table around this space the ministers were seated, and the remainder of the tables at that end were occupied with brethren and in front by sisters, until all were seated. Then the remaining seats at the table were filled up with those attending the meeting and all ate together."[42] Evidently both position in the church as well as gender factored into the seating arrangements, though the attendant commensality was intended to erase lines of division and foster unity and harmony among all. As in medieval English guild feasts, this feast's "defining rhetoric of honorable equality and commensality enabled new relationships to be legitimately forged, often between participants of markedly different background or economic status."[43] While the homogeneity of the typical Brethren in Christ congregation would not have required those of "markedly different" backgrounds to find common ground with one another, the commensality the congregants enjoyed at these feasts surely did help to forge new bonds between diners who otherwise would not have known each other very well, either because of age difference, geographical distance between their homes, or religious difference, the latter in the case of "worldlings" visiting the congregation from outside the church community.

SPIRITUAL FEASTING

While church members relayed in their diaries and later rehearsed in interviews their delighted memories of what they physically ingested at their love feasts, in more formal church records, like the *Evangelical Visi-*

tor, church members place much more emphasis on the spiritual feasting that accompanied the physical feasting. Indeed, a gustatory language fully pervades these accounts of spiritual development, even while church members remain reticent about what they actually ate. They clearly saw their spiritual and physical refreshment as intertwined, perhaps reflecting a form of belief in the "somatomorphic soul," because the vocabulary to which these writers turn to describe this refreshment of their souls is frequently bodily oriented.[44] S. G. Engle, for instance, remembers the love feast as a "feast to our souls" and muses that through the love feast "Heaven may come to us. We need not like Moses, when upon Pisgah's Mount, could view [*sic*] a land of milk and honey which he dared not enter, nor like Baalam view the tents of Jacob, in which he had no interest, but we can here in this vale of tears, eat of the fruits that grow upon the hill-top of glory."[45] Similarly reflecting on the relationship between physical and spiritual dining, Jesse Engle makes a point of referencing both the Hebrew and Greek etymologies of the love feast to assert that even though the communion meal might consist only of two small elements it is indeed still a *feast* and not merely a "full meal," for "when we hear of some who say, that, to take a small slice of bread, and a sip of wine, could not possibly constitute a feast (deipnon), we must conclude that such have a very limited knowledge of the body, and blood of Christ."[46] A feast need not be represented by quantity, he implies, but rather by its ability to fulfill, sustain, and provide joy. Even more explicitly, he later notes, "When we celebrate the Lord's Supper, and enter by the Spirit, into the essence of the mystical body of Christ, we do not only have a supper (as the amount we eat, does not make the supper, but the *time* in which we participate), but we have much more than a supper, we celebrate one of the greatest feasts, that the Christians can celebrate on this side of millennial glory."[47] The communion meal is thus a climactic meal of physical *and* spiritual feeding.

HOSPITALITY AND EVANGELIZATION BY FOOD

Many Brethren in Christ congregations, though not all, hoped that they could reach others outside their immediate communities by extending to them love feast hospitality. While at some points in church history certain congregations practiced "closed communion," not allowing "worldlings" to participate in their feasts, this was not standard practice in the church as a whole, and much more common was the view like that expressed by S. G. Engle, who framed the feast as an open, accessible, and inviting event, not as an exclusionary meal that separated believers from non-believers or church members from those not members of the church.[48] Monroe Dourte, for example, approvingly remembered, "Many of the unsaved folks would say, and I quote, 'we want to go to Lovefeast to eat.'"[49] If love feast and its food attracted visitors and had the potential to evangelize them in addition to feeding them and unifying the congregation itself, so much the better. In Sallie K. Doner's account of a love feast held at Mapane Mission, South Africa, she happily notes that the "natives and workers" gathered together for a love feast. Her mention of both categories of churchgoers points out that they were united in the feast, yet simultaneously marks her awareness of them previously existing in different categories within the church.[50] The love feast at least initiated a process of further unification that had not existed to such an extent prior to the event.

Love feasts also provided opportunities for evangelization. Congregants requested prayer "that God's presence may be made manifest . . . by leading sinners out from the world of sin into the ark of safety and divine protection," that "the ungathered sheaves" not go to "waste," or that congregants allow themselves to be used "in rescuing the lost of the earth."[51] Such mention at first tended not to be a part of love feast descriptions, as the focus of the love feasts was on community and unity, not separation.[52] However, in some cases, the love feasts did draw visitors from outside the church, sometimes simply visitors from other denominations, and the feasts became tools of evangelization.[53] With the advent of revivalism in the Brethren in Christ denomination in the late 1880s, which accompanied similar and often even more aggressive revivalist movements in other local churches, the Brethren in Christ began to try to develop a "more outgoing ministry, both within and without the church's boundaries."[54] Congregants' growing attention to and documentation of the effects of love feasts upon visitors suggest this increasingly outward-looking perspective or awareness of a world outside their own churches.

THE COMMUNION MEAL

The Brethren in Christ church ascribed to a memorialist understanding of the communion meal. Most laity contributing to the *Evangelical Visi-*

tor described the meal in terms such as those used by Alvin H. Berry, who remarked on the meal as a "beautiful memorial service whereby we can remember His suffering and death and the great price that was paid that we might have eternal life through the blood which flowed on Calvary's Hill."[55] *Memorial, memory, remembrance,* and *commemorative* recur throughout these accounts, reiterating the church's Protestant and rather nonsacramental, or even antisacramental, understanding of the holy meal as symbolic and emblematic only and not consisting of transubstantiated elements. Communion was practiced by men and women simultaneously, though separately, and communicants used strips of unleavened bread and, historically, drank from a common cup. Communicants broke off their own small pieces of bread from the larger piece, passing the larger piece to their neighbors while saying, "Beloved Brother [Sister], 'The bread which we break is the communion of the body of our Lord and Savior, Jesus Christ.'" As they passed the cup, they repeated to their neighbor, "Beloved Brother [Sister] The cup which we drink is the communion of the blood of our Lord and Savior, Jesus Christ.'"[56] These addresses reinforced the symbolism of the elements as well as the sense of familial unity that this commensality was intended to promote.

Of course, the communion meal, even more than the fellowship meal, fostered spiritual feeding and not just physical feeding in communicants. Among *Evangelical Visitor* contributors, Sister L. stands out as uncharacteristically verbose or personally revelatory in her recollections of her spiritual response to this meal. After communing, she remembers, "It seems to me I could, with faith, look up and see our dear Lord and Master led to Calvary's hill in the garden of Gethsemane nailed to that rough tree, to see him bleed and die for you and me. Not only you and me, but for the whole world. I often think of that dark and doleful night when the Savior of this world was crucified for the sins of the whole world."[57] She then turns to the more typical commentary on the communal response to the love feast as a whole, noting that the next day Sabbath meeting "began with experiences," as "brethren and sisters told how they had been built up by coming there, to the meeting, and their desire to still go on in this narrow way and live for the Master while life shall last."[58] Their love feast meals had sustained and even fortified these congregants not only physically but spiritually.

A gustatory language of spiritual refreshment reverberates throughout these *Evangelical Visitor* accounts. One anonymous participant in a Harrisburg, Pennsylvania love feast comments that "the seasons of testimony were times of refreshing, the testimonies having a clear ring, as regards the enjoyment of salvation through Jesus Christ."[59] The particular selection of the word *refreshing* echoes the language of gustatory theology as far back as colonial America, when Puritan writers sought affirmation of their spiritual development through literal gustatory change and bodily experience of "refreshment" upon reading Scripture, hearing the preaching of the Word, or praying.[60] In "Love Feast at Springfield, O.," one *Evangelical Visitor* contributor remembers the "time of enjoyment" prompted by the distribution of "the bread of life" and, in a related passage praising the entwining of bodily and spiritual pleasure, comments that the "testimony services" were so "inspiring" as to prompt love feast attendees to raise their hands in prayer.[61] The love feasts encouraged what in these rather restrained accounts passes almost for effusiveness, as congregants expressed deep pleasure in these communal experiences. These are "good feasts," "season[s] of refreshing," and times that prompt "rejoic[ing] on account of the feast" that "greatly refresh and strengthen the brotherhood."[62] When F. K. Bowers comments "we were truly fed," it is not at all clear whether this refers to spiritual feeding or physical feeding, presumably because for this author the distinction between the two types of feeding is unimportant or impossible to make, for the love feast feeds both body and spirit.[63] Indeed, citing a plethora of biblical verses about eating and drinking, participants in love feasts expected to experience the "lifegiving—and vitalizing," "all cleansing, and refreshing," "soul-quickening, and soul-reviving power" of the "everlasting *feast*."[64] This was eating and drinking unlike that typically experienced at any other time of the church year.

LOVE FEASTS REFLECTIVE OF THE LARGER CULTURE

The unique or special qualities of the love feast meals demanded a kind of behavioral and spiritual commitment that other meals would not have required, and interestingly it is these behavioral qualities that evidence the participation of Brethren in Christ church members with late nineteenth- and early twentieth-century culture outside their own church. In an attempt to prevent the love feast rituals from becoming "mere performance—in which case there can be no blessing to the partaker," one *Evangelical Visitor* contributor exhorts congregants to make sure "they 'worship . . . in spirit and truth'" and walk with Christ in "love" and "light," bearing "the fruit of light which 'is in all goodness and righteousness and truth.'" This done, "we shall see him as he is and be like him. 'And every man that hath this hope set on him purifieth himself even as he is pure.' (I. John 3:3 R.V.)"[65] This writer's concluding emphasis on purity, a quality that binds together the preparatory portion of the love feast, with its time of self-examination and feet washing, then the fellowship meals that follow, not only draws on a biblical language of purity but also invokes another language of purity common in the nineteenth-century American sanitation movement. A language of purity, particularly bodily purity, often gestures toward anxiety about maintaining class and economic divisions.[66] A church may focus on purity as related to the bodies of believers because these bodies are "centers of transcendent faith" that function "as instruments of spiritual salvation" and as a "channel of belief."[67] Many nineteenth-century American churches grappled with how to respond to new medical and scientific understandings of hygiene that could affect how congregants took the bread or cup, who touched it and when, and who could touch it after them, and the implications of all this for maintaining both unity and social division with the church. Beginning in the 1870s, the American public had become increasingly more aware of recent scientific discovery of the germ theory of disease transmission, which many churchgoers and clergy soon applied to the circumstances of communion, wondering if they were passing disease by drinking from the same cup or touching the bread that another had touched.[68] The physician William Baker, in an *Evangelical Visitor* article titled "Religion and Sanitation," quoted C. O. Probst, secretary of the Ohio State Board of Health, to explain the biblical basis for interest in sanitation. He then went on to himself assert that "it is just as scriptural for the minister to pour the wine in a separate cup for each communicant as to have it passed from lip to lip."[69] While many Brethren in Christ congregations embraced the advent of individual communion cups for reasons of hygiene, some of their members regretted what they perceived to be a dismantling of the unifying purpose of their communion table commensality.[70]

Concern about behavioral expectations for the love feast could be particularly acute among the more diverse Brethren in Christ congregations. In her account of a South African mission love feast, for example, Sallie K. Doner remarks, "We again met and commemorated the suffering and death of our dear Savior. Thirty-seven partook of the Lord's Supper. Sunday evening Sister Frey gave a talk on etiquette."[71] Why give an etiquette talk as part of a love feast? Perhaps Sister Frey intended this talk specifically to instruct the native peoples participating in the feast, who presumably were perceived as needing education on proper civilized behavior, and, just as likely, the talk was additionally targeted toward the etiquette of the Lord's Supper meal or love feast itself, as it stood at the nexus of the spiritual and physical practices of Brethren in Christ belief. Similar references to conduct and etiquette appear in other accounts of love feasts. Henry Davidson notes with pleasure that "general conduct was good" at the love feast he attended at Brother Zerchus's home, where the crowds grew so large that services expanded from the barn to outdoors, and he similarly finds that "the behavior of the people" during a love feast in North Dickinson County, Kansas, in 1892, was "exceptionally good," while "conduct" at a love feast in Belle Springs, Kansas, was likewise "very good."[72] Most strikingly representative of nineteenth-century concerns with hygiene as related to particular behavior and etiquette at the communion meal are the comments of *Evangelical Visitor* contributor Asa Bearss. He writes, in an 1891 submission titled "Some Things We Like to See and Some Things We Don't," that

> we like to see members clean and tidy. . . . We like to see all the members forward and participate in the ordinance of feetwashing and wiping to show that we are willing to hold still to each other and all will be wiped away. But we don't like to see members handle boots, shoes and stockings and then break the bread to each other with unwashed hands, especially those that officiate on the occasion; hence the necessity of a basin of clean water on hand, as "cleanliness is next to godliness and godliness with contentment is gain."[73]

His sentiments were echoed by physician William Baker, who also recommended that church deacons provide "a wash-basin, water and towels" for congregants to wash their hands after feet washing.[74] Some church members even advocated the use of individual foot tubs for reasons of hygiene.[75] If the corporate touching of communion bread generated controversy and contention because of classist assumptions overlaid on congregational and ministerial hands, the potential for even more controversy and contention existed in the Brethren in Christ church when both hands *and* feet factored into this ceremony of unity.

The elements of the communion meal likewise drew some comment from later writers about love feasts, once again pointing out that the broader religio-alimentary concerns of nineteenth-century churches in general touched the lives of the separatist Brethren in Christ, too. Throughout the nineteenth century, many Protestants churches, their clergy and their laity, wrangled with the implications of the temperance movement for the practice of the communion meal. Should they use fermented wine, unfermented wine, make their own wine, or purchase one of the new unfermented grape juice products? What, exactly, did Jesus drink? Did Jesus and/or the Bible teach against immoderate consumption of wine or promote complete abstention from alcohol?[76] In a column titled "Temperance," which immediately precedes another column charging congregants to announce their love feasts in the church paper well in advance of the feasts themselves, Henry Davidson remarks on "the terrible consequence of indulging in this dangerous beverage [alcohol]" and the lamentable results of drinking beer, whiskey, or wine, "a terrible experiment which may prove fatal to your earthly hopes and may finally destroy both soul and body."[77] Explicitly contrasting secular consumption with sacred consumption, Charles Cocklin writes in the same issue of the newsletter of "the love" he felt as "the effects of the love feast," in contradistinction to his growing conviction that "tobacco and liquor" should have no place in his life, after which he "shunned" these substances and "received the blessing."[78] Jesse Engle, in "The Lord's Supper," even more clearly spells out a connection between temperance and the meaning of the love feast, as he draws on portions of 1 Corinthians 11 to argue that the apostle Paul clearly had to correct the early Corinthian church's practice of the Lord's Supper, as they had fallen into their pre-Christian, "idolatrous" ways and made of the meal a disordered, disorganized, and drunken feast. Such behavior, particularly drunkenness, he argues, has no place in this sacred rite, even if wine is present, not just because drunkenness interferes with the sacred but also because it destroys the witness of the church to the poor and visitor, who might walk away from such bacchanalian displays disillusioned with how the church had stewarded its resources.[79] The issue of whether to use fermented wine, as had been the practice of the early Brethren in Christ church, or unfermented wine, which became increasingly more popular in the church in the 1880s, repeatedly came before the church governing body. The General Conference ultimately decided to recommend that the unfermented kind be used "as much as possible," but that each congregation could resolve this issue at their own discretion, with "forbearance" of each other's preferences and beliefs being practiced by all.[80] Attempting to sustain the spirit of unity characteristic of the love feast, the church hierarchy refused to make into doctrine their stance on alcohol as communion element if such a ruling would introduce divisiveness into their congregations.

The love feasts of the late nineteenth- and early twentieth-century Brethren in Christ church thus reflect both the unique distinguishing characteristics of this generally separatist church, such as humility and unity, as well as their participation in the conversations of nineteenth- and twentieth-century American culture at large, such as those about hygiene and temperance. The church developed a simply stated and simply practiced, though complex, gustatory theology, through which they bound themselves to one another, both in their home districts and in other counties, states, and countries, as well as extended hospitality and evangelized others through the means of food. Their faith was profoundly embodied, even as they looked to this physicality as a means by which to experience spiritual development and God's grace. While their love feasts clearly could not erase all church division, whether of class, economy, gender, or ethnicity, they certainly did promote a spirit of harmony and peace and gave congregants practical methods such as feet washing and commensality by which they could physically enact the love they knew they should feel and be able to demonstrate as fruit of their faith. At their love feasts they made clear to themselves and to others how they could fully realize the metaphors of the body of Christ and Christian brotherhood that their Brethren in Christ community so valued.

Notes

I would like to thank Glen A. Pierce, director of the Brethren in Christ Historical Library and Archives, for his time, expertise, and attentive assistance, as well as Rachel Yaegle, Messiah College English department work study student, for her help with photocopying and sorting through archival materials. I also appreciate the scholarship grant that Messiah College provided to me for the purposes of researching and writing this article.

1. For a history of the Brethren in Christ church, see Wittlinger, *Quest for Piety and Obedience;* and Climenhaga, *History of the Brethren in Christ Church.*
2. Davidson, "Love Feast" and "Untitled Submission" (June 1893). Davidson reports in the former that approximately three hundred communicants participated in Saturday evening ordinances, and Sunday attendance at the love feast was estimated at one thousand

people. He also outlines the "usual order" of the love feast events. In the latter report, attendance figures for a love feast in Belle Springs, Kansas again stand at three hundred communicants at the "commemorative ordinances" and eight hundred to one thousand at Sunday dinner. One *Evangelical Visitor* article reports of a love feast that attracted four thousand participants and at which over one thousand people were fed at one meal. Davidson, "The Brethren Conference."

3. Some congregations intentionally eliminated Sundays as potential days for love feasts because of the work it would take them to host the feast on what was supposed to be a holy day of rest. Their feasts thus were one-day affairs, rather than two-day events. Monroe Dourte, "Love Feast at Mastersonville, Rapho District: 1898," unpublished MS, 1898, Brethren in Christ Historical Library and Archives, Messiah College, Grantham, Pennsylvania, 1, and "Mastersonville, Rapho District," 2.

4. "Communion Seasons"; and Dourte, "Love Feast at Mastersonville," 1.

5. See, for example, Brubaker, "Anticipating the Future."

6. All of these narratives are now housed in the small Brethren in Christ church archives located in Murray Library, on the campus of Messiah College, in Grantham, Pennsylvania.

7. Puskar-Pasewicz, "Kitchen Sisters and Disagreeable Boys."

8. For this phrase, see Juster, *Doomsayers,* 103–104.

9. Lindman, *Bodies of Belief,* 2.

10. While the love feast was indeed a profound physical as well as spiritual experience, that physicality rarely, if ever, took the form of expressing sexual or erotic love. The love feasts, like most church events, fostered a degree of socialization and thus allowed young people to meet one another and perhaps to initiate the process of courting. However, there would have been little opportunity and certainly no expectation, but rather strong censure, of sexual encounters of any kind during the love feast. Male and female sleeping accommodations were separate, and there was no cross-gender kissing or feet washing. While the church papers occasionally included church members' complaints about disruptive behavior, such as lack of hygiene, at love feasts, there is no record of complaints about sexual behavior. Only brief expressions of "filial" or "brotherly" love appear with frequency in church documents. Even church members' descriptions of their love feast encounters with or experiences of the Divine are not marked by the ecstatic, erotic vocabulary or overtones that one might find in mystic or some late nineteenth-century or early twentieth-century communal societies' accounts of love for or with the Transcendent. Moreover, food at the love feasts is described by terse cataloguing, rather than by sensual, savoring detail, so this spiritualized gastronomy is paradoxically nonsensual, at least in print, though surely not in experience.

11. Ahlstrom, *A Religious History,* 731–762; Boyer, *Urban Masses;* and Hatch, *The Democratization of American Christianity.*

12. Brown, *Foul Bodies,* 9, 11, 291, 325–326, 361.

13. Sack, *Whitebread Protestants,* 9–59; Ahlstrom, *A Religious History,* 733; and Boyer, *Urban Masses.*

14. Ahlstrom, *A Religious History,* 733, 743.

15. Beahm, *The Brethren Love Feast,* 3–4.

16. Engle, "The Lord's Supper," 68–69. See also this same article in Engle, *A Treatise on the Lord's Supper.*

17. Emerging from German Radical Pietism, and with an Anabaptist view of the church, the Dunkers were much like the Brethren in Christ theologically and culturally, and certainly influenced them, though the two groups were not directly related. The Dunkers, whose name was derived from the obsolete German word *tunken,* or "to immerse," were called such because of their manner of baptizing adults by trine, forward-motion immersion. They were also sometimes called "Dunkards" or "Tunkards," as well as German Baptists or German Baptist Brethren, though they were unrelated to Baptist denominations. For more information on the Dunkers or the Church of the Brethren, see Durnbaugh, *The Church of the Brethren,* and *Fruit of the Vine;* and Gordon, "Brethren Groups." For a brief comment on the difference between Brethren in Christ and Dunker love feasts, see Wittlinger, *Quest for Piety and Obedience,* 66–67.

18. Ramirez, *The Love Feast,* 16.

19. Sider, *Messiah College,* 9–11.

20. Engle, "Love Feast at Philadelphia Mission."

21. "Miscellany."

22. Theophano, *Eat My Words,* 86.

23. Davidson, "Our Visit East," 185.

24. George Detwiler, "Untitled Submission," *Evangelical Visitor* 28 (June 1915): 4.

25. Engle, "Love Feast at Philadelphia Mission."

26. Davidson, "Church News."

27. Sister L., "Our Love Feast," 347.

28. Steckley, "My Experience."

29. Beahm, "The Brethren Love Feast," 6–7.

30. Zook and Zook, "On Our Mission."

31. Eyster and Eyster, "Lovefeast at Intokozo," 13.

32. Cocklin, "Let Us Be Careful."

33. Hess, "The Brethren-in-Christ Love Feast," 10; Dourte, "Love Feast at Mastersonville," 2, and "Mastersonville, Rapho District," 3.

34. Kipe, "Report of Early Love Feasts," 1.

35. Dourte, "Mastersonville, Rapho District," 3.

36. Woloson, *Refined Tastes,* 2–6.

37. Plaisted, "Mid-Atlantic Region," 2:90–98; and Zanger, "German American Food."

38. Williams, *Food in the United States,* 4, 6; and Elias, *Food in the United States,* 2.

39. Williams, *Food in the United States,* 27.

40. Plaisted, "Mid-Atlantic Region," 2:92–93; Zanger, "German American Food," 563; Elias, *Food in the United States,* 12; and Williams, *Food in the United States,* 33, 39–40, 206–209.

41. Wittlinger, *Quest for Piety and Obedience,* 85.

42. Baker, "Early Customs of the Church in Canada."

43. Rosser, "Going to the Fraternity Feast," 432.

44. Bynum, *The Resurrection of the Body,* 11, 295, 306.

45. Engle, "Love Feast at Philadelphia Mission," 437.

46. Engle, "The Lord's Supper," 69.

47. Ibid., 70.

48. Wittlinger, *Quest for Piety and Obedience*, 64–66.
49. Dourte, "Love Feast at Mastersonville," 2.
50. Doner, "Untitled Submission," 5.
51. Winger and Winger, "Untitled Submission."
52. E., "Love Feast at Rosebank"; and Doner, "Untitled Submission," 5.
53. Correspondent, "Love Feast at Springfield"; and Winger and Winger, "Untitled Submission," 4.
54. Sider, *Messiah College*, 12.
55. Berry, "Untitled Submission."
56. Wittlinger, *Quest for Piety and Obedience*, 64.
57. Sister L., "Our Love Feast," 347.
58. Ibid.
59. "Miscellany," 2.
60. Lee, "'The Hungry Soul.'"
61. Correspondent, "Love Feast at Springfield."
62. Aaron Ebersole, "Untitled Submission," *Evangelical Visitor* 21 (November 1907): 4; Davidson, "Our Visit East," 186, "Love Feast," 184; and "Communion Seasons," 362.
63. Bowers, "Love Feasts."
64. Engle, "The Lord's Supper," 70.
65. "Miscellany," 2.
66. Douglas, *Purity and Danger,* 126–127.
67. Lindman, *Bodies of Belief,* 5.
68. Sack, *Whitebread Protestants*, 9–59.
69. Baker, "Religion and Sanitation."
70. Kipe, "Report of Early Love Feasts," 3; and Climenhaga, *History of the Brethren in Christ Church*, 317.
71. Doner, "Untitled Submission," 5.
72. Davidson, "Our Visit East," 186, "Love Feast," 184, and "Untitled Submission," 184.
73. Bearss, "Some Things We Like to See," 106.
74. Baker, "Religion and Sanitation," 210.
75. Kipe, "Report of Early Love Feasts," 3.
76. Sack, *Whitebread Protestants*, 9–59.
77. Davidson, "Temperance," 264.
78. Cocklin, "Let Us Be Careful," 195.
79. Engle, "The Lord's Supper," 69.
80. Wittlinger, *Quest for Piety and Obedience*, 64–65.

METAPHYSICS AND MEATLESS MEALS

WHY FOOD MATTERED
WHEN THE MIND WAS EVERYTHING

Trudy Eden

In the United States in the latter half of the nineteenth century, a number of Protestant sects arose that had deep roots in mysticism and the hermetic tradition and shallower roots in the thoughts and practices of Emanuel Swedenborg and spiritualism. Although these sects varied significantly, they gathered under the general term *New Thought*. They believed in a united universe in which the Spirit, or Mind, constituted the complete reality of human existence. This Spirit was omnipresent and good. To adherents of New Thought, the body—and the evil, pain, suffering, illness, and mortality connected with it—were really only erroneous but correctable beliefs. The New Thought movement counted among its many adherents Mary Baker Eddy and her Church of Christ, Scientist, based in Boston; the Hopkins Metaphysical Association based in Chicago, the Church of Divine Science in San Francisco, Religious Science in New York, and the Society of Silent Unity in Kansas City, which became the Kansas City Unity Society of Practical Christianity in 1903 and later the Unity Church of Christianity. Today it is known as the Unity movement. The role of Christ and Christian principles varied among these sects and changed over time. In all of them, however, Christ served at the very least as a role model and reminder of the ability of all humans to reject the wrong thinking that centered on materiality and to claim their rightful place within the Divine Mind.[1]

The extension of this basic New Thought tenet led to the belief that the relief of pain and suffering and the eradication of illness could be accomplished mentally. The most prominent historical practitioner of this belief was Mary Baker Eddy, who had been a student of Boston healer Phineas Parkhurst Quimby. Others, some of whom were students or followers of Eddy, were Warren Felt Evans, Julius Dresser and Annetta Seabury Dresser, Emma Curtis Hopkins, Mary Plunkett, H. Emilie Cady, Charles Fillmore, and Myrtle Fillmore.[2] From the end of the nineteenth century to the beginning of the twentieth, mental healing attracted tens, hundreds, even thousands of new members to New Thought churches. It was a dominant activity of church leaders and staff. Newsletters, books, personal correspondence, and personal appearances helped to spread the New Thought philosophy as, of course, did successful cures.

Despite their heavy emphasis on metaphysics, some New Thought advocates paid close attention to the body and its care and feeding. The Unity Society of Practical Christianity, founded by Charles Fillmore and Myrtle Fillmore, was one of those groups. In what seems to be a flat contradiction to the basic tenet that the mind could correct all, Unity did not insist, but strongly advocated, that its followers practice vegetarianism. Was this belief and advocacy of vegetarianism a conflict in philosophy? After all, if the proper thinking could transcend all earthly woes, why did it matter what one ate or how one lived one's life? As the chapters in this volume make clear, food has been a useful tool for Christians since the Middle Ages: the uses to which it has been put are many. Three of those uses practiced by the Fillmores are evangelization, the use of the commensal power of food for group coherence, and the sacramental use of food to achieve spiritual regeneration. Compared to Christians in centuries before them, the Fillmores had a modern approach and styled these common elements of Christianity to their own liking. The practicalities of vegetarian eating in the early twentieth century—the acquisition of special food items and the preparation of meatless meals—attracted many people to Unity and held them there. The commensality of the shared meals at the Unity Inn and the common philosophical beliefs attached to those meals bound the faithful together as a group and gave them an identity.[3] In addition, Unity founders embraced vegetarianism because they believed it enhanced rather than undermined their metaphysics, which included a strong belief in an all-pervasive life force. Meatless meals mattered because they enabled spiritual growth in a way that meat-filled meals simply could not. More importantly, the Fillmores' vegetarianism bridged the divide between traditional Christian, even Catholic, practices and the still developing modern Christianity. The structure of that bridge was the most fundamental Christian belief, the taking of the sacrament, which assisted believers in their journey toward spiritual redemption. The style and the substance of the bridge, however, were Unity's own. Whereas earlier Christians might consider the bridge to be assistance from Christ, Charles Fillmore felt it was assimilation to "Christ Consciousness."

Charles Fillmore and Myrtle Fillmore, who founded the Society of Silent Unity in 1889, are excellent examples of how right thinking could turn personal suffering into health and wealth. Born in northern Minnesota in 1854, Charles fell while ice skating at age ten and broke his hip. Infections from the injury and numerous unsuccessful medical procedures to heal it left him with a right leg several inches shorter than his left and with what doctors believed was a fatal case of osteotuberculosis. By adulthood his health had improved, although he walked with a brace. Myrtle, born in Ohio in 1845, contracted tuberculosis at some point in her adult life and had struggled with it as well as stomach troubles and hemorrhoids for years. In 1877–78 she met Charles in Dennison, Texas, while seeking a tuberculosis cure. He lived there with his mother and worked as a railroad clerk. Charles and Myrtle married three years later and lived in Colorado and Omaha, Nebraska. They moved to Kansas City in 1885 where Charles became quite successful in real estate. By that time they had had three sons.[4]

In 1886 Myrtle and Charles attended a short course on Christian Science practice. Myrtle felt it changed her life. She applied what she had learned to her own illness, teaching her body that it was "full of vigor and energy," "energetic, strong and intelligent," and "no longer infested with ignorant ideas of disease, put there by [her]self and by doctors." She became convinced that her body was "all athrill with the sweet, pure, wholesome energy of God." It worked. Her achievement of curing her own, considerable, health problems led Myrtle to the conclusion that her mission in life was to become a spiritual healer. Myrtle's practice and success spurred Charles to his own exploration of New Thought beliefs. By the end of the decade, after much study, prayer, and meditation, he, too, accepted the divine internal presence.[5] As he worked out his ideas carefully through speaking and writing, he came to believe that "God is Spirit, the Universal Mind in whom we 'live, move and have our being.' This Mind is Omnipotent, Omniscient and Omnipresent."[6] It presided within all humans, giving them divine potential, and those who became conscious of it would be happy, healthy, and prosperous. Those who did not succumbed to evil, unhappiness, and ill health. Charles referred to this consciousness as "Christ Consciousness" because he believed that Jesus was the only human who had fully utilized his divinity through conscious thought.[7]

Between the two of them, Charles and Myrtle developed and led a circle of like-minded individuals. Their adherents soon numbered enough to be a church, and by the early 1890s they employed others to help with their important work. In addition, Charles edited periodicals as well as running the company that published them. He also founded the Unity Book Company and the Unity Tract Society, creating a correspondence course and then a regular school. By 1909 the Fillmores headed a worldwide movement with a staff that included their three sons, Lowell, Rickert, and Royal, and numerous employees.[8]

Charles Fillmore and Myrtle Fillmore converted to vegetarianism in the 1890s and incorporated their belief in it into their religious activities. So strongly did they believe in the benefits of vegetarianism, they started a vegetarian cafeteria in their church in 1906, the Unity Inn, and followed it with a store, the Unity Pure Food Company, from which anyone could purchase hard-to-get foods. In 1920 the church built a new Unity Inn, at the time one of the largest vegetarian cafeterias in the world, serving as many as ten thousand meals a week and offering free round-trip transportation to workers in downtown Kansas City between the inn and their workplaces. Although the Unity Inn has moved, it is still in existence at Unity Village in Lee's Summit, Missouri. As early as 1903, Charles published an article on metaphysics and meat eating in *Unity Magazine*. In 1906 and 1907 the magazine offered a column on diet written by Lowell Fillmore and on October 25, 1911, Royal Fillmore began a column, "The Vegetarian," in the newspaper *Weekly Unity*, which he authored until his death in 1923 under the pseudonym Veg.[9]

One would expect a successful real estate developer to be a skilled promoter of a church he founded, but Charles Fillmore's energy and creativity were entrepreneurial if not exemplary. In its early years, the Unity Society occupied a building in Kansas City. The Fillmores and some of the staff were vegetarian, and they cooked and ate their lunches at the church office. The idea of the Unity Inn grew out of this practice and the natural human tendency to offer food to visitors and friends. In 1906 Unity completed the construction of its first building and its first restaurant space. Diners gave freewill offerings for their meals, except for the Sunday dinner, which in 1909 cost thirty-five cents. Built in the Italianate architectural style, the building was bordered by terraces and enclosed by a hedge. The central dining room had a large fountain, red tile floors, and bay trees, with French doors opening onto the terraces. The first floor, which housed the cafeteria, seated two hundred diners and had a soda fountain. The second floor accommodated banquets. It had a fabric-draped ceiling, elaborate chandeliers, and a formal stage.[10]

The Unity Pure Food Company furnished customers foodstuffs unavailable in grocery stores or markets, including Millennium Extract, a vegetarian extract that tasted like beef; Kaola and Konut, coconut butters; cotton seed oil, sold as "Wesson's Snowdrift Oil"; Unity brand peanut butter; and coffee substitutes.[11]

The Fillmores followed up their food sales efforts with plenty of written promotional pieces. The Unity Tract Society published its first vegetarian cookbook in late 1909. An earlier advertisement stated that it would " surpass any cook book of this kind . . . in size, number of recipes, convenience, beauty and novelty." Designed to hang on the wall, each of its recipe pages had "a motto in red beside terse understandable recipes in large type."[12] Unity's strongest written promotions were the little notations Royal Fillmore included in his weekly columns, particularly those fleeting mentions of the Unity Inn cook, Mrs. Walmsley, whose recipes and menu suggestions, including recipes, appear in the column throughout the years. On February 7, 1912, she recommended her "exceptionally fine" recipe for "Macaroni and Millennium." On May 22, 1912, she suggested the novel idea of combining fresh strawberries, lemon juice, and vegetable gelatin for a "treat." The society also published the menus of their banquets on holidays and other occasions. They solicited menus from their readers and answered the questions on cooking they received.

All of these food-related activities emphasized the commensal benefits of Unity's food agenda, an aspect that must have been especially comforting to members living within and outside of Kansas City who found themselves not only practicing a nonconforming faith but a nonconforming diet as well. Every week Royal's columns spoke to readers as if they were all sitting in a room together. The descriptions of the banquets suggested that readers would have been there had something not prevented them. The dietary recommendations themselves, while separating Unity members from the larger society, united members by association in the small, tightly knit group.[13] Any time people share a similar diet, or even dine at the same meal, a connection forms between them. Christian churches have used this fact in their efforts to isolate their adherents from the larger society and identify them as part of a special group as well as to create a bond between them. Dietary restrictions such as meatless Fridays or Lenten restrictions, festivals, church suppers, and even foods raised or processed by Christian groups have all served this purpose.

With their foray into the arena of nutrition advice and advocacy, the Fillmores, in addition to participating in a new Protestant wave, joined a group of what can only be described as formidable health reformers. Their vitas matched those of their colleagues. Experiencing histories of illness caused by an injury, bad habits, or weak constitutions, they renounced their self-indulgence, searched for and found the ideas and practices that rewarded them with health, and began to publish their ideas. They were, after all, at the height of the Progressive period in American history, that time when no speck of dirt was too small to ignore and no industrial morass too large to tackle because a clean environment and a healthy populace offered nothing less than utopian rewards. Already by the time the Fillmores began their publications, John Kellogg had become famous with his sanitarium and his breakfast cereal, Horace Fletcher was extolling the benefits of careful chewing, and scientists at universities large and small were working to develop the science of nutrition and literally change the shape of the nation forever. Moreover, the Fillmores's Unity philosophy aligns with what historian James C. Whorton has defined as a hygienic ideology. All such ideologies rest on the belief that nature is good and should be trusted. Because most people do not do so, they cannot enjoy the degree of vitality and longevity of which they are naturally capable. The illnesses they suffer, therefore, are unnatural but can be reversed through proper action. Once achieved, physical health results in mental and moral perfection in individuals as well as in societies when it is practiced en masse. Finally, because personal and social purity are achievable, to refuse or fail to do so is moral failure.[14]

By the first decade of the twentieth century, many people advocated and practiced vegetarianism. Their rationale for doing so combined traditional justifications—some centuries old—with modern scientific ideas. Like all food philosophies, vegetarian thought dwelt on the food itself, the eater, and the physiological effects of any particular food once it was digested. In regard to the food, vegetarians offered a two-pronged argument. One prong attacked meat, the other uplifted vegetables. Criticisms against meat rested on economics, morals, and health concerns. Meat was and always had been a more costly foodstuff than vegetables, although, at different times and places, certain cuts of meat may have been less expensive than certain vegetables. The United States at the turn of the nineteenth century and into the twentieth did not break that tradition. Advocates of meatless living offered numerous scenarios and economic comparisons to support their arguments, although basic common sense would have done just as well.

Their moral arguments required more finesse, even though those discussions, too, represented a long tradition. A few advocates combined economics and ethics to question the justness of a relatively small percentage of the world's population commandeering resources to raise animals for food when a much larger proportion of the world starved. In a United States that at the time offered free land for homesteading and perceived itself to be a breadbasket of the world, that argument was not compelling. However, the killing of animals as well as the brutality with which it was often performed, did garner the attention of meat eaters and vegetarians alike. Some vegetarians joined forces with antivivisectionists to attempt to abate animal cruelty of all kinds. To those reasons, advocates added the unhealthy and cruel conditions in which livestock were forced to live.[15]

The ethics of the treatment of animals elided into health concerns when contemporaries discussed the issue of meat's cleanliness. At the dawn of the discovery of germs and with the simultaneous publication of Upton Sinclair's famous exposé of the packinghouse industry, *The Jungle*, all eaters concerned themselves with the cleanliness of slaughterhouses. Their attitudes toward cleanliness had strong tones of purity and pollution that went beyond mere dirt. Many vegetarians believed that even meat from animals raised and processed hygienically polluted the body because of its very nature and/or because, from the moment the animal was killed, it began to rot. They believed that neither chemicals nor refrigeration could completely forestall that corruption and that decayed meat caused diseases. Closely related to the theme of corruption was the idea, existing as early as the ancient Greeks, that the animal nature of meat prompted animal behavior in humans, particularly violence, lust, and anger as well as physical diseases.[16]

A meatless diet eliminated all ethical concerns. Most vegetarians insisted, in addition, that vegetables, even those pulled from the soil, possessed an innate purity unattainable by meat, had more vitality, and decomposed much more slowly. These qualities made plant foods easily digestible. Because advocates considered vegetables to be more nutritious than meat, they thought vegetables took longer to digest, which they believed to be an asset rather than a detriment.[17] Proponents of meatless living insisted that the design of the human digestive system, including the teeth, indicated that man's natural diet was plants, particularly grains. Although meat eaters argued that vegetables lacked the ability to provide eaters with the stamina, strength, and body warmth associated with the perceived "innate heat" of meat, vegetarians offered numerous testimonials and studies, some by prominent scientists, that concluded otherwise.[18]

Unity publications from 1903 to 1916 explain numerous reasons why what you ate and how you lived your life were important in a mentally constructed world in which sin, evil, illness, and even death could be eliminated through thought. Some justifications, particularly those written by Charles Fillmore, grapple head-on with the tough problem of metaphysics and meatless meals. Others, such as morality, filth and purity, animal cruelty, the Bible, and history, constituted the stock-in-trade of their vegetarian heritage, to which Royal Fillmore added a package of the popular science of digestion, health, endurance, and nutrition all loosely tied with metaphysical string. Recognizing the difficulty of converting from a meaty to a meatless diet in the early twentieth century (in one of the slaughterhouse capitals of the United States, no less), he also offered moral support and, always, a wide array of recipes.[19]

Veg began writing his column, "The Vegetarian," in *Weekly Unity* at age twenty-two. He was a likely and an unlikely candidate for the task. Having grown up in Unity, he certainly was familiar with its philosophies and practices. As early as age ten he wrote a piece for *Wee Wisdom*, the children's magazine founded by his mother Myrtle. A few years later he had his own column in the periodical and he took over its editorship in 1912. Contemporaries described him as the Fillmore son who would most likely have succeeded his mother and father at the helm of the movement, had he not died in 1923, because of his charisma and his strong determination to implement the teachings of Jesus in everyday life. The image of Royal Fillmore on paper, however, did not fit that of the flesh. He was obese since childhood. At age seven he weighed one hundred pounds, earning him the schoolyard nickname of "Baby Elephant." By the time he reached college, he weighed three hundred pounds. He died at age thirty-four of complications arising from hypertension and arteriosclerosis.[20]

The strong, lively character of Royal Fillmore drives "The Vegetarian." At times sophisticated, at times melodramatic, he hammered home the joys and imperatives of vegetarianism. Sometimes he relied on ancient wisdom, as when he published "Plutarch's Morals of Eating Flesh."[21] Other times he featured the works of contemporary authors, as when he presented the philosophy of Alfred McCann, a contemporary nutritionist and journalist.[22] Most of the weekly columns, though, came straight from Royal's pen. His recurring themes of morality, hygiene, economics, character development, Christianity, love, and personal spirituality intertwined with each other in numerous ways.

In its vivid prose and direct questioning, few modern essays have surpassed Plutarch's on the morality of eating flesh. *Unity Weekly*'s translation asks readers how the first man to eat meat endured the "blood of the slaughtered, flayed and mangled bodies." How could this "nastiness" not "offend his taste while [he] chewed the sores of others, and participated in the saps and juices of deadly wounds?"[23] For Plutarch, as for Royal Fillmore, the taking of an animal's life was the primary moral concern of meat eating. Royal often repeated stories about the companionship, love, and service animals offered humans to highlight the treachery involved in the eating of meat. The following story is representative. Royal met a "very refined and cultured woman" who showed a great deal of interest in "the law of Love," although she approved the killing of animals for "food and fur." She laughingly told him of her friend who, having acquired some chicks, raised them "to love her, to come at her call, to eat from her hand, and jump on her shoulder to caress her." One day, when the chickens were grown, the friend received unexpected company and, having nothing else to serve them, slaughtered her chickens. As she lifted the hatchet, she proclaimed, "This is enough to make me a vegetarian." But, of course, it wasn't. To Royal, that was the saddest part. He wrote: "Each of the pets put its trusting head upon the block and laid down its life that the perverted taste of some thoughtless guests might be pampered. . . . I did not smile. I was thinking, and my mind connected unconsciously the act of severing those three innocent heads with the pages of our daily papers, filled with accounts of heartless murders and atrocious crimes."[24] Animals, he believed, at the very least were God's creatures and at the very most our brothers and sisters with souls less developed than ours. To kill them to eat, when our planet provides us with more than enough plants, was immoral.[25]

Joined to this theme of immorality is that of love. Royal believed that the most commendable vegetarians were those who did so out of love. He defined it as the "unified feeling that we are all God's children, and therefore should share equally the great bounties which he has bestowed upon us."[26] A basic tenet of the Unity philosophy was that of the inter-connectedness of the universe and the necessity of love. It "oiled" every "delicately fitted part" of life, it "eliminate[d] vermin, diminishe[d] friction and heat" and was the "remedy for every social and moral evil." To talk about love was not enough. It had to be demonstrated, and killing our "earthmates" did not do so. Although Unity members did not accept the divinity of Jesus Christ, they did believe he had, through his thoughts and actions, achieved perfection and was a person to emulate. This "Christ Ideal" was "the road of Love, away from all struggle and pain, away from the stain of blood."[27]

The Bible caused Royal to express some degree of consternation. Frustrated with those people who misquoted it ("The devil can cite scripture for his purposes"), he insisted that Unity faith followed the spirit of the law and the principles of Christ's teachings, not simply isolated passages.[28] Having said that, however, he did resort to explicit passages himself on occasion. Citing Genesis 1:27–30, he concluded that God's plan was for mankind not to eat flesh. Genesis 9:4–5, he thought, indicated that, if the Bible became law, packinghouses would have to go out of business.[29] Quoting a modern translation of Romans 14:19–22, he encouraged his readers to "not undo God's work for the sake of what [they] eat, for if [they] put a stumbling block in the way of others," they were doing wrong. The "stumbling block," here, is death and "brothers," fellow creatures.[30]

Related to the issues of morality, love, and the Bible were those of character and spiritual development, especially of children. Good character came from living and acting in accordance with one's moral beliefs.

One could not profess the doctrine of love while, at the same time, encouraging, indeed paying for, murder at the meat market. Such hypocrisy was not consistent with good character. In this area, meat eating had another dimension. As already stated, many people believed that meat fostered negative emotions in humans.[31] "Meat steals away our love, our affections, our spiritual instincts and leaves in their place a passion, a lust, a restlessness which drives us on and on," wrote Royal on January 1, 1913.[32] Along with these negative emotions went certain vices. He was not alone in his belief that meat eating caused alcoholism and cautioned his readers to avoid meat for the sake of their own lives and those of their children. Parents, he cautioned, who would do anything to prevent their children from "taking up vice" or "being alcoholics *pave their way* to these ends with the meats they serve."[33]

Like other vegetarians of and before his time, Royal also justified meatless meals with arguments about hygiene, laced heavily with themes of purity and pollution. Barnyard hogs with "dirty snouts" that ate anything "from manure to ashes," and slaughterhouses that echoed with squeals of terror and flowed rivers of blood, in some ways, were not as bad as the meat-filled table and the eaters seated around it.[34] From that perspective, the local butcher was an assassin and the eaters hypocrites and accomplices to murder. He wrote: "We attend church, pray for love, mercy, peace and good-will, then go home to feed upon the fruit of carnage. We ask a blessing on our food and sink our teeth into the body of some poor animal. We smack our lips and remark on the state of decay that has rendered the flesh tender and rich in flavor."[35]

In contrast to the filth and pollution of meat, "The Vegetarian" offered the purity of vegetable foods. In addition, vegetables pacified the mind and gave strength to the body without any transfer of undesirable characteristics. When eaten in combination, they provided all the essential nutrients needed for health, strength, and long life.[36]

Alongside the theoretical arguments and exhortations in "The Vegetarian" lay practical information and advice. Numerous issues offered economic justifications for vegetarianism, some in the form of testimonials. Topics covered household and social economics, focusing on the extravagance of getting necessary nutrients via animal flesh instead of straight from vegetables.[37]

Although Royal Fillmore produced hundreds of weekly columns between 1911 and 1916, keeping his readers abreast of current and historical vegetarian rationale, he was, from the point of view of metaphysics, a backup to the star of the show, his father Charles. The contrast between the writings of the two on meatless meals couldn't be more vivid. While Royal was loquacious, Charles used his words sparingly. While Royal threw at his readers every traditional rationale for vegetarianism and then some, Charles stuck to metaphysics and that all-important issue of assimilation, the act of food becoming flesh. While Royal flamboyantly dwelt on the carnage of the slaughterhouse, the stench of scorched corpses, and the hypocrisy of those who celebrated Christmas with the dead bodies of murdered turkeys, Charles quietly enthralled his readers with the majesty of the transfer of life from one cell to another, the celestial importance of that transfer, and the ability of all humans to regenerate body and soul to achieve a higher spiritual consciousness. And he did it all in one essay, published for the first time in 1903.

In that essay, "As to Meat Eating," Charles stated that in 1887, when he began studying New Thought ideas (what he referred to as "the Truth"), he was told that thought, not food, dictated his well-being. That dictum proved correct as long as his spiritual growth remained within his conscious mind. However, after some time of study and effort, he began to experience "vibrations" in his "sympathetic nerve centers," feelings that he attributed to the quickening of his subconscious mind. As he put it, he "was becoming a conscious vital battery," witnessed by the dramatic growth in his "vital currents." His appetite, passion, and emotions became so strong he could hardly control them. Unsure of how to manage these increased life forces, he "set up a system of communication with the higher realms of consciousness" through which he learned what his body did with the food he fed it. Upon receiving food, the body put it through a "process of regeneration" to get it to the "condition to be built into the new body in Christ." This regeneration, he learned, took place in the numerous "subconscious centers" of the body.[38]

Physical and spiritual regeneration lay at the heart of Unity philosophy. Both Charles and Myrtle believed they could, through sustained spiritual effort, regenerate the cells in their bodies and in so doing cure illness, avert old age (perhaps even reverse the aging process), and even regenerate whole body parts. The ultimate act of regeneration—something Charles thought entirely possible for those highly practiced and spiritual persons—was dematerialization. Accomplishing such a feat, one could avoid death altogether. Charles worked all his life on regeneration. He believed he had successfully restored lost hearing in one ear and had made great progress with his tubercular leg. After years of spiritual practice, he discarded his leg brace. Decades later, shortly before his death in 1948 at age ninety-four, he stated that he had succeeded in restoring length and bulk to his leg, but had not entirely healed it. Disappointed that he had not been able to escape death, he believed that he would reincarnate and perhaps be successful in a future life.[39]

Regeneration of the body occurred at the cellular level. Charles called the cell a "mind battery vibrating with intelligence, force and substance."[40] Living cells in food had these same characteristics. Charles and others believed that plant foods retained their life after harvesting. Meat, on the other hand, because it was the substance of a dead animal, was life interrupted. Meat cells did not exhibit the "vigor and force of the animal" and were "only a festering mass of dead cells without a single animating principle." Furthermore, these cells could not regain "upbuilding" life until they had "pass[ed] through earth and the vegetable kingdom to the animal" (197–198).

Vitality was essential in food because humans, indeed all living organisms, ate to sustain life. As Charles emphatically put it, "*life* is the object of eating. Every form in existence is a manifestation of life, and the life idea that pervades it is its source. If that life idea is for a moment withdrawn the form collapses. Hence we do not eat matter, but *life*" (195). When a person ate, his body "appropriated" the food's cells and they became a part of his consciousness, the degree to which depending on the eater's ability to consciously regenerate the cells. The body, by itself, could extract only a small amount of energy from food cells, without the mental assistance of the eater to "build up and sustain" it for years, but this "thread of life [was] frail and its texture coarse" (196). The eater could change that tenuous state through conscious regeneration.

One can see then why food was so important to Unity metaphysicians. Meat, which they thought consisted of decaying "corpse-cells that tend to disintegrate," burdened the body. Furthermore, those cells retained the animal's negative states of consciousness, such as fear, suffering, violence, ignorance, anger, and lust, all of which transferred to the eater. Charles told a story of a group of diners who, after eating a beef dinner, became violently ill. The meat was not tainted, but, on further investigation, physicians discovered that the steer had fought for its life for an hour after its slaughter. He believed that during this time the animal transferred its anger and terror to its cells and that those negative qualities caused the diners' illnesses (198). Charles advised eaters to choose foods with the most vibrant vitality. Once their bodies assimilated such food into their cells, eaters must daily subject them to the "refining" process of regeneration. Such effort, Charles believed, "established a new body built up as designated by Jesus in the symbology of the New Testament" (197).

This metaphysics of meatless meals appears in a scattershot manner in "The Vegetarian" column, although readers unaware of Charles's important essay, or any other synthetic New Thought treatment of the subject, must have had difficulty synthesizing the difficult philosophy. "Every cell has a state of vibration . . . that is controlled by the mind of the organization to which the cell belongs," wrote Veg on January 24, 1912, and the eater had to "attune" those vibrations to his own. In other columns he explained that carnal cells had "low" vibrations that took a great deal of energy for the eater to overcome. They antagonized the body and so were not a true food. He called meat a "nutrio-stimulant," because, upon being digested and assimilated, it "disorganize[d] the proper body channels" as did alcohol, tobacco, tea, drugs, coffee, and cocoa. This effect countered the natural life forces in humans and degraded "man's organism" to the carnal plane.[41] In addition, "The Vegetarian" suggested that the participation in death attending all meat eating somehow factored into the metaphysical process. "Death is the breaking up of the unity between soul and body," he wrote. "If we do not wish to experience it ourselves, we should be careful not to be a party to it." To participate not only altered the body: it injured the "Universal Life" within us which "demands protection for all other life."[42]

In contrast to meat, vegetables had "negative vibrations," which made them easily assimilable and increased the body's receptivity to regeneration. Vegetables could give life to eaters if eaters allowed them to do so. They were man's natural food and possessed the wisdom to convert that which was not food—in other words, soil and the air animals exhale—and turn it into food pulsating with life. In addition, vegetables cleansed not only the blood of animals from the eater's body and mind but also the thoughts and actions that blood provoked.[43] Vegetables that grew below the ground were "of a more material state" but still contained one of the highest forms of energy. Fruits and nuts, on the other hand, were filled with sunshine, and their energy was easily set free. They exemplified the truth that, because everything was an aspect of mind, the more spiritual the thought realm in which a thing was produced, the better adapted it was for food.[44]

Royal Fillmore devoted most of the space in his column to the practicalities of daily vegetarianism. Occasionally he pulled back from the dishes and the drama to remind his readers of the true task in which they all engaged themselves—"to transforming human sepulchers into Temples of the Living God." Although food constituted the building material and vegetables were by far the superior choice, food, nevertheless, remained material until the eater "permitted the great harmonious Spirit of Truth to shape it into living substance."[45] This phrase nicely sums up the essence of Unity beliefs and why food mattered when the mind was everything. Mind, the body, and the food one ate were not disparate entities or ideas. The mind was not simply ethereal and the body and food merely substantial. Rather, they were unified by the fact that all three were, as Charles Fillmore expressed it, *"life."* No Cartesian dualism existed where organic matter without a residing soul was mere matter. Rather, all organic forms contained in their cells the power and majesty of the connected universe. If they were plants, that power rested in their seeds, and they mysteriously multiplied it with soil, water, sunshine, and air. If they were animals, they got it at generation and they lost it when they died. Between that beginning and end, only humans could consciously utilize this life when they digested their vegetable food and directed it to their cells to engage it.

In the hands of Charles Fillmore, the Unity philosophy retains the Christian tradition of the sacrament in that it is an act that imparts, at the least, a spiritual benefit and, at the most, divine grace. The taking of the sacrament is perhaps the most unusual food practice among Christians in the early twentieth century. A "meal" partaken of bread and wine, Catholics believed it was transformed through prayer by a priest into the literal body and blood of Christ. Protestants, on the other hand, believed the ritual taking of the two foods to have spiritual benefits. Despite this difference, both groups believed the regenerative power of the consumed bread and wine to be connected to the divinity of Jesus Christ. Charles Fillmore rejected that divinity along with its ability to spiritually regenerate. However, he believed in the human perfection of Christ and endeavored to provide his followers with the method through which they could attain it. A modern self-help philosophy with the highest rewards, it incorporated the ancient, sacred, and essentially Christian ritual of communion. Special food eaten as a part of a spiritual practice brought about desired spiritual growth. The traditional Christian practices implicate Christ in that growth; the Unity practice exemplifies Christ and requires the eater to achieve the same goal. Communion employs bread and wine; Unity uses vegetable foods. Communion was and is strongly associated with the divine, Unity's philosophy with the natural and the human.

In eliminating the divinity of Christ, Unity philosophy necessarily had to do away with the traditional communion practices of Christian churches that relied on such divinity. Those practices made no sense in a faith in which Christ was a human, albeit a perfected one. The removal of the ritual did not mean, however, that regeneration of the spirit through food disappeared as well. In fact, Charles Fillmore's philosophy quite clearly stated that regeneration of the spirit as well as the body was altogether possible and, like other aspects of New Thought religion, could be achieved on one's own, without the intervention of minister, priest, or god. The transformative force that the communion bread and wine were believed to be, or to represent, was the life force found in the cells of live organisms. Consumption of those cells was necessary for humans who wished to regenerate their spirits, their flagging bodies, and even, according to Charles Fillmore, their damaged or missing body parts. For early Unity practitioners, then, the daily act of eating vegetables that possessed the "life force" constituted a "communion" in which their consumption equaled the taking of blessed bread and wine, and their mental concentration on their bodily cells the accompanying prayer. It was the bridge that enabled them to cross the deep chasm between their old sickly or sinful selves and their new "Christ Consciousness."

In the nineteenth century, American Protestant beliefs fused with democratic ideas, spawning many new sects that practiced direct communication with God. The U.S. version of European romanticism, transcendentalism, strengthened that belief and urged Christians to look within themselves as well as to nature for personal growth. Unity took American Protestantism a step further when, insisting on the human superiority of Christ, it pronounced humans not only to have the same potential within themselves but to have to *achieve* it by themselves. A vehicle of this new empowering faith was food. The right foods, vegetables, possessed the life force necessary for spiritual regeneration. In addition, vegetarianism offered a wealth of possibilities for bringing the interested seeker and the adherent together at the Unity table, enabling the commensal bond and group identity so helpful in a young and growing congregation located in the meat-filled world of early twentieth century Kansas City. Thus, while Unity offered some novel ideas on the properties and power of food, it relied on age-old customs to implement those ideas.

Notes

1. Albanese, *A Republic of Mind and Spirit*, 303–317; Vahle, *The Unity Movement*, 145.
2. Albanese, *A Republic Mind and Spirit,* 303–317.
3. Rapport, "Eating for Unity."
4. Vahle, *The Unity Movement,* 6, 33–34.
5. Ibid., 6–8, 34–39.
6. *Unity,* November 1, 1895, 9, as quoted ibid., 39.
7. Vahle, *The Unity Movement,* 39–46.
8. Ibid., 145–148.
9. "Ready Reference File."
10. "Unity Inn Timeline"; "The Unity Inn—901 Tracy Avenue"; "The Convention," *Unity Magazine* (September 1906): 214–215.
11. "The Vegetarian," *Weekly Unity,* December 6, 1911, 4; and *Weekly Unity,* September 25, 1909, 1; *Weeekly Unity,* February 3, 1915, 1; and *Weekly Unity,* August 7, 1920, 1–2.
12. *Weekly Unity,* September 25, 1909, 1.
13. Rapport, "Eating for Unity."
14. Wharton, "Physiologic Optimism."
15. Iacobbo and Iacobbo, *Vegetarian America,* 125–154.
16. Ibid.
17. The length of digestion and assimilation (the repair and replacement of worn out body parts) concerned scientists and eaters alike at the time. The longer the process, the healthier and longer lived would be the eater.
18. Wharton, "'Tempest in a Flesh-Pot.'"
19. On theology and vegetarianism in general for this time period, see Calvert, "'Ours Is the Food That Eden Knew'"; and Gregory, "'A Lutheranism of the Table.'"
20. Vahle, *The Unity Movement,* 201–203.
21. "The Vegetarian," *Weekly Unity,* January 20, 1915.
22. "The Vegetarian," *Weekly Unity,* May 19, 1915.
23. "The Vegetarian," *Weekly Unity,* January 20, 1915.
24. "The Vegetarian," *Weekly Unity,* December 11, 1912.
25. "The Vegetarian," *Weekly Unity,* June 25, 1913, January 20, 1915, March 24, 1915, September 4, 1915, December 25, 1915, March 4, 1916.

26. "The Vegetarian," *Weekly Unity,* August 22, 1912.

27. "The Vegetarian," *Weekly Unity,* January 1, 1913 (quote), July 16, 1913, February 25, 1914.

28. "The Vegetarian," *Weekly Unity,* April 3, 1912 (quote), May 15, 1912.

29. "The Vegetarian," *Weekly Unity,* March 15, 1912.

30. "The Vegetarian," *Weekly Unity,* January 8, 1913.

31. "The Vegetarian," *Weekly Unity,* September 4, 1912, September 18, 1912, October 23, 1912, January 1, 1913, June 11, 1913, July 9, 1913, August 20, 1913.

32. "The Vegetarian," *Weekly Unity,* January 1, 1913.

33. "The Vegetarian," *Weekly Unity,* October 23, 1912.

34. "The Vegetarian," *Weekly Unity,* May 1, 1912.

35. "The Vegetarian," *Weekly Unity,* May 20, 1916.

36. "The Vegetarian," *Weekly Unity,* July 2, 1913, September 3, 1913, April 1, 1914, June 3, 1914, January 6, 1915, January 8, 1916, April 17, 1912.

37. See, for example, "The Vegetarian," *Weekly Unity,* August 7, 1912, October 30, 1912, May 5, 1913, April 16, 1913, April 22, 1913, May 19, 1915, and May 26, 1915.

38. Fillmore, "As to Meat Eating."

39. Vahle, *The Unity Movement,* 57–63.

40. Fillmore, "As to Meat Eating."

41. "The Vegetarian," *Weekly Unity,* January 24, 1912, June 10, 1914, September 2, 1914, October 23, 1914, February 28, 1914, April 24, 1912.

42. "The Vegetarian," *Weekly Unity,* March 20, 1912.

43. "The Vegetarian," *Weekly Unity,* January 24, 1912, February 28, 1912, October 22, 1913, March 10, 1915.

44. "The Vegetarian," *Weekly Unity,* February 12, 1913.

45. "The Vegetarian," *Weekly Unity,* February 25, 1915.

CHAPTER 9

Fasting and Food Habits in the Eastern Orthodox Church

Antonia-Leda Matalas, Eleni Tourlouki, and Chrystalleni Lazarou

This chapter examines fasting and the influence of Greek Orthodoxy on food habits from three perspectives: from literature and the literary, from information gleaned from account books of the nineteenth century reflecting ordinary and elite habits, and finally from an examination of the so-called Mediterranean diet as practiced in the mid twentieth century. Concluding remarks consider the impact these traditions may have had on present dietary patterns.

The Influence of the Christian Orthodox Faith on Food Habits

The following passage has been paraphrased from the Greek novel *The Two Loves* by Theotokis (1873–1923) and illustrates the importance of voluntary fasting as a special form of devotion in the Orthodox Church.[1] In the novel Arghyris Spatharos is an artist who paints saints and lives in a small village with his wife and son on the Greek island of Corfu. The story opens with a discussion of Easter food and what they plan on eating.

> "What did you cook today?" asked the artist.
> "For us, Easter food, but for you, who fasts for her sake, you will taste bread and olives," the wife replied humbly.

"OK . . . ," he replied contently. "And our son, he is downstairs?"

"Yes," she replied.

They both went downstairs to the basement. There, in a row, against the wall, stood three large barrels full of wine. Next to them, two containers—the first contained oil, the other, olives. Opposite the wall, through the door, was a table, on it, a lonely plate with olives and a loaf of bread. Sitting, relaxed on a log, was the son of the artist, and with a spoon he was mixing food and tasting it carefully, checking if it was seasoned well, as he chewed his mouthful. He was young, twenty-two years old, with a thin moustache, and he wore "European" clothing, as did all the youngsters in the village.

"Welcome master . . ." the son said with a grin, as he turned his head.

"Hello George," his father replied kindly, as he sat down at the table, and began crossing himself slowly.

George poured the mixture into a deep bowl, while the old man cut the bread, which was yellow inside like gold. George brought it to the table and sat across from the old man. His mother sat down close to him, bringing a large pitcher full of diluted wine and only one cup. The food was red with chili pepper; it was steaming and smelled good. The mother and son crossed themselves, and each took a piece of bread, and the three began to eat.

The old man chewed his bread and olives slowly with his damaged teeth, while the others, first the mother then the son, sharing a single spoon, took from the deep bowl, and dipped their bread into the red sauce.

"Master," said the son as if his first hunger pains were appeased. "Won't you taste some of ours?"

"No my child," he refused. "You eat, and don't you worry about me."

"And what would I gain if I gave up now? When I was young, I liked living the good life, but since then, I have devoted myself to the Madonna—I worship her name—I will fast until I depict her. The Virgin will help me, and I will finish the icon quickly, and there will be miracles for the Greeks . . ." said the old man.

The old man expresses his love and devotion to the Virgin Mary by taking an oath to fast while painting the icon. An oath calls on one or more gods to witness an assertion, a denial, or a promise.[2] The oath he took was a promise that forbade him from eating certain foods until he finished an icon of the Annunciation (*Evangelismos*). The old man kept his oath strictly and dismissed tantalizing offers of food made by his son and wife. He no longer desired the "good" life and instead swore to fast for her sake. Though in Greek Orthodox practice there are three lengthy regularly scheduled fasts during the year, the faithful may also choose a voluntary fast in order to seek divine favor. Pious individuals with various afflictions may fast in hope of relief. The old man in this story fasts for the sake of the Virgin Mary because he believes she will perform miracles for the Greeks on the Ionian Islands, who at the time were under British rule.

For lunch he eats bread and olives, observing a form of *xerophagia*—a strict fast in which one eats only "dry" food. "Dry" fasts exclude olive oil which is permitted on most fasting days. In effect when individuals abstain from olive oil, they forgo all main courses since olive oil is the foundation of traditional Greek cooking. Moreover, the fact that only one cup is brought out suggests that he also abstains from wine. Although permitted on most fasting days, there are some during which both oil and wine are prohibited.[3] But in this case, the more extreme form of fasting is a conscious personal choice.

The passage, written at the turn of the twentieth century, depicts traditional attitudes toward fasting. The old man practices self-control as a means of achieving perfection in his portrait of the Madonna and with this hopes to improve the circumstances of his compatriots through the intercession of the Virgin. Self-denial lies at the heart of Greek religious doctrines concerning food. The following excerpt further illustrates this notion. A Greek priest, Papa-Nicholas Planas, recites the following conversation he had with a nun who visited him on Clean Monday to confess.[4]

"Did you eat meat during the 'Cheese Week' my child?"

"Yes, and I ate today as well father!"

Priest Nicholas was in awe . . . since he and his companions, for three days, were not allowed to put a piece of crumb in their mouths, not even water!

"What can we have done father, let them throw food away?"

He says to her, "My child you have weighed food on one side of the scale and your soul on the other, and the weight of scale tilted towards the food?"

These two passages show the significance of fasting in the life of an Orthodox Christian. Fasting serves the dual purpose of preparing the faithful physically and mentally. It cleanses the body and soul while people anticipate an upcoming feast, helping them to focus on its true meaning.[5] True fasting is not merely a physical practice, but involves spiritual transformation as well. Self-restriction in Christianity constitutes a chosen lifestyle that enables disciples to bolster their willpower, but also to "reach" God.[6]

FOOD HABITS AND EASTERN ORTHODOXY IN THE NINETEENTH CENTURY

Food choices are largely shaped by one's culture. Orthodox dietary rules require periodic vegetarianism through the avoidance of all animal food, with the exception of mollusks and crustaceans, which are permitted on many fasting days.[7] Some plant-based foods such as wine and vegetable oil are also prohibited during some fasting periods. Historically, there has not been a general consensus among church leaders on exactly which foods were permitted during particular fasting days. The frequently revised editions of ecclesiastical rules and related literature reflect this confusion. A long-lasting dialogue has created controversy over which foods may be consumed during Wednesdays and Fridays and during the four Lents.[8] For instance, a number of theological texts written in the Byzantine era ruled that fish eggs do not constitute a "pure" food suitable for the fast. This view however, was in direct contrast to the common practice of lay people in Greece, for whom fish roe is an important food even during Lent. Though fasting proscriptions on seafood and plant-based foods (oil and wine) are less stringent, there has always been consensus on the avoidance of meat and meat products.

The Greek Orthodox religious calendar includes four extended fasting periods before each of the principal feasts: Lent (preceding Christmas—in the West called Advent), Great Lent (preceding Easter), Fasting of the Apostles (after Pentecost), and the two weeks preceding the feast of Assumption of the Theotokos [Mary] on August 15. In addition, meat is prohibited throughout the year on Wednesdays and Fridays. Fasting is prescribed for a total period of 150–180 days a year. The duration of fasting periods can range from seven weeks, in the case of the Great Lent, to a single day.

Though fasting has been a regular practice among Christians through-out history, few accounts survive that describe the manner and to what extent religion has influenced the food habits of ordinary people. Two nineteenth-century logs provide detailed information on the aforemen-tioned issues. The first is the log of a Greek merchant brig, the *Konstanti-nos*, that was discovered on the Aegean island of Chios.[9] This *katastichon* contains a register of all expenses, including detailed food purchases, supplied for the crew throughout their Mediterranean travels, from Au-gust 1865 to January 1868. The *Konstantinos* was officially registered as a Greek ship, and all the sailors were Greek Orthodox. Date-specific food purchases furnished by the ship's log can be used to determine how re-ligious practices influenced the crew's everyday eating habits. Detailed procurement data including dates, quantities, and regions where items were purchased have been described previously. The second log is the *katastichon* of an affluent urban family from the island of Syros written in 1837.[10] It should be noted that food patterns recorded in the second log do not exemplify conventional eating patterns of the general populace at that time, but food habits of the elite upper class.

In contrast, the sailor's eating habits while in port can be taken as being representative enough of the habits of the common male popula-tion. The most commonly recorded purchase was bread, in frequency and sheer volume, compared to all other food and nonfood commodities, amounting roughly to 450 grams per sailor daily. The average daily in-take of fresh meat has also been estimated at about 100 grams per sailor during nonfasting periods. Eggs contributed little to the sailor's diet; only ten dozen eggs were purchased throughout the twenty-nine-month voyage. A variety of preserved fish is recorded in the log, among them salt cod, salted and smoked mackerel, tiny salted female mackerel, salted sardines (consumed most frequently), and smoked little tunny (*lakerda*), while unidentified fresh fish was also regularly consumed while at port. Cheese was also a typical component of the crew's diet and was pur-chased in larger quantities when in the Black Sea and the lower Danube. Potatoes were eaten when the ship anchored in the Aegean Sea and in the Western Mediterranean, but not in the Bosporus or in the Black Sea. The crew consumed several types of legumes, haricot beans, chickpeas, fava beans, and lentils. Vegetable and fruit consumption varied according to season. During winter months, cabbage, celery, endive, leek, wild greens, and other unidentified "salad items" were consumed, while eggplant, okra, pepper, tomato, zucchini, figs, and grapes were more frequently consumed during summer months. Eggplant, peppers, and tomato were commonly purchased with meat or intestines, suggesting that the sailors often cooked meat and vegetable stews. During stays at port, wine consumption ranged from 50 to 80 grams per sailor, while raki (a type of eau de vie) and rum were also purchased regularly.

The log of *Konstantinos* also includes dates of food purchases, allowing for a comparison of foods procured during fasting and nonfasting periods. Purchases made during the Great Lent in 1867 (February 28 to April 15) and after (April 16 through April 30,1867) reveal the effect of fasting on the sailors' dietary pattern. It should be noted that during the seven weeks of Great Lent preceding Easter the diet should have only included legumes, vegetables, fresh and dried fruit, bread, olives, nuts and sesame, and invertebrate seafood.[11] All other foods of animal origin would have been prohibited.

A distinct difference between foods procured on fasting and nonfasting days emerged from this analysis. Bread, for example, was purchased thirty-seven times during Great Lent but only six times in the fifteen-day period following the fast. This is not surprising considering fasting restrictions, there would have been a need to substitute calories lost from meat and animal products with large quantities of other foods. Procurement data suggests that bread was one of these; it was the most frequently purchased item. Daily use of bread holds significant functional meaning in the Greek diet. Bread could accompany olives, cheese, tomatoes, fruits, coffee, or wine to form a proper meal and bread was at the core of traditional eating habits. J. L. Stephans presents a tourist account, about a man traveling with two Greek boatmen from the island of Zakynthos to the Greek mainland, that illustrates the traditional reliance on bread.[12] In this case, bread with eggs constituted the whole meal:

> We had been on and almost in the water since daylight, exposed to a keen wind and a drizzling rain, and now, at eleven o'clock, could probably have eaten several chickens apiece; But nothing came amiss, and, as we could not get chickens, we took eggs, which for lack of any vessel to boil them in, were roasted. We placed a huge loaf of bread in the middle of the floor, and seated ourselves around it, spreading out so as to keep the eggs from rolling away, and each hewing off bread for himself.

Seafood, in particular fish roe, caviar, mussels, and oysters were also an important component in the sailors' diets during Great Lent. Specifically, oysters, and mussels were purchased ten and twenty-three times respectively during this period and then never again to the end of this particular trip. The *katastichon* records three purchases of fresh fish during the Great Lent in the year 1867. The church permitted fish to be consumed on two occasions during the Lent: on March 25, the day of Annunciation of the Virgin, and on Palm Sunday.

From the *katastichon* of the *Konstantinos,* it becomes clear that the sailors ate more olives during the Great Lent compared to the nonfasting periods. In general, the Greeks ate olives throughout the year, but more so during fasting periods, even when olive oil was not permitted. In the past, olives formed, together with bread, the main meal for the peasants working in the fields. According to Christian Orthodox doctrines, olive oil and wine were the only vegetable foods the devout should remove from their diet during Lent days. The Greek diet was, above all, characterized by the use of olive oil. It was highly esteemed and considered a very nutritious food by the Greeks since medieval times, but, at the same time, it was an expensive commodity since its production required a low-yield and laborious process.[13] Olive oil's liberal consumption was considered a privilege only for rich people. Olive oil was sold in the Greek cities at prices 2 to 4 times higher than the price of meat, 1.5 times higher than the price of cheese, and 5 to 12 times higher than the price of wine.[14] The widespread belief that spilling olive oil brings bad luck illustrates the scarcity of the product.[15] Archival sources from the monastery of St. George Ragousi, located on the island of Chios, from the mid eighteenth century provide evidence that the quantity of olive oil secured for the operational needs of the church (i.e., as fuel for oil candles) surpassed the quantity that was used for the nourishment of the ten monks (61.5 kg/year versus 46 kg/year).[16] It has thus been proposed that the tradition of consuming the olive, but not olive oil, during Lenten fasts was intended to promote greater demand for the raw material, the olive, which was more abundant, at the expense of the secondary product, the oil, which was of limited availability.[17]

Sesame, in the form of the sweet sesame paste known in the East as halvas, was one of the most prevalent Lenten foods. Halvas, however, was eaten only during the winter and spring fasts, and never during the summer, as summer heat prevents its preservation. Other foods that were purchased more often during Lent fasting were lemons (likely to have been used to season seafood), wild greens, and various other salad items. Eggs were not eaten during fasting periods. However, eggs purchased on Saturday April 15, that is, the very last day of the Great Lent, were in all likelihood used as part of the Easter tradition. Hard-boiled eggs are dyed red on Thursday prior to Easter day, the day Jesus was nailed to the cross, to represent the blood of Christ that was shed.

Fruit procurement data during the fifteen-day fasting period of the Dormition of Mary and the subsequent fifteen-day nonfasting period have been examined. Figs, grapes, and melon were all purchased more frequently during the fasting period compared to the subsequent fifteen-day nonfasting period. Watermelon was the only fruit purchased more frequently during nonfasting days (once) than fasting days (twice). Fruit, naturally, was appreciated most during summer fasting periods, and, throughout the log, fruit procurement patterns are indicative of seasonality. During the Great Lent (February 27 through April 15, 1967), fruit was not procured.

The log of *Konstantinos* clearly documents a shift in purchases from nonfasting to fasting foods during Great Lent. Bread, seafood, leafy greens, wild greens, fruits, salad items, and halvas characterize the food purchases throughout the forty-nine-day fasting period. The pattern of the Greek sailors can be compared and contrasted to the pattern of an affluent urban family that lived on the island of Syros in the Aegean Sea three decades earlier. Food habits of the urban family have been analyzed and interpreted from a procurement log containing information on everyday purchases of food and nonfood items.[18] The log consists of forty-one handwritten pages detailing items, prices, and dates of purchases made from Monday, December 28, 1836, through December 28, 1837. The family consisted of six members, and resided in the city Hermoupolis, the capital city of Syros.

The procurement data of this urban family reveal food habits that differ considerably from those of the sailors. The consumption of meat (264 times a year), followed by butter and caviar, were most characteristic of this family's food habits. Contribution of meat to dietary regimen varies according to the economic environment and the degree of affluence. Meat consumption patterns of this particular family correspond to a high level of affluence. Meat was commonly consumed with rice (227 times a year). Occasionally, rice was eaten with butter or tomatoes as a meal on its own, possibly during periods of fasting. Available evidence suggests that rice consumption was associated with a high socioeconomic status on mainland Greece. The present family had a live-in worker, which may also suggest economic affluence. After rice, meat dishes were most commonly served with potatoes (74 times a year) and pasta (28 times a year), however, during warmer months, vegetables such as eggplant, zucchini, and okra accompanied meat dishes. Vegetables were eaten frequently; throughout the year, they were purchased 680 times (otherwise quantified as two purchases of vegetables per day) and were usually eaten raw in the form of a salad or cooked in a stew. Tomatoes (128 times a year) were eaten regularly, followed by leafy greens, potatoes, and okra. Green vegetables and salads, of which the islands of the Aegean have a plentiful supply, varied according to season. Wild greens, however, are never mentioned in this log. We know that wild greens were sold in urban markets throughout the Greek mainland and the Aegean Islands in the nineteenth century, but were generally considered a lesser food item by urban Greeks.

Procurement data suggests that the present urban family did not strictly adhere to fasting prescriptions and fasted no more than 30 of the 150 fasting days. Intake of caviar and halvas, foods considered appropriate for fasting, reflect changes in consumption between fasting and nonfasting periods. Around the months of April, August, and December (the months that correlate to the three lengthy fasts), intake of caviar and halvas increased. The log reports no consumption of halvas during the summer months, which is expected, as it is a difficult food to preserve in warm conditions. The family ate fish frequently, roughly once every three days. Caviar was consumed 122 times throughout the year, and was sometimes purchased twice in the same day. Wine accompanied meals daily. Fruit was consumed 179 times a year, whereas grapes (77 times a year) and figs (36 times a year) were consumed the most. In particular, grapes and figs comprised more than half (56 percent) of all fruit consumed by the family throughout the year. Annual consumption of fruit is a reflection of availability. Figs and grapes tolerate the dry Greek climate and have been traditional and abundantly available fruits of the Mediterranean since time immemorial. Additionally, though the family consumed butter and oil frequently throughout the year, the intake of butter declined, while oil intake increased during fasting periods. Butter, though preferred by this affluent family during fasts, replaced Noby the traditional olive oil, a vegetable fat. In summary, animal products, namely, meat, fish, and butter, dominated the diet of this prosperous urban family, while fasting was seldom observed.

FOOD HABITS AND EASTERN ORTHODOXY IN THE MID TWENTIETH CENTURY

Greeks have received widespread attention during the past decades owing to their traditional, semivegetarian diet. Information on the diet followed in Greece in the late 1940s through the early 1960s has formed the basis of an eating pattern that epidemiologists have coined the Mediterranean Diet,[19] touted as the prototype of a prudent and health-promoting lifestyle alternative. Two surveys, the Survey of Crete and the Seven Countries Study, explored food habits among peasants on the islands of Crete and Corfu and have substantiated the notion of a healthful Greek-Mediterranean Diet.

The Survey of Crete: 1948

The Survey of Crete was conducted by representatives from the Rockefeller Foundation from May 19 to November 15, 1948.[20] It was an investigation into the feasibility of raising the standards of living in an undeveloped area and explored ways in which knowledge and skills from industrialized countries could benevolently assist underdeveloped areas such as Crete. According to seven-day diet records, foods of vegetable origin, such as cereals, vegetables, fruits, and olive oil, primarily characterize the Cretan diet. Olives were used throughout the year in large quantities and typically consumed as oil. Grapes were eaten in substantial amounts, in addition to other fresh fruits such as apples, melons, and pomegranates. During the winter months, pulses and nuts were consumed considerably, potatoes were used extensively as well. Meat, fish, milk, eggs, and sweets were scarcely consumed. Including only a small amount of meat, poultry, game, or fish in various dishes was common practice. Rice and milk were considered important commodities in Crete, the former recognized as a treatment for gastrointestinal disease, and the latter may have gained significance because of extensive child-feeding programs that had been established in the area. *Hondros* (crushed wheat and milk, salted, cooked together, and then spread out in thin sheets and dried in the sun) was consumed by three-fifths of all families. Because of fuel and cooking equipment scarcity, there was a tendency to cook one-dish meals. Main cooking methods included stewing and boiling, and approximately half the families cooked once daily. When tomatoes were unavailable, tomato paste was used to cook vegetables and stews. It was recorded that Cretans had the habit of dipping bread into the sauce of stewed or braised dishes. Seasonal fresh fruit was the preferred dessert at the end of the meal.

The researchers observed that the degree of observing fasts varied from family to family and by age group. Children were often not expected to observe long or strict fasts, whereas the older people were more likely to fast for lengthy periods. Some carried out fasting on Wednesdays and Fridays, but this may had been merely abstention from meat. The following (in decreasing order of importance) were named as foods eaten by the Cretans during fasts: fresh vegetables, including tomatoes and potatoes, legumes, olives, bread, rice, and pasta, fish roe, shrimp, squid, honey, halvas, must syrups, fresh fruit, tea and sugar, sesame paste, and *hondros.*

The Seven Countries Study: 1960s

The Seven Countries Study, initiated in the late 1950s, investigated the relationship between food intake patterns and long-term incidence of coronary heart disease and overall mortality. The study included sixteen cohorts from seven countries.[21] The Greek sample consisted of individuals from the islands of Crete and Corfu, Greece. Dietary data showed that Southern European cohorts, including Crete and Corfu, were characterized by a dietary pattern high in cereals, legumes, vegetable products, oils, and wine, whereas intakes of meat and animal products were low. Further analysis revealed that the main source of fat was olive oil. Throughout the duration of this study, data did not differentiate between fasters and nonfasters, and, therefore, the effect of Greek Orthodox fasting practices on dietary habits remains unknown. More recently, Professor Aravanis (the investigator who designed the Seven Countries Study methodology) confirmed that fasting practices might have significantly influenced dietary habits. Following a personal communication with Professor Aravanis, Sarri and Kafatos report that 60 percent of the Cretan study participants were fasters who not only fasted during the seven weeks of Lent but also strictly adhered to other Greek Orthodox Church fasting guidelines.[22]

Prevailing dietary patterns in the mid-twentieth century suggest a relationship between the Orthodox religious dietary pattern and a traditional diet whereby meat and animal products are eaten in small amounts and foods of vegetable origin are eaten regularly. However, the surveys did not record any information regarding fasting compliance, and it remains unclear to what extent observed patterns were influenced by Orthodox fasting decrees.

FASTING PRACTICES IN THE LATE TWENTIETH AND EARLY TWENTY-FIRST CENTURY

Fasting is still a common practice among Greek followers of the Eastern Orthodox Church. On the basis of various observational studies conducted since the 1980s that examined fasting practices among Greeks, we may conclude, though, that the length of periods observed is less than that of previous decades.

During the years 1988–90 we conducted a field study on the island of Chios in the Aegean Sea with the purpose of investigating the eating habits of rural and urban residents.[23] Our findings indicate that fasting practices differed according to economic environment. Fasting was a common practice among women who lived in the poor, mountainous areas of North Chios, as two-thirds of them reported observing at least fifty days of fasting year-round. These poor peasant women also adhered to a weekly "protocol" of food choice for planning their family's main dish during nonfast periods: they typically cooked meat or poultry as their main meal on Sundays and Thursdays, fish on Saturdays and Tuesdays, and legumes or vegetables (stewed) on Mondays, Wednesdays, and Fridays. This customary protocol facilitated observing the fasting rules on Wednesdays and Fridays. Peasant women in the prosperous villages in the South and urban women living in the island's main town, on the other hand, exhibited different rates of fasting; only one-third of these women reported having fasted for more than fifty days during the previous year. Among the Chian men, fasting was even less common: only one out of six, among both peasant and urban men, had observed more than fifty days of fasting during the previous year, while the majority reported fewer than twenty-five days of fasting.

Further information on the fasting practices of contemporary urban Greeks is provided by the ATTICA study, a Greek epidemiological survey that collected dietary and other lifestyle information in a representative sample of some three thousand adult men and women living in the greater Athens area in the early 2000s.[24] Almost half of urban men and women observed religious fasts of just one or two days, while only 4 percent reported having fasted more than thirty days during the year.[25]

The CYKIDS, a study that was conducted in 2005 among 1,140 school children between nine to thirteen years old in Cyprus provides information on how fasting rules are put into practice among the very young.[26] The findings show that one out of four Greek-Cypriot children is a *regular faster. Regular fasters* were classified as children who reported that, during the previous year, they had observed most of the fast days of Lent and Great Lent as well as Fridays and Wednesdays. It is informative to examine how frequencies of food consumption between children who only fasted occasionally (*nonfasters*) and children who were *regular fasters* differed.[27] Looking at the 0.05 level of statistical significance, we found the following differences: children who were regular fasters consumed eggs, milk, fish and seafood, vegetables, and soy protein products more often compared to nonfasters, while they consumed sweets and various convenience foods, such as candy, chocolate, and "junk" food, less often. No differences were found with regard to the use of meat, legumes, bread, and fruit. At first glance, it may seem that, compared to their counterparts who do not fast regularly, children who fast regularly consume eggs, milk, and fish more often, whereas they also consume meat as often. One may argue, however, that fasting among these children and their families is also indicative of adherence to more traditional dietary habits. This trend is expressed by a decreased use of processed, convenience items, such as potato chips and candies, rather than by a reduction in conventional animal products, such as meat, fish, and milk.

The CYKIDS study also documents the use of novel Lent foods; children substituted soy milk and soy meat substitutes for dairy milk and meat during fasting periods. Among children who fasted regularly, 14 percent reported drinking soy milk at least twice a week as opposed to only 6.5 percent among children who were classified as nonfasters. For use of soy meat substitutes by the children, similar rates of 16 and 7 percent, respectively, were found.

The data indicates that, in contemporary time, a rather small portion of the Greek population complies with the traditional fasting regime of the Orthodox Church. The evidence suggests that urban Greeks are less likely to observe extended periods of fasting compared to their rural counterparts. In addition, the rules about foods permitted during Lents have been enriched with novel interpretations such as the use of vegetable meat and dairy substitutes.

Nineteenth-century dietary patterns compare with those of the early twentieth century where meat was seldom consumed and bread, wine, and olive oil were key components of the diet. The eastern Mediterranean dietary reliance on plant food sources is dictated by the dry climate and mountainous landscape, which can only support small-scale husbandry. Agriculture in this part of the world developed at a very early time and has since dominated peoples' livelihoods and customs. Ancient religious rituals and practices were preserved during the Christian era, and they were given new meanings. What's more, the Orthodox Church introduced an annual schedule of fasting that concentrates on the frequent avoidance of animal food. The periodic abstinence from meat and dairy is viewed as a form of asceticism to strengthen personal willpower and discipline, enabling one to overcome his or her passions. Through this the Church also implemented a policy that may have sustained other natural resources and inadvertently contributed to overall health.

Notes

1. Konstantinos Theotokis, *Oi Dyo Agapes* [The two loves] (Athens: Epikairotita, 1997 [1910]).
2. Mathew Dillon, "By Gods, Tongues, and Dogs: The Use of Oaths in Aristophanic Comedy," *Greece and Rome* 42, no. 2 (1995): 135–151.
3. Wine and olive oil are forbidden on all Wednesdays and Fridays throughout the year. The only exceptions are the following: Wednesdays and Fridays of Bright Week, after Christmas, and of the Publican and Pharisee Week (three weeks before the beginning of Great Lent), after Easter until Pentecost, on certain name days of Great Saints, during the Cheese fare (the week before the beginning of Great Lent), Christmas, and in the years when the Dormition of the Theodokos happens to be on Wednesday and Friday. We are thankful to Father Ioannis Kyprianou (Saint Nicholaos, Engomi, Nicosia, Cyprus) and to Mr. Xenophon Lazarou (Nicosia, Cyprus) who provided the information on fasting days and periods.
4. Nikolaos Pournaras, *Philokalia* (Thessaloniki: Pournara, 2002), 287–288.
5. Sotiropoulos, "The Pre-holiday Fasting of the Orthodox Christian Church."
6. Jackson, "Fasting."

7. The avoidance of all animal and animal products is completed on the following fasting days and periods (with few exceptions throughout the year): Wednesdays and Fridays, the Great Lent (forty-nine days prior to Easter), the Lent (forty days, November 15 through December 23), Fasting of the Apostles (the period after Pentecost until June 28; length varies from one to six weeks), Fasting of the Dormition of the Theotokos (from August 1 through August 14), January 5—Theophany (Epiphany) Eve, August 29: the Beheading of Saint John the Baptist, and September 14—the feast of the Exaltation of the Holy Cross.

8. Matthaiou, "Dietary Taboos During the Ottoman Occupation."

9. The *katastichon* is available in the archives of Chios, found in the Korai Library, city of Chora, island of Chios (document accession number: 1225B). Matalas and Grivetti, "The Diet of Nineteenth-Century Greek Sailors."

10. Kremmydas, "Urban Dietary Patterns."

11. Imellos and Polymerou-Kamilaki, "Traditional Material Life of the Greek Populous."

12. Stephans, *Incidents of Travel*.

13. Lydia Sapounaki-Drakaki and Zenon Mathas-Demathas, "Olive Oil in Nineteenth-Century Greece: Consumption and Prices," in *Olive Tree and Olive Oil* (Athens: ETBA Foundation, 1996), 155–163.

14. Efthemia Liata, "Prices and Commodities in Athens (1839–1846)" (Athens: National Bank Educational Institute, 1984), 92–106.

15. Philip Argenti, *Manuscripts of Chian Folklore*, vol. 2 (Chios: Historical Archives of Chios, 1890).

16. Provided in the Monastery Code of Saint Georgios Ragousis for the years 1711–1866, Historical Archives of Chios, manuscript no. 215.

17. Matthaiou, "Olive Oil and the Fast."

18. Kremmydas, "Urban Dietary Patterns."

19. Willet, "The Mediterranean Diet."

20. G. Leland Allbaugh and George Soule, *Crete: A Case Study of an Underdeveloped Area* (Princeton: Princeton University Press, 1953), 107.

21. Mennoti et al. "Food Intake Patterns and Twenty-Five-Year Mortality from Coronary Heart Disease."

22. Sarri and Kafatos, "The Seven Countries Study in Crete."

23. Matalas, Franti, and Grivetti, "Comparative Study of Diets and Disease Prevalence."

24. Panagiotakos et al., "Status and Management of Blood Lipids."

25. Personal communication with Demosthenes Panagiotakos.

26. Lazarou, Panagiotakos, and Matalas, "Dietary and Other Lifestyle Characteristics of Cypriot Children."

27. Chrystalleni Lazarou, unpublished data.

CHAPTER 10

DIVINE DIETING

A CULTURAL ANALYSIS OF CHRISTIAN WEIGHT LOSS PROGRAMS

Samantha Kwan and Christine Sheikh

Over half a century ago, in 1957, Presbyterian minister Charlie Shedd introduced his book *Pray Your Weight Away*. In it he attributed overweight/obesity to personality flaws in people with these body types including, as he stated in an interview with Patsi Farmer, "a guilt complex[,] inferiority complex, resentment toward the world in general, hatred for one person or group of persons, escapism or just plain loneliness."[1] Shedd's solution to this web of pathology was a regimen of exercises, set to the rhythm of verses from Psalms and Proverbs, coupled with acknowledgment of how inner spiritual turmoil becomes externally manifest in what Shedd understood to be the sinful fat body. Not one to mince words, Shedd famously remarked in *Pray Your Weight Away* that "we fatties are the only people on earth who can weigh our sins."[2]

Since the publication of Shedd's best-selling book, followed by two more best sellers, *The Fat Is in Your Head: A Life Style to Keep It Off* and *Devotions for Dieters,* an entire Christian diet culture has flourished. Hundreds of Christian weight loss programs have inundated a forty-billion-dollar-a-year secular diet industry,[3] inspiring an array of questions for sociological and cultural inquiry. In her ground-breaking work, R. Marie Griffith examines the role of religion in the history of U.S. weight-loss culture, paying special attention to gender, class, and race.[4]

This chapter builds on her work in that, while Griffith offers an exhaustive analysis of how various forms of Protestant Christianity in the U.S. engage diet and fitness discourses in ways that are novel and mundane, this chapter examines how contemporary Christian elites use secular diet and body discourses to foment an ostensibly unique Christian identity. We thus address several questions: What do these diets say about the body and health? How do these diets differ from and/or resemble conventional diets? How do Christian leaders who developed these diets engage religion to promote their messages? Finally, what do these diets say about bodies and religion, including the reproduction of gendered beauty norms?

Five prominent Christian diets contain answers to these questions. They are Neva Coyle and Marie Chapian's Free to Be Thin diet, George Malkmus's Hallelujah Diet, Jordan Rubin's Maker's Diet, Gwen Shamblin's Weigh Down Diet, and Carol Showalter's 3D Plan Diet.[5] These diets were and continue to be highly visible, clearly articulated, and extensive in scope. Most came or still come with elaborate Web sites and offer workshops, workbooks, support groups, and/or inspirational talks. The books accompanying each diet have also been labeled best sellers. Simply put, these were and still are leading Christian diets.

This chapter thus presents an analysis of these diets with an eye toward a critical cultural understanding of health, beauty, body, and religion. It begins with an overview of two camps in which these diets can be classified, followed by a discussion of several mainstream assumptions about fat bodies, health, and beauty. An analysis of these Christian diets then illustrates how they both embrace and reframe these secular assumptions. The chapter closes by examining the social significance of these diets for understanding gendered bodies and hegemonic cultural norms.

CHRISTIAN DIET TYPOLOGY: SUCCESS WITH GOD AND GARDEN OF EDEN DIETS

An analysis of Christian diets suggests that they can be classified into two camps. On the one hand, like secular diets, Christian weight loss programs draw upon a simple algorithm for weight loss: weight loss is inevitable if one reduces caloric intake and maximizes caloric output. Both secular and Christian diets profess some variation of this equation, differing only in the type and amount of food and exercise recommended. However, these Christian weight loss programs are unique insofar as followers are told to turn to God for success. In other words, religious faith lies at the heart of these regimens. For example, participating in Coyle and Chapian's Free to Be Thin diet means entering into a covenant with God. In their words: "You are making a commitment with the Lord today regarding how you treat your body."[6] Drawing on the Holy Spirit through prayer and devotion brings strength in times of temptation and weakness; God will provide followers with the discipline needed to lose weight. Shamblin's Weigh Down Diet, along with Showalter's 3D Plan Diet, urges a similar core method: Trust in God and weight loss is forthcoming. These modes of Christian dieting can be referred to as Success with God.

On the other hand, Rubin's Maker's Diet and Malkmus's Hallelujah Diet can be labeled Garden of Eden diets. While these diets also emphasize faith, Scripture, and God as key sources of empowerment, discipline, and inspiration, they differ from Success with God diets in that they are also characterized by a nostalgic return to an "ancient" style of eating. For example, the Maker's Diet encourages Christians to purge their bodies of processed or artificial foods and preservatives and adopt what is thought to be a more natural way of eating. The Hallelujah Diet advises even greater restrictions, in part resembling a raw foods vegan diet. Malkmus, formulator of the Hallelujah Diet, likens our civilization to a modern Babylon.[7] His diet plan, which he also refers to as a "Genesis 1:29 diet,"[8] stresses the foods Adam consumed in the Garden of Eden—foods derived directly from the earth such as fruits, vegetables, seeds, and nuts. According to Malkmus, individuals are overweight because God-given systems of immunity and self-healing do not work to their maximum potential when individuals fuel their bodies with the Standard American Diet (SAD). The SAD lacks nutrition because foods are cooked, processed, and devoid of life. Returning to a more natural and blessed way of eating thus promises health and weight loss. Notably, Garden of Eden diet proponents maintain that their diets cure not only "obesity" but also an array of health maladies—from cancer to irritable bowel syndrome to depression and anxiety.

THE FAT BODY: SECULAR ASSUMPTIONS

Western body discourses make various assumptions about fat and fat bodies that construct the discursive milieu in which Christian elites generate their own uniquely Christ-centered understanding of the appropriate body. Gaining a nuanced understanding of Christian diets, then, requires a more general grasp of how fat bodies are understood within Western culture.

First, as Susan Bordo maintains, the external body functions as a metaphor for internal processes in which the fat body represents unconstrained desires, impulses, and the appetite.[9] Despite biological limitations and structural constraints such as access to affordable healthy foods and leisure time for exercise, there is a pervasive belief in Western cultures that individuals can change their bodies. Fat bodies are seen as a choice and considered a product of laziness and a lack of will or discipline. These "moral models of fatness" emphasize personal responsibility and are prominent in Western societies.[10] This ideological outlook means that fat individuals are admonished for their supposed weakness and for making poor decisions. Indeed, research suggests that this individualistic ideology correlates with size-based discrimination.[11] For example, fat individuals are treated more negatively when others assume they are responsible for their physical condition.[12]

Second, contemporary body discourses sometimes assume that weight gain is a result of psychological stress or disorder. Specifically, fat individuals are thought to suffer from some form of psychological emptiness such as loneliness or depression.[13] To deal with this void, individuals turn to food as a source of comfort and/or control, and this behavior potentially results in an "overweight" or "obese" body. Others have argued that eating disorders at either end of the spectrum, that is, extreme weight gain or weight loss, are a reaction to social oppressions such as hetero/sexism and racism.[14] In both perspectives the fat body is a problematic response to psychological or social stressors, whereby individuals employ food as a coping mechanism. In secular discourses, addressing this problematic response may involve some form of therapy, working with nutritionists to develop "better" eating habits and/or turning to the services and products of commercial programs like Weight Watchers, NutriSystem, and Overeaters Anonymous.

Third, Western medical discourses deem fat unhealthy. Public health messages promoted by the medical community claim that it is unhealthy to be overweight or obese—conditions defined using the Body Mass Index (BMI).[15] According to the Centers for Disease Control, these conditions can increase an individual's risk of type 2 diabetes, stroke, and hypertension.[16] The medical community encourages fat individuals to lose weight by eating healthily and exercising daily.[17] This medical perspective remains pervasive despite assertions by Health at Every Size and fat acceptance advocates who challenge the obesity-health risk link; these advocates also contest the claim that the fat body is itself unhealthy.[18] Indeed, the social power of the medical establishment,[19] the medicalization of obesity,[20] and the multibillion-dollar-a-year weight loss and diet industries all help to legitimate the dominant medical paradigm that equates fat with unhealthiness.[21]

Lastly, mainstream U.S. culture generally deems the fat body unattractive. Despite the celebration of the voluptuous body by seventeenth-century painters such as Peter Paul Rubens, contemporary Western aesthetic norms typically dictate that, to be desirable, women should strive for slim bodies and men should pursue a muscular Adonis physique.[22] Feminist scholars have identified the socially and politically debilitating effects of this aesthetic ideal,[23] the numerous and harmful body modification practices associated with it,[24] and the innumerable ways the beauty industry has profited from women's body insecurity.[25] Nevertheless, these ideals remain ubiquitous and function as taken-for-granted hegemonic norms.

THE FAT BODY: UNIQUELY CHRISTIAN ADAPTATIONS

Western body discourses thus make several assumptions about the overweight body including the beliefs that fat people lack will or discipline and make poor choices that affect their weight; overeat or eat compulsively to fill an internal emptiness; and are unhealthy and unattractive, but can become healthy and more attractive by losing weight. These assumptions are not only embedded in secular talk, but are directly mirrored in American Christian dieting discourses. However, while Christian leaders adopt these assumptions, they *also* uniquely reframe them in Christian rhetoric. In the frameworks presented in these Christian diet programs, attaining a healthy body becomes a *religious* obligation where God provides the motivation and proper guidelines for body transformation.

CHOICE, WILL, AND DISCIPLINE

For example, like other Christian diets, Showalter's 3D Diet Plan stresses individual choice. Thus, similar to mainstream thinking, Showalter presumes the fat body is caused by poor lifestyle decisions. She embraces the attitude that individuals can control their weight and, in fact, make "right" choices. As she states of herself: "The problem was me, not God. I loved to eat—I just hated to gain weight. And even after 'willing' the weight off through Weight Watchers, I still chose to begin eating the wrong foods again. . . . If I ate what I wanted, when I wanted to, I was going to get fat again. . . . The problem was me!"[26] Coyle and Chapian take an even stronger position on poor personal eating habits. They ask followers to consider whether their unhealthy eating habits are actually sinful, especially when nutritious and healthy food is available.[27] Essentially, they frame eating unhealthy foods not only as a poor choice but as a sin that ultimately violates the sacred temple of the body.

Again resonating with mainstream diet gurus, these Christian authors connect the fat body to individual moral fiber. Overweight Christians, like overweight nonbelievers, are thought to be lacking in character. These authors argue that overweight individuals overeat and/or fail to exercise because they lack the will and discipline to do so. Without discipline and a firm rootedness in biblical imperatives, they easily succumb to worldly desires. As Rubin writes of his Makers Diet: "we have allowed food to become our idol. Too many people admittedly 'live to eat.' . . . In our promiscuous society, we say yes to virtually every whim and desire of our palate, resulting in the national dilemma of becoming overweight, sedentary, and an increasingly sick population."[28] At the same time Christian diets individualize weight problems in this secular manner, they also claim that the answer is found in one's relationship to God. True weight loss success, they argue, requires turning to God for strength and discipline. Indeed, this is a key dimension of Showalter's 3D program—discipline (the other two are diet and discipleship). So while Christian diet leaders profess that inadequate character manifested in laziness and poor choices leads to the overweight condition, the solution ultimately lies with God. For example, in both the earlier and recent versions of her 3D Diet Plan,[29] Showalter admonishes herself for relying upon her individual will, rather than God, for weight loss. It is God, she argues, who is the long-missing element of her weight loss journey. Showalter is explicit that one must rely upon God for successful weight loss. Or, as Coyle and Chapian say of their Free to Be Thin diet, their diet is a formula for success since *"God cannot fail."*[30] Trusting in God and turning to Him through prayer and devotion will provide the strength and knowledge necessary for weight loss.

EMPTINESS

Embedded in this discussion of overeating and poor choices, which ostensibly characterize the production of the fat body, is the conjecture that
these poor habits are motivated by internal emptiness. While secular discourses presume that individuals overeat because of social stressors, emotional neediness, depression, and unfulfilled lives, Christian leaders use
the concept of emptiness to highlight spiritual deficiencies. Whereas secular authors suggest that fat people require therapy or some other intervention to uncover the roots of their ostensibly poor eating habits, Christian authors intimate that fat individuals attempt to fill the God-shaped
holes in their hearts with food. While Christian weight loss programs,
mirroring mainstream discourse on the fat body, also tie poor eating habits to loneliness, histories of abuse, or other kinds of trauma, they ultimately still argue that overweight/obesity is born of distance from God,
idolatry of worldly things, and other problems that can only be remedied
by seeking to please and draw closer to God rather than to the self.

For example, Shamblin talks expressly about the emptiness she believes
motivated overeating. In her Weigh Down Diet she describes "two empty
holes"[31]—one in the stomach, which requires food, and one in the heart,
which she describes as a proxy for emotional and spiritual needs. Shamblin makes her argument about human emptiness clear by including a dia-
gram of the human form with two empty spaces in it, one shaped like a
stomach and the other like a heart. Of the heart, she notes: "The person
who attempts to feed a longing heart with food will stay on the path to
overweight."[32] The solution to the dilemma of overeating to fill an empty
or "longing" heart, Shamblin argues, is to "relearn how to feed or nourish the longing human soul with a relationship with God."[33] Her Weigh
Down program focuses on teaching followers how to distinguish between
actual physical hunger and the longings of an empty heart. Ultimately
Shamblin argues, "if you love and trust the Lord, you will feed yourself
the appropriate amount, and you will not indulge in desire eating."[34]

Like Shamblin, Showalter assumes that being overweight is caused by
excessive eating. Showalter implicitly ties this "lack of discipline," an oft-
used phrase in her books, to unresolved emotional and spiritual troubles.
She invites readers to "be open to new understandings of your weight
struggles,"[35] with said "understandings" being an analysis of willful-

ness and rebellion vis-à-vis one's food consumption. Showalter argues that "food, like everything else, needs to come under the Lordship of Christ. . . . The whole area of food brings out rebellion, fear and anxiousness, and it reveals a lot about who we are inside."[36] She also includes an assignment during week 6 of the program, advising readers: "Examine your [eating] journal for clues of rebellion regarding food. How can you constructively deal with resentment, rather than with food?"[37] Thus like secular diets, Christian diets offer a set of strategies for dealing with pathological eating habits, although it is now framed in terms of accepting God's love into one's heart. In the end, Christian leaders argue, it is only by so doing that the spiritual emptiness at the root of overeating may truly be remedied.

HEALTH

One dimension of striving to live in obedience to God is trying to discern what God wants for and from human beings. A few of the Christian diet authors suggest that God does indeed have a "natural state" intended for humans in which they eat the appropriate kinds and amounts of food. This line of thought was identified earlier as the Garden of Eden model of Christian dieting, which rests on the assumption that human beings do in fact have a primordial state where they may live according to God's plan by consuming natural whole foods. Eden enthusiasts argue that contemporary modes of food production, such as the development of manufactured preservatives and artificial ingredients, produce foods that are toxic to the body and run counter to the natural state in which God wants his creation to exist.

Rubin, for example, bemoans the state of contemporary foodstuffs, the majority of which he argues is a departure from the idyllic diet intended for humans by their creator: "We have departed so far from the wisdom of our forefathers that fully 55 percent of the American diet is 'new food'—not designed by the Creator or eaten by our ancestors. . . . We must leave behind our disease-producing diets and lifestyle and return to our Creator's dietary guidelines, as incorporated in the Maker's Diet!"[38] Similarly, in his Hallelujah Diet, Malkmus maintains that modern innovations in food production are an insidious corruption of how human beings were intended to live by God. His Hallelujah Diet, is comprised of mostly raw foods (85 percent living foods and only 15 percent cooked foods). It also focuses on the elimination of toxins, emphasizing clean air, clean water, moderate sunlight, exercise, and rest.

All the Christian weight loss programs analyzed here rest uncritically on modern medicine's declaration that fat is directly linked to poor health outcomes, despite evidence that the location of fat on the body matters and that fat may even serve a protective function against certain diseases.[39] Indeed, Showalter explicitly accepts the most standardized version of health definitions by including the BMI chart in her books and advising program followers to calculate their BMIs and figure out what their "healthy"—that is, normal—weights should be. Shamblin too includes charts for her readers to use when tracking weight loss and decreases in measurements.

These Christian diet advocates also demonstrate their belief that fat is unhealthy by including an array of illustrative vignettes and success stories in their books. For example, in 1977 Showalter recalls being scolded for her weight gain by a doctor who tells her that she is too young to weigh almost 170 pounds. She quotes him as saying that "young mothers fall into depression from being overweight [and] older people literally die from overweight."[40] Thirty years later, Showalter retells this story with no revision or critical commentary, tacitly accepting the doctor's assertion that being overweight is essentially a death sentence.[41]

In the Maker's Diet, Rubin refers to obesity as a "disease," and the book includes several testimonials from those whose health problems are essentially defined by what they consider to be excess weight. Five of the seven "success stories" explicitly describe weight loss as a key to improved health. The theme of thin as healthiness and fat as sick and diseased is also evident in Coyle and Chapian's Free to be Thin Diet when they tell followers that weight loss indicates that one is "on your way to a healthier you."[42] The conflation of obesity with poor health is thus a thread that runs throughout the Christian diet programs examined here. Like their secular counterparts, Christian diet authors profess the fat body to be a diseased body a priori and offer their readers tools to become healthier by losing weight.

BEAUTY

Lastly, Christian and secular diets both engage, albeit through different lenses, beliefs about fat aesthetics. While mainstream diets tend to embrace hegemonic norms that celebrate thin and muscular aesthetic ideals, for women and men respectively, Christian authors warn their audiences not to fixate on external beauty. Coyle and Chapian ask followers to reflect on their motives for weight loss. Chapian admits that her life only changed when she made "the decision to stop pursuing thinness and become dedicated to health and wholeness instead" (21). Christians should be motivated by a desire to "feast on God's precious Word" (23) since "in all these things we are more than conquerors through him who loved us" (Romans 8:37). As Coyle and Chapian put it, "food abuse, pigging out on unhealthy junk food . . . lying in bed all day with an overeater's hangover" can all separate believers from Christ's love (24).

They concede, however, that there is "nothing wrong with wanting to look attractive" and note a fine line between wanting to look good and the vanity that can hinder God's work in a Christian's life (26). The Free to Be Thin diet reminds followers of Philippians 2:3: Do nothing out of selfish ambition or vain conceit (26). In addition, Shamblin's Weigh Down Diet emphasizes that "the motivation to be thin is not vanity—it is natural. God has programmed us to want the best for our bodies."[43] In fact, Shamblin makes clear that God "programmed" individuals to desire a "right weight" and that health problems suffered by overweight individuals reinforce this desire. Similarly, Showalter rebuffs external beauty as a motivator to weight loss and criticizes her previously self-centered dieting motivations. As she puts it: "I dieted so I could wear nicer clothes, get more attention from my husband and family, and have a good self-image. I was at the center, but the center of my life was supposed to be God."[44] In sum, these diets all frame external beauty as prideful and unchristian. Thus both Success with God and Garden of Eden diets agree that Christian weight loss should focus on physical, emotional, and/or spiritual wellness.

The emphasis on inner beauty ties in part to the Christian's view of the body as a temple that must be pleasing to God. All the weight loss programs examined here refer to 1 Corinthians 6:19–20 or similar passages that underscore the body as a sacred temple: "Do you not know that your body is a temple of the Holy Spirit, who is in you, whom you have received from God? You are not your own; you were bought at a price. Therefore honor God with your Body." Like the Eden diets, to honor God with one's body is to keep it pure by not ingesting modern, anthropogenic, processed, and artificial foods or preservatives. These impure contaminants are, both literally and metaphorically, toxins. Honoring God with one's body also comes in other forms. For example, Rubin warns readers against getting tattoos, citing Leviticus 19:28,[45] and Malkmus rebukes options such as surgery, radiation, chemotherapy, drugs, and other medical interventions, arguing that they are not God's answer to sickness.[46] Like other Christian diet gurus, Malkmus relies on Romans 12:1–2, stating that, "your bodies [are] a living sacrifice, holy, acceptable unto God."[47] Similarly, honoring God with one's body means not engaging in self-harm, particularly through overeating.[48] Indeed the four themes are interconnected.

This analysis of five prominent Christian weight loss programs examines the various ways in which these programs adapt mainstream assumptions about the fat body. While secular discourses claim that fat individuals are fat because they lack will and make poor choices, experience some form of emptiness, are unhealthy, and are aesthetically displeasing, Christian leaders encourage their followers to turn to Scripture and the Holy Spirit—rather than food—to fill this emptiness, overcome weakness, and develop strength. The goal is a body that is sacred, healthy, and pleasing to God. Even though external beauty is not in and of itself an unholy motive, Christians are reminded that vanity and conceit are ungodly; holy motives include a desire for spiritual, emotional, and/or physical well-being.

Discussed elsewhere,[49] these subtle yet powerful Christian adaptations of mainstream tenets are among several means that evangelical leaders take to solidify a collective Christian identity. They do this by employing various cultural resources in their available "cultural toolkits" such as religious doctrine and Scripture,[50] while simultaneously promoting body modification—an end that can be deemed a superficial, anti-Christian, and antimodern goal.[51] By doing so, Christian weight loss programs reframe parts of mainstream culture to resonate with Christian discourses. Diet talk is no longer secular, but simply another dimension of how Christians can live a uniquely Christian life.

These Christian adaptations, along with Christian leaders' general condemnation of the "obesity epidemic" and the fat body, have solidified and expanded the realm of control over the fat body. Despite the various meanings of fat and recent challenges to mainstream understanding of the fat body,[52] Christian body messages undeniably reproduce the conventional view that fat is both unhealthy and unattractive.[53] Christian weight loss programs thus continue to reinforce a traditional body hierarchy that privileges thin and conventionally beautiful individuals and stigmatizes and discriminates against those deemed physically unattractive.[54] This cultural hierarchy becomes even more firmly entrenched and difficult to dismantle now that it is has the support of a powerful social institution, the Christian church. Christian weight loss programs can therefore contribute to ongoing fat phobia, a phobia that is distinctly gendered in Western culture.

These observations can also be contextualized within today's culture of food as well as the history of Christianity. Practicing food restraint and dieting in general has become a widespread norm, particularly for women.[55] This food restraint occurs, however, in a rather paradoxical cultural context that simultaneously promotes overindulgence and overconsumption.[56] While individuals encounter countless opportunities and temptations to consume, they are expected to exercise restraint. This is especially true for women.[57] Indeed, it is well documented that cultural body norms affect women more significantly than men. The thin body ideal is one means by which women "do gender."[58]

Yet, even through the highly gendered scripts of mainstream body discourses, Christian weight loss programs tend to exhibit a form of gender neutrality.[59] Despite occasional gendered talk about, say, losing weight to find or please a husband, Christian diets target both women and men in their transformation efforts. It is worth noting that the diets selected in the current analysis were promoted by both female and male figures. However, most leading Evangelicals, including those who discuss weight loss, are men. When promoting their weight loss programs, these men often share the difficulties they encountered trying to achieve health and/or a certain weight. Their visibility as dieters is, in and of itself, a challenge to gendered body rules.

This rather remarkable gender neutrality is particularly evident in Showalter's program. In her more recent 2007 work she excises a section from the 1977 book in which she locates the roots of her personal overeating in the childhood competition between herself and her older brothers for parental attention. In 2007 Showalter also includes reference to male participation in her 3D groups as well as a comment box called "Tips for Men" authored by nutritionist Maggie Davis. This contrasts with the earlier version of the 3D Plan that assumed a solely female participation in the program. Undoubtedly, a key difference between the two versions is the gender neutral nature of the latter, while the earlier text is primarily oriented toward the experiences and needs of women, particularly those living gender-traditional lives as primary caretakers for husband and children.

In conclusion, one key strategy by which the American Protestant Christian subculture successfully creates a distinct collective identity is by selectively engaging and appropriating mainstream cultural discourses. Christian weight loss programs provide a compelling case study of how Christian cultural producers encourage their consumers, that is, both Christian women and men, to perceive themselves as striving for uniquely Christ-centered lives while simultaneously sharing the goals and interests of mainstream secular culture. This dynamic of cultural consumption and co-optation, considered extensively by Christian Smith,[60] lends greater complexity to the concept of secularization, whether it is understood in its classic form,[61] in terms of differentiation into separate spheres of society,[62] or as the diminishing of religious authority.[63] Religion, as Emile Durkheim famously noted, is "destined to transform rather than disappear."[64] Indeed, rather than disappearing or retreating to the dark corners of contemporary society, Christian cultural producers are adeptly engaging mainstream culture in ways that are simultaneously conventional and uniquely Christian.

Notes

1. Patsi Farmer, "Minister Loses 100 Pounds by Praying Weight Away," *Sarasota Harold-Tribune*, February 28, 1957, 13.
2. Griffith, *Born Again Bodies*, 162.
3. "The Diet Industry a Big Fat Lie," *Business Week,* January 2008, http://www.business week.com/debateroom/archives/2008/01/the_diet_indust.html.
4. Griffith, "There Seems to Be a Growing Interest"; see also Griffith, *Born Again Bodies.*
5. While both Peter Shockey and Stowe Shockey contribute to Malkmus's *The Hallelujah Diet,* we reference Malkmus solely hereafter as he is the key proponent and formulator of this diet.
6. Neva Coyle and Marie Chapian, *The All-New Free to Be Thin Lifestyle Plan* (Minneapolis: Bethany House, 1993), 17.
7. Malkmus, Shockey, and Shockey, *The Hallelujah Diet,* 36.
8. Genesis 1:29: "Then God said, "Behold, I have given you every plant yielding seed that is on the surface of all the earth, and every tree which has fruit yielding seed; it shall be food for you" (New American Standard Bible).
9. Bordo, *Unbearable Weight.*

10. Sobal, "The Medicalization and Demedicalization of Obesity."

11. Crandall et al., "An Attribution-Value Model of Prejudice"; Puhl and Brownell, "Bias, Discrimination, and Obesity."

12. DeJong, "The Stigma of Obesity"; Weiner, Perry, and Magnusson, "An Attributional Analysis of Reactions to Stigmas."

13. Markowitz, Friedman, and Arent, "Understanding the Relation Between Obesity and Depression."

14. Orbach, *Fat Is a Feminist Issue;* Thompson, *A Hunger So Wide and So Deep.*

15. U.S. Department of Health and Human Services, *The Surgeon General's Call to Action.*

16. Ibid.

17. For specific guidelines see Centers for Disease Control and Prevention, "Physical Activity for Everyone"; U.S. Department of Agriculture. *MyPyramid.gov.*

18. Bacon, *Health at Every Size;* Campos, *The Obesity Myth;* Campos et al., "The Epidemiology of Overweight and Obesity"; Gaesser, *Big Fat Lies.*

19. Conrad, "Medicalization and Social Control."

20. Sobal, "The Medicalization and Demedicalization of Obesity."

21. Fraser, *Losing It.*

22. Pope, Phillips, and Olivardia, *The Adonis Complex.*

23. Wolf, *The Beauty Myth.*

24. Gimlin, *Body Work;* Sprague-Zones, "Beauty Myths and Realities."

25. Fraser, Losing It.

26. Showalter, *3D,* 12–13.

27. Coyle and Chapian, *The All-New Free to Be Thin Lifestyle Plan,* 11.

28. Rubin, *The Maker's Diet,* 32.

29. Showalter, *3D;* and Showalter, Davis, and Shannon, *Your Whole Life.*

30. Coyle and Chapian, *The All-New Free to Be Thin Lifestyle Plan,* 16.

31. Shamblin, *The Weigh Down Diet,* 1.

32. Ibid., 2.

33. Ibid., 3.

34. Ibid., 187.

35. Showalter, Davis, and Shannon, *Your Whole Life,* 5.

36. Showalter, *Members Plan,* 9.

37. Showalter, Davis, and Shannon, *Your Whole Life,* 133.

38. Rubin, *The Maker's Diet,* 49.

39. See, e.g., Gaesser, *Big Fat Lies,* 117–134.

40. Showalter, *3D,* 7.

41. Showalter, Davis, and Shannon, *Your Whole Life,* 19.

42. Coyle and Chapian, *The All-New Free to Be Thin Lifestyle Plan,* 29.

43. Shamblin, *The Weigh Down Diet,* 5.

44. Showalter, Davis, and Shannon, *Your Whole Life,* 39.

45. Rubin, *The Maker's Diet,* 86.

46. Malkmus, Shockey, and Shockey, *The Hallelujah Diet,* 55.

47. Ibid., 55–56.

48. Coyle and Chapian, *The All-New Free to Be Thin Lifestyle Plan,* 22.

49. Kwan and Sheikh, "Paradoxes."

50. Swidler, "Culture in Action," *Talk of Love.*

51. Kwan and Sheikh, "Paradoxes."

52. Kwan, "Framing the Fat Body."

53. The Christian critique of external beauty can be interpreted as a progressive challenge to cultural assumptions. For example, Coyle and Chapian's 1979 emphasis on physical, emotional, and spiritual wholeness over thinness per se can be seen as a critique of the dominant medical paradigm, which tends to equate a high BMI with health risk and a lower BMI with healthiness, regardless of other risk factors. As Annemarie Jutel has pointed out, an oppressive "aesthetics of normality" says more about our culture's standards of beauty than about health and has resulted in health and social disparities. See "Does Size Really Matter."

54. Kwan and Trautner, "Beauty Work."

55. Rodin, Silberstein, and Streigel-Moore. "Women and Weight."

56. Bordo, *Unbearable Weight.*

57. Ibid.

58. McKinley, "Ideal Weight/Ideal Women"; Rothblum, "The Stigma of Women's Weight"; West and Zimmerman, "Doing Gender."

59. Because of limited space, this chapter does not analyze the role of race in depth. The Christian diet pundits considered here are all white, and, in general, with the exception of African American pastor T. D. Jakes, who has written a weight loss book (see *Lay Aside the Weight!*), Christian weight loss programs have been developed by white men and women. The prominent Hispanic evangelical Reverend Luis Cortés Jr., president and CEO of Esperanza USA, focuses primarily on economic and immigration issues and has not yet promoted a specific diet program.

60. Smith, *American Evangelicalism.*

61. Berger, *The Sacred Canopy.*

62. Gorski, "Historicizing the Secularization Debate."

63. Chaves, "Secularization as Declining Religious Authority."

64. Durkheim, *The Elementary Forms of Religious Life,* 432.

CHAPTER II

EATING IN SILENCE IN AN ENGLISH BENEDICTINE MONASTERY

Richard D. G. Irvine

THE EATING HABITS OF ENGLISH BENEDICTINES

B enedictine communities are shaped by a timetable of shared prayer, work, and eating. This chapter explores the role of meals within that timetable and examines the relationship between food and monastic life in Downside Abbey, a contemporary Catholic English Benedictine monastery.

Over tea one spring afternoon, a monk spoke of a letter he had received from a man asking to stay in the monastery through Lent so that he could experience the rigors of severe fasting. "I hate that kind of thing. I wrote back and told him that if he was interested in fasting, he probably wouldn't find much of it here."[1] He defiantly munched on a biscuit, and his frustration with the assumption that the monastic life must be characterised by extreme austerity was palpable. Benedictine life was, for him, not about pushing those kind of limits. Certainly, the monastery observed elements of fasting; on Friday, in commemoration of the day of the week on which Christ was crucified, the community abstained from meat and substituted soup for one of its meals. In so doing, of course, the community was not behaving in an exceptional manner, but only sharing in the abstinence of the wider Church[2]—even if participation in what is colloquially known as the "Friday fast" has lost its universal character as a mark of Catholic living following the Apostolic Constitution *Paenitemini* in 1966, which allowed the hierarchy of bishops in each region to make a decision to substitute other forms of penitence for eating restrictions. Since 2009 the monastery has also reduced the amount eaten on Wednesdays, again substituting one of its meals for soup. In fact, this was not wholly an ascetic impulse—the decision was taken because many of the community wanted the opportunity to have soup containing meat as part of their dietary repertoire, as the soups served on Friday obviously contained no meat. Nevertheless, in their choice of Wednesday as a "soup day" we see the contemporary monastic community consciously reconnecting itself with the practice of the early church, with fasting on Wednesdays and Fridays referred to in the *Didache*, a pastoral document from the late first or early second century. There is also a reduction in food consumed in the monastery during the season of Lent.

Beyond this, however, the eating patterns of English Benedictine monks do not differ radically from those of the wider English population. The monks eat three meals a day. A breakfast of porridge and, for those who wish, cereal, bread and jam or a boiled egg, is provided in the refectory at 7:30 A.M. after the first two services of the monks' daily liturgy, Vigils at 6 A.M. and Lauds at 7:10 A.M. A lunch, usually consisting of a meat dish (fish on Fridays) with vegetables, accompanied by cold salads, and followed by a pudding, is served at 12:40 P.M. after the Midday Office (sometimes referred to as Sext). The monks are able to take tea in the refectory at 4:15 P.M., and outside of Lent there is sometimes a slice of cake to go with their beverage. A meat and vegetable dish (replaced with soup on Wednesdays and Fridays) is served once again for supper at 6:45 P.M. There is generally no reduction in the number of meals served throughout the year, although, as previously noted, there is some alteration in the amount and nature of food served on fast days.

The following examples of meals served during a week in June 2006 offer an impression of the community's typical fare: on Thursday lunchtime the monks were served chicken korma and rice with mixed vegetables, followed by apple crumble and cream, and at supper they were served quiche Lorraine and green salad. On Friday the monks were served fish, chips, and peas for lunch and vegetable soup for supper. Other foods served to the monks included macaroni and cheese, minced beef with Yorkshire pudding, and chicken and mushroom pie. As in many households up and down the country, the monks are served the traditional Sunday lunch of roast beef or lamb served with roast potatoes and gravy. The Sunday lunch has been described as "one of the central icons of British-ness,"[3] a ritual act that connects the national community, so in eating their roast the monks are participating in the wider food culture of British society.

The monks' diet and their timetable of meals are clearly at some variance with the eating habits set out in the sixth-century Rule of Saint Benedict, upon which the government and daily practice of the monastery is based. There we read that the monks are to take two meals on all Sundays and on nonfast days during the summer months from Easter to mid-September, a single meal during the winter and on fast days,[4] and that all are to abstain from the flesh of four-footed animals.[5] The apparently lax observance of contemporary monasteries in this area has attracted some comment. One notable critic has been the monastic historian and Benedictine monk Adalbert de Vogüé, whose work *To Love Fasting* is both a personal reflection on the experience of fasting and a comment upon the decline of fasting as a monastic practice. Noting the widespread abandonment of Saint Benedict's meal program, de Vogüé speaks instead of fasting as "an expansive and liberating practice,"[6] describing his own routine of waiting until the evening to eat his only meal of the day, consisting of eggs or fish, vegetables, salad, and fruit, with cheese on occasion,[7] and his wish to press further to find the "truly necessary minimum."[8] However, the monks at Downside were wary of such ascetic excesses—in place of austerity they stressed the importance of moderation. One monk pointed out that undereating came with its own spiritual dangers: "the vanity which causes you to eat too little can be just as dangerous as being greedy and always wanting to eat too much. Both of these things are a kind of self-obsession, really, aren't they?"[9] Another drew a contrast between the "superhero" saints who sought God through the most extraordinary feats and the simplicity of a Benedictine life where God is sought (and, he believed, found) in the ordinary and the everyday.[10]

In this emphasis on moderation, the monks follow in a tradition of thinking about the Benedictine life that can be traced to earlier English Benedictines. In *Consider Your Call*, the 1978 report of a Commission of English Benedictine monks and nuns examining the key principles of their monastic life in light of the Second Vatican Council, we are told that "the monk has traditionally sought to train and discipline himself by voluntary acts of self-denial. Historically this custom often led to exaggerations. . . . An exaggerated emphasis on negative ascetical practices often makes people gloomy and irritable, whereas the result of true love is always a spirit of mercy, peace, and joy."[11] Cuthbert Butler, abbot of the community between 1906 and 1922, also set out a contrast between Benedictine moderation and the deliberate hardship of earlier modes of monasticism. He described the Desert Fathers, in fourth century Egypt, each prolonging their fasts, pushing for greater and greater feats of endurance: "Before St Benedict the practice of these bodily austerities had been looked on as a chief means for attaining the spiritual end of the monastic life. But he prescribed for his monks sufficient food, ample sleep, proper clothing."[12] Crucially, for Butler this was a contrast between spiritual individualism and the communitarian ideal of the Benedictine Rule. He wrote of the Desert Fathers that "they loved to 'make a record' in austerities, and to contend with one another in mortifications,"[13] whereas Benedict broke with the past through "the elimination of austerity and . . . the sinking of the individual in the community."[14]

So English Benedictines take a pragmatic view of the dietary restrictions in the Rule. Of course, the interpretation of the Rule in this area has historically been a source of great division; we see, for example, that in the twelfth century Bernard of Clairvaux criticized the variety and extent of the food consumed by monks in his day and saw the rigorous application of the dietary instructions of the Rule of Saint Benedict as a key aspect of the Cistercian reform and as a point of major contrast with Benedictine foundations in his day.[15]

Avoidance of meat in accordance with the Rule of Saint Benedict remains a key aspect of Cistercian identity in particular and is also presented as an important part of Benedictine tradition in some monasteries.[16] For example, the best-selling cookbook *From a Monastery Kitchen*,[17] which consists of recipes by a monk of Our Lady of the Resurrection monastery, La Grangeville, New York, contains no meat recipes (but some fish recipes), on the grounds that this reflects a monastic diet which follows the Rule. The English Benedictines, however, have not tended toward a legalistic approach to this question, and this shapes the moderate reading of the Rule provided by Cuthbert Butler. So, for example, Butler does not necessarily see abstinence from meat as being to the benefit of the modern monk, going so far as to quote a seventeenth-century English Benedictine who wrote that the effects of vegetarianism were that "monasteries are made rather hospitals of sick persons than places to sing with joy the praises of God."[18] Butler's approach to the Rule is, therefore, pragmatic, as two current members of the community have pointed out: "When no problem exists, Abbot Butler does not turn to the Rule to create one."[19]

De Vogüé directly criticized Butler,[20] deeming it an error to argue that Benedict eliminated corporal austerity. Of those who emphasize the Rule's moderation, de Vogüé wrote: "On the one hand, they praise the Father of monks for having admirably tempered the traditional austerities so that little or nothing of them remains. On the other hand, they do not even mention that his meal program, reputed to be so easy, is in fact completely ignored."[21] Against Butler's emphasis on the role of community life, he argues that "however precious these communitarian values . . . the personal ascesis of fasting and other analogous bodily practices remain irreplaceable, being of another order."[22] Yet, as one monk explained, this goes against a principle that he believed was essential to the proper understanding of Benedictine life: "you have to remember that living in community is the first and primary mortification."[23] It was suggested that, when reading de Vogüé, one should bear in mind that his account was not that of a monk centered in community, living a life shared in common according to the Rule. Indeed, de Vogüé explained that his life was that of a hermit, going into the monastery only for an hour each day to pick up his mail, books from the library, and food from the kitchen.[24] He suggested that the intensity of communal life limits the capacity to fast,[25] and noted the benefits of a life of isolation: "To speak, to adapt to others, to be on time, to take account of one or several neighbours at every moment—all this keeps one in a state of constant, though unconscious, tension."[26] Yet the monks believed that it was *precisely* this work of learning to live with one another that lay at the heart of their identity as Benedictines—for them, the life of the community was the path to Christian humility and charity. By contrast, the work of taking on individual austerities could be self-defeating, inasmuch as it might lead a monk to egotism and pride.

Here we see a reflection of the teaching of Augustine Baker (1575–1641), an English Benedictine who acted as spiritual director to the nuns at the monastery of Our Lady of Consolation, Cambrai, and whose instruction on prayer and mortification remains influential within English Benedictine monasteries. In a commentary on Saint Benedict's Rule, discussing Benedict's eighth degree of humility, to "forbear all acts of singularity,"[27] Baker gives the example, "he who would out of devotion forbear flesh, where all others by ye orders of ye house do eat it, doth offend against this degree of humility,"[28] and explains that such singularity "is naughty & hurtfull in two respects; first to ye party himself, by causing & nourishing self-will & pride in him; 2dly by raising scandal & troubles to others, to ye prejudice of ye common peace and to ye endangering of others, that are indeed unable for it, to undertake ye like, or if they do not, to be daunted or discouraged that they cannot."[29] Here we see the rejection of voluntary mortifications on the grounds that they do more harm than good, both to the individual and to the community. The central concern here is the humility gained from yielding to the common way of life. To return to the words of the monk I quoted earlier: "living in community is the first and primary mortification." And so, in the daily life of the monastery, the focus was not on *cutting out* food but on *sharing* food.

MEALTIME AS RITUAL

In the monastery, eating is connected to the work of prayer. A connection between the daily liturgy and the meal is made visible as the monks make their way along the cloister, moving from the abbey church to the refectory. Each meal follows a period of prayer and can be seen as a continuation of that prayer. Breakfast follows Lauds, and lunch follows the Midday Office, while supper follows the half-hour period of private prayer after Vespers. The use of the refectory as a ritual space reflects the use of the abbey church in a number of respects. Like the abbey church, the refectory is treated as a space of silence and prayer, and, as in the choir stalls, monks are seated in a specific order reflecting their place in the community; novices and juniors (monks in the early years of their membership of the community who have not yet made their solemn profession) are seated at one table, and the rest of the community sits along the tables in the order in which they received the habit, with the exception of the abbot, prior, and sub-prior, who are seated together at the end of the room.

Prayers are chanted before lunch and supper (at breakfast the monks individually say grace in silence before eating.) The hebdomadary (the monk appointed to intone prayers for that week in both the abbey church and the refectory) begins by chanting *Benedicite* (Bless you), with the community chanting *Benedicite* in response. The hebdomadary then intones the grace (I give the grace before lunch for ordinary time as an example here), with the community joining in after the first two words:

Oculi omnium in te sperant, Domine:
et tu das escam illorum in tempore opportuno.[30]

The doxology is then chanted, with the monks bowing in honor of the Trinity during the first half, just as they would when the doxology occurs within the Divine Office:

Gloria Patri et Filio et Spiritui Sancto:
sicut erat in principio et nunc et semper
et in secula seculorum. Amen.[31]

The monk who has been appointed for that day to read to the community during the meal then asks the abbot to bless him: all respond amen after the abbot chants the blessing. At this point all sit and a Scripture reading for the day, drawn from the Liturgy of the Word at the community mass, is read out. At supper, the necrology of saints is also read out, giving brief lives of the saints whose anniversaries fall on the coming day. Only after this is the food served.

Guests staying at the monastery are the first to be served. It is worth noting that guests are *built into* the structure of the monastery. The guest wing, providing room for around ten guests, occupies a floor above the monastic refectory and faces the living quarters of the monks across a courtyard. The guests' quarters in the east wing and the monks' quarters in the west wing are linked by the cloister, upon which monks and guests converge in order to reach the refectory and abbey church where they eat and pray together (although they are seated separately). We therefore see that the built environment of the monastery assumes that there will be a near constant presence of guests.[32] On the desk in each guest room is a printed information sheet that begins with a quotation from chapter 53 of the Rule of Saint Benedict: "Let all guests be received in the Person of Christ, so that He will say to us: 'I was a stranger and you received me.'"[33] It is clearly significant that guests are to be welcomed as Christ, since in offering this welcome the monks express and act out the ideals of charity and humility which are central to their own vocations and central to their understanding of the Christian life. The importance of this ideal of hospitality is highlighted by Benedictines who have written about the reception of guests,[34] and the invitation to share food with the monks at mealtimes is an important part of this welcome. So when the guest is the first to be given food it is a demonstration of respect and charity. Nevertheless, in allowing guests into the enclosure, the community opens itself to potential disruption. For this reason, the guest is an ambivalent presence, and in the refectory the community needs to maintain its boundaries. The guest is invited to participate in the life of the community, yet he is seated at a separate table in order to be spatially segregated from the monastic community in the refectory, as in the abbey church, and in sleeping quarters. Furthermore, some guests cannot be welcomed into the refectory at all. The constitutions of the English Benedictine Congregation designate the refectory as part of the monastic enclosure,[35] and women are not ordinarily allowed within this enclosure according to the norms of the house. In fact, it should be noted that this is not a complete restriction. The monastery, along with the adjoining school run by the monastery, employs a number of staff members to assist in the kitchens along with cleaning, and, as some of the staff are female, they do on occasion enter the refectory in the course of their work. However, while such a female presence is clearly treated as expedient on occasion, the refectory is a male-marked area during mealtimes.

As well as being an occasion on which to serve guests, mealtimes are also occasions for the community to serve one another. All able-bodied monks are obliged to take their turn as reader or server in the monastic refectory according to a rota, and novices in particular are heavily involved in the duties of serving as part of their formation. The American Benedictine Rembert Sorg has remarked at length on the signifiance of Saint Benedict's insisting that work be part of the daily routine for everyone in the monastery. Work was not something to be shirked, but something that all monks, regardless of social background, must accept and embrace in the service of God and of others.[36] That which was considered menial comes to be considered holy. This helps us to understand the significance of the work of serving in the refectory. A common connection is made between the importance of servility and Christ's example in washing the feet of his followers.[37] Around Maundy Thursday, discussing the symbolism of the act of washing his parishioners' feet in the service for that day, one monk directly linked this ritual with the importance of serving the rest of the community at mealtimes in the refectory: "It's like a little Maundy Thursday . . . it's Christian charity as it should be, really. We're all servants of one another, after all."[38]

Nevertheless, while the importance of work within Benedictine life is visibly demonstrated in the refectory, the route by which the meals arrive on the table is less clearly illustrative of the idea that the monks should work for themselves. Food is typically sourced commercially and prepared by hired caterers (in conjunction with the catering carried out for the adjoining school). Thus, while monastic service is visible in the ritual at mealtime, this is made possible by the service of others.

Knowles, sketching the ideal of the monastery as presented in the Rule, wrote that "economically and materially it contained within its walls and fields all the necessaries of life and the means of converting them to man's use."[39] Yet the extent to which such self-sufficiency is achievable by monasteries is questionable, especially as a variety of activities make competing demands upon the monks' time. Sorg has argued that the clericalization of monks was the primary cause of the abandonment of manual labor,[40] and in Downside, where all of the monks are ordained priests or are in the process of training for the priesthood, and therefore have pastoral work on parishes and in the school to attend to, it is difficult to allocate time to provide and prepare the food needed for the community.

The problem of the the compatability of manual work with other activity in the monastery is a recurrent one in monastic history. As Applebaum explains in his outline of the monastic contribution to the concept of work, one of the tensions which led to the Cistercian reform movement in the twelfth century was the argument that monks had turned their back on manual labor to attend to increasing ritual commitments and that, in doing so, they had moved away from the teaching of the Rule.[41] Yet the Cistercians themselves relied on a division of labor between choir monks, with a greater focus on prayer, and lay brothers, with a greater focus on manual work, and gradually hired other laborers to supplement the work of the lay brothers.[42] So the dependence of monks on work carried out by those outside the community is by no means a new historical development. Nevertheless, it is a situation that has generated comment within the monastic community both now and in the past.

In 1933 an unsuccessful proposal was made by several monks within the community to establish a new foundation which would be substantially different in practice to the mode of life at Downside; this proposal specifically sets out the ideal of greater self-sufficiency and an increased emphasis on manual labor, with a decreased focus on pastoral work. "The aim would be to be as self-supporting as possible with dairy produce, eggs, vegetables and fruit, and perhaps in time to increase all these forms of produce for the market."[43] The proposal was ultimately rejected, and this would lead to several monks parting company with the community.

In recent years new monastic recruits have once again expressed a desire that the community should grow all its own vegetables and prepare its own food, and some steps have been taken in this direction, with asparagus, lettuce, garlic, herbs, tomatoes, strawberries, and raspberries now produced in the monastery gardens. However, at the present time, these items are only a small supplement, with the bulk of the food still needing to be externally sourced.

THE SILENCE IN WHICH TO LISTEN

Except on feast days, when the monks are given special permission to talk after grace has been chanted, the monks remain silent throughout the meal. This condition of silence is striking. Food sharing might be seen as an ideal setting for conversation, with such talk considered an ingredient of the meal as important as the food itself in its capacity to create and maintain social relationships. Commensality is clearly central to the life of the monastery, yet the community is brought together in the act of sharing food without any accompanying exchange of words. There is, in fact, a sign language which the monks occasionally use when, for example, they wish someone to pass the butter. However, this is limited to a series of specific signs relating to food and other items in the refectory. I will record these signs, as described in a list provided by the novice master; a customary of 1935 describes essentially the same set of signals:

> *Bread:* palm of hand placed flat on the table.
> *Butter:* forefinger drawn along the surface of the table.
> *Cheese:* hand extended at right angles to the table, like a knife.
> *Sauces, custard, jam:* circle drawn in air close to the table with forefinger.
> *Salt:* thumb and forefinger held downwards and rubbed together.
> *Sugar:* thumb and all fingers held upwards and rubbed together.
> *Vegetables:* clenched fist placed down on the table.

Salad: fingers of hand shaken in air close to the table like leaves.

Fruit: fist is clenched in air close to the table, as if picking fruit.

Beer: forefinger held out.

Cider: two fingers held out.

Water: three fingers held out.

Anything else in a jug: clenched fist turned as if pouring.

Plate: forefinger drawing circle over table in the place of the plate.

Cutlery: forefinger drawing line over table in the place of the absent item.

Cruets: little finger extended and crooked, moved as if raising the cruets.

This list covers a useful vocabulary and allows the monks to make a number of practical requests without speaking. However, it should be noted that it comes nowhere near the elaborate sign systems used by the monks of medieval Cluny, as described by Scott Bruce,[44] or the sign language recorded by Robert Barakat among twentieth-century American Cistercians.[45] These languages demonstrate a breadth of vocabulary and a capacity for articulation, with monks able to string together several signs in a row to communicate more complex ideas. In those settings, with a much wider condition of silence going beyond mealtimes, signing can stand as a proxy for spoken conversation. By contrast, the sign system described here is very much a restricted code for mealtimes. It is not a nonverbal means for conversation, but a practical tool which maintains silence while restricting communication in the refectory to only that which is necessary.

While the monks eat in silence, one of the community, seated at the lectern, begins to read from the book chosen by the abbot or prior. The books to be read are not necessarily of an overtly "religious" character, although some selections, such as Pope Benedict XVI's encyclical *Deus Caritas Est*, are clearly chosen on the basis that they represent the teaching of the Church, this is not always the case. The current abbot of the monastery is a historian, hence there is a particular bias toward historical books at mealtimes. Books are read continuously over the course of months, with the reader picking up each day where he had left off the last time. As a result, the books become a part of the everyday life of the monastery, creating a shared focus during the meal and generating remarks and conversations outside mealtimes. They can also occasionally become a source of laughter within the community. The selection of Jonathan Fenby's *Penguin History of Modern China* as a reading led to various jokes around the monastery about liturgical innovations representing a "great leap forward" or "cultural revolution." On another occasion, listening to Andrew Marr's *A History of Modern Britain*, the reader had reached a point where Marr explains how Ian Fleming's loving description of American food in the James Bond novel *Live and Let Die*—hamburgers, fries, salads with Thousand Island dressing, ice cream!—would have titillated the British readership, who were still on postwar rations. As the community and guests listened to the words and contemplated the distance between the delights being described and what they found on their own plates, the monks began to laugh. The reader, unable to suppress his own amusement, had to stop, and Andrew Marr's words about the culinary fantasies of ration-time England were met with an understanding which had not been anticipated.

So, throughout the meal, the monks share a common focus: they listen to a common text. The importance of remaining silent is made clear in this setting. They cannot rely on the back and forth of chatter as a way of building up social connections. They do not break up into pairs or small groups in order to talk to one another; they do not dwell on what they have to say themselves. Together, as a group, they focus on hearing what the reader is saying. Through keeping silent, the monks share in the act of listening.

The importance of listening within the culture of the monastery becomes apparent in *lectio divina*,[46] a particular style of reading taught and practiced within the community, described as the "slow, contemplative praying of scripture, through which God talks with a still small voice."[47] *Lectio*, as practiced within the monastery, involves reading through a short passage, usually a few verses from the Bible, slowly, "hearing each word in your mind as though you were reading aloud,"[48] eventually finding a "resonance" within the words upon which to meditate and through which to pray. The idea that you should *listen* to the words you were reading, as though they were being spoken, was a recurring theme in the monks' advice. One monk within the monastery has explored this in a practical guidebook he has written on *lectio*: "Perhaps the first step in learning to listen to the scriptures as the word of God is to think of ourselves, as it were, in the synagogue in Nazareth, listening to Jesus read them to us."[49] I would say that this approach to reading makes sense if we consider the role of listening in the life of the monastery. In both the abbey church and the refectory, to read is to hear. The monks encounter the psalms verse by verse as they chant and listen alternately. Reading in the liturgy is reading aloud or listening to someone reading aloud. And, as we have seen, at mealtimes the monks hear books—sacred and secular in subject matter—read to them. In the monastic culture of reading aloud, the individual loses control over the text. He does not set the pace for reading; he does not dart from place to place in the text. "Listening, we have to take it as it comes; someone else is in charge of the words."[50]

THE IMPORTANCE OF COMMENSALITY

Commensality lies at the heart of English Benedictine identity. The refectory stands alongside the abbey church as a gathering place in which the monks join together as a single household of Christian living and prayer. Of course it has to be recognized that pressures of work and other commitments draw individual monks away from the common timetable, leaving empty spaces in the refectory and the choir stalls. Yet the ritual importance of the meal, giving spiritual significance to the material act of eating, remains central to the daily life of the monastery.

Historical studies of Christian ascetic practice have illustrated well the potential disruption to the domestic domain caused by asceticism. Caroline Walker Bynum, for example, in her account of the religious significance of food to medieval women, provides numerous cases in which women's fasting was seen as threatening to the stability and unity of a household. Indeed, she suggests that the fasting practices of medieval women may be understood precisely as rejection of a "cozy domesticity."[51] Stepping away from food can have a notable impact on others in the household. Husbands, for example, could be shamed by their wives refusal to cook or eat at the table with them, as in the story of the fourteenth-century Englishwoman Margery of Kempe. "Margery's husband, who had married her in an effort to rise socially in the town of Lynn and was obviously ashamed of her queer penitential clothes and food practices . . . finally agreed to grant her sexual abstinence in private if she would return to normal cooking and eating in front of the neighbors."[52] As we have seen, one of the reasons English Benedictine monks avoid individual fasting and instead follow the prescribed moderation is because to do otherwise would be considered disruptive, so Bynum's observations in a different historical and social setting provide a useful illustration of why this might be the case: "If women's food distribution or food avoidance became acute enough to disrupt their role as food preparer, it could wreak havoc with social relations."[53]

Bynum makes the point quite clearly that rejection of commensality was seen as a rejection of the family, who often responded to such refusal with great hostility. "A family is a group of people who reside—and especially eat—together. To refuse commensality is both to refuse the meal as symbol of familial bond and to refuse the most basic support that a father's money and a mother's household can provide."[54] In the monastery we see domesticity not as something to be rejected but as the very substance of the monastic life. The monks identify themselves as a household. This is very clearly expressed in the following account from a life history interview: "I came from a secure home, yes, I'd say a happy home. And I think I always took with me some idea of that stability. It was loving, I think it's reasonable to say there was the love of God there, I'm not talking about piety you understand, yes they were church going, yes but love of one another. . . . So yes, a loving family, loving . . . and I think that coming here wasn't a break from that for me but a continuation of that. This is a family home, a household . . . household in Christ."[55]

Inasmuch as commensality might be central to the identity of the household in England, it is often invoked as a thing of the past. As the sociologist Anne Murcott has noted, it is very much associated with the nuclear family and is presented as part of a narrative of "crisis" and fragmentation of that family unit, which belong to a "golden age" now departed.[56] True to their commitment to the ideal of the household, monks sometimes locate their own meals within this narrative. Over tea I asked one of the community members, who had used the term *household* in conversation, what it was that made the monastery a household. He replied, "Oh, you know, little things, obviously living together and sharing but little things, like don't let the sun go down on your anger, that's Paul of course, but it's good household advice."[57] Later he continued, "eating together, taking the time to eat together, that's very important. . . . It's such a shame that so few families do now, with pressures of work and television. So the real question for me is, is a family a true household if it doesn't eat together? And families are breaking up . . . no home life, of course."[58] So it is clear that the monks do not depart significantly from the usual food habits of the wider English population in *what* they eat. Rather, in their efforts to eat *as a household* they invoke a particular ideal of the English meal as a family occasion, and this family occasion becomes a central feature of Christian social life.

As we have seen, the key characteristic toward which the monks turn when asked to explain their vocation is the ideal of community. An example of this self-representation comes from a talk given to a group of retreatants who were discerning their own vocations: "The first and, I would say, most important thing is that St Benedict is writing for *cenobites*, that is, monks who wish to live in community, according to a rule, under an Abbot . . . so the Rule is not for the eremitic lifestyle of the desert monks of the early Christian centuries, living in some kind of spiritual solitary combat, but a cenobitic lifestyle, praying together, eating together, serving one another."[59] What we see, the retreatants were told, is Saint Benedict setting out a stall for the communal life in distinction to various forms of spiritual individualism.

The goal, as described by Cuthbert Butler, is "the sinking of the individual in the community." When the monks eat together in the refectory they move toward this goal.[60] The meal involves a renunciation of self-will, which has been traced out here in three ways. First, the monks accept a common timetable of meals and a common diet. As described, individual austerities are discouraged. Instead, the primary mortification is to live in community. Second, during the meal, the monks act as "servants to one another." Third, the monks sit in silence and listen to a common text, letting someone else take charge of the words.

The refectory is an important ritual space within which the monks seek to demonstrate the ideals of Benedictine life. It has a significance in the monks' daily timetable as a space of ritual, prayer, and service. We see that the monks reject excesses of asceticism in their attitudes toward food and focus instead on the importance of commensality, joining together as a household for breakfast, lunch, and supper. It is in this way that the monks grant sacred significance to the act of eating and food sharing and seek God not through isolation but through learning to live with others.

Notes

1. Conversation in the monastery, recorded in field notes, March 17, 2006.
2. For a discussion of the social significance of the Friday fast and an account of its decline in England, see Douglas, *Natural Symbols,* chapter 3.
3. Ashley et al., *Food and Cultural Studies,* 84.
4. Rule of Saint Benedict, chapter 41; for a modern translation, see, for example, *RB 1980: The Rule of St. Benedict in English*, ed. Timothy Fry (Collegeville, MI: Liturgical, 1981), 63–64.

5. Rule of St Benedict, chapter 39; see *RB 1980,* 61–62.

6. de Vogüé, *To Love Fasting,* 11.

7. Ibid., 6.

8. Ibid., 15.

9. Interview with a member of the community, May 15, 2006.

10. Conversation in the monastery, recorded in field notes April 17, 2006.

11. Rees and English Benedictine Congregation, *Consider Your Call,* 151–152.

12. Butler, *Benedictine Monachism,* 40.

13. Ibid., 13.

14. Ibid., 45.

15. For a discussion of this controversy, see Bazell, "Strife Among the Table-Fellows."

16. For a Cistercian reflection on vegetarianism, see Cawley, "Vegetarianism, Abstinence and Meatless Cuisine."

17. d'Avila-Latourrette, *From a Monastery Kitchen.*

18. Butler, *Benedictine Monachism,* 308.

19. Richard Yeo and Leo Maidlow Davis, "Abbot Cuthbert Butler, 1858–1934," in *Commentaria in S. Regulam,* ed. Jean Gribomont (Rome: Pontificio Ateneo San Anselmo, 1982), 91–108.

20. De Vogüé, *To Love Fasting,* 100.

21. Ibid., 94.

22. Ibid., 101.

23. Conversation in the monastery, recorded in field notes February 2, 2006.

24. Ibid., 5.

25. Ibid., 71.

26. Ibid., 14.

27. Rule of Saint Benedict, chapter 7; see *RB 1980,* 37.

28. Baker, "St. Benedict's Rule," 441.

29. Ibid., 445.

30. "The eyes of all creatures look to you, Lord: and you give them their food in due season" (Psalm 145:15).

31. "Glory be to the Father, and to the Son, and to the Holy Spirit: as it was in the beginning and now and always and for ages of ages. Amen."

32. The guest wing is only closed to visitors for a period during the summer around the time when the monks are making their own annual retreat.

33. See, for example, *RB 1980,* 73.

34. See Seasoltz, "Monastic Hospitalit."; and Fortin, "The Reaffirmation of Monastic Hospitality."

35. *Constitutions of the English Benedictine Congregation* 1997, item 108.

36. Sorg, *Towards a Benedictine Theology of Manual Labor.*

37. John 13:1–15.

38. Interview with a member of the community, April 12, 2006.

39. Knowles, *The Monastic Order in England,* 9.

40. Sorg, *Towards a Benedictine Theology of Manual Labor,* 54.

41. Applebaum, *The Concept of Work,* 205–208.

42. Ibid., 206.

43. The proposal has been published as an appendix to Morey, *David Knowles*.

44. Bruce, *Silence and Sign Language in Medieval Monasticism*.

45. Barakat, *The Cistercian Sign Language*.

46. This term can be translated as Divine Reading or Sacred Reading, although in practice the Latin term (or its abbreviation *lectio*) was used around the monastery.

47. The words "still small voice" are themselves taken from Scripture; they are used in the King James Version of the Bible to describe how the voice of God was heard by Elijah in 1 Kings 19:12. Talk given by a member of the community during a day of recollection for laypeople of the diocese, recorded in field notes, November 4, 2005.

48. Interview with a member of the community, February 9, 2006.

49. Foster, *Reading with God*, 21.

50. Ibid., 19.

51. Bynum, *Holy Feast and Holy Fast*, 240–241.

52. Ibid., 221.

53. Ibid., 192.

54. Ibid., 223.

55. Interview with a member of the community, May 8, 2006.

56. Murcott, "Family Meals."

57. Ephesians 4:26.

58. Conversation with a member of the community, recorded in field notes, April 3, 2006.

59. Talk given by a member of the community, recorded in field notes, March 17, 2006.

60. Butler, *Benedictine Monachism*, 45.

Abad, Reynald. "Une indice de déchristianization? L'évolution de la consommation de la viande à Paris en carême sous l'Ancien Régime." *Revue historique* 641 (1999): 237–275.

Abercrombie, Thomas A. *Pathways of Memory and Power: Ethnography and History Among the Andean People*. Madison: University of Wisconsin Press, 1998.

Acosta, José de. *Natural and Moral History of the Indies, Chronicles of the New World Order: Latin America in Translation/en Traducción/em Traduçào*. Trans. Frances M. López-Morillas. Durham: Duke University Press, 2002.

Acts of the Parliament of Scotland, 1127 to 1707. Printed by the Command of His Majesty King George the Fourth in pursuance of an address to the House of Commons of Great Britain. 1844–1875.

Ahlstrom, Sydney E. *A Religious History of the American People*. New Haven: Yale University, 1973.

Albala, Ken. *Eating Right in the Renaissance*. Berkeley: University of California Press, 2002.

——— "To Your Health: Wine as Food and Medicine in Mid Sixteenth-Century Italy." In M. Holt, ed., *Alcohol: A Social and Cultural History*, 11–24. Oxford: Berg, 2006.

Albanese, Catherine L. *A Republic of Mind and Spirit*. New Haven: Yale University Press, 2007.

Andrews, Philip. *No Fear of Rusting*. Rotorua: Rotorua and District Historical Society, 2001.

Andry, Nicolas. *Traité des alimens de caresme*. Paris, 1713.

Appendices to the Journals of the House of Representatives, 1862.

Applebaum, Herbert. *The Concept of Work: Ancient, Medieval, and Modern*. Albany: State University of New York Press, 1992.

Ashley, Bob, Joanne Hollows, Steve Jones, and Ben Taylor. *Food and Cultural Studies*. London: Routledge, 2004.

Ashwell, Benjamin. "Letters and Journals." MSS and Archives A-72, University of Auckland Library.

Bacon, Linda. *Health at Every Size: The Surprising Truth About Your Weight*. Dallas: BenBella, 2008.

Baker, Augustine. "St. Benedict's Rule." Ed. John Clark. *Analecta Cartusiana* 119, no. 24 (2005).

Baker, Samuel. "Early Customs of the Church in Canada," *Evangelical Visitor* 2 (November 1888): 26.

Bibliography

Baker, W[illiam] O. "Religion and Sanitation," *Evangelical Visitor* 16 (July 1893): 209–210.

Baldwin, Frances. *Sumptuary Legislation and Personal Regulation in England.* Baltimore: Johns Hopkins University Press, 1926.

Barakat, Robert A. *The Cistercian Sign Language: A Study in Non-Verbal Communication.* Kalamazoo, MI: Cistercian, 1975.

Bazell, Dianne M. "Strife Among the Table-Fellows: Conflicting Attitudes of Early and Medieval Christians Toward the Eating of Meat." *Journal of the American Academy of Religion* 65 (1997): 73–99.

Beahm, William M. *The Brethren Love Feast.* Elgin, IL: Church of the Brethren General Offices, n.d.

Bearss, Asa. "Some Things We Like to See and Some Things We Don't," *Evangelical Visitor* 4 (April 1891).

Beattie, H. "Traditions and Legends: Collected from the Natives of Murihiku (Southland, New Zealand)." *Journal of the Polynesian Society* 29 (1920): 115.

Bell, Rudolph. *Holy Anorexia.* Chicago: University of Chicago Press, 1985.

Bennett, Judith M. *Ale, Beer and Brewsters in England: Women's Work in a Changing World, 1300–1600.* New York: Oxford University Press, 1996.

Benzoni, Girolamo. *History of the New World.* Trans. by William Henry Smith. No. 21. London: Hakluyt Society, 1857.

Berger, Peter. *The Sacred Canopy: Elements of a Sociological Theory of Religion.* New York: Anchor/Doubleday, 1967.

Berry, Alvin H. "Untitled Submission," *Evangelical Visitor* 24 (June 1910): 4.

Bordo, Susan. *Unbearable Weight: Feminism, Western Culture, and the Body.* Berkeley: University of California Press, 2003.

Bossy, John. *Christianity in the West, 1400–1700.* New York: Oxford University Press, 1985.

Bowers, F. K. "Love Feasts," *Evangelical Visitor* 23 (November 1909): 9.

Boyer, Paul. *Urban Masses and Moral Order in America, 1820–1920.* Cambridge: Harvard University Press, 1978.

British Parliamentary Papers—Colonies New Zealand. Vol. 10.

Brittan, S. J., G. F., C. W., and A. V. Grace, eds., *Pioneer Missionary Among the Maoris, 1850–1879: Being Letters and Journals of Thomas Samuel Grace.* Palmerston North: Bennett, 1928.

Brockliss, L. W. B. "The Medico-Religious Universe of an Early Eighteenth-Century Parisian Doctor: The Case of Philippe Hecquet." In Roger French and Andrew Wear, eds., *The Medical Revolution of the Seventeenth Century,* 191–221. Cambridge: Cambridge University Press, 1989.

Brown, Kathleen M. *Foul Bodies: Cleanliness in Early America.* New Haven: Yale University, 2009.

Brown, Peter. *The Body and Society: Men, Women, and Sexual Renunciation in Early Christianity.* New York: Columbia University Press, 1988.

Brown, Rev. Alfred Nesbitt. "Journal, 1835–1859." MSS and Archives A-179[19/9/01], University of Auckland Library.

Brubaker, John Arthur. "Anticipating the Future," *Evangelical Visitor* 108 (July 1995): 30.

Bruce, Scott G. *Silence and Sign Language in Medieval Monasticism: The Cluniac Tradition, c. 900–1200*. Cambridge: Cambridge University Press, 2007.

Butler, Cuthbert. *Benedictine Monachism: Studies in Life and Rule*. London: Longmans, Green, 1919.

Butler, John. *Earliest New Zealand: The Journals and Correspondence of the Rev. John Butler*. Ed. R. J. Barton. Masterton: Palamontin and Petherick, 1927.

Bynum, Caroline Walker. *Holy Feast and Holy Fast: The Religious Significance of Food to Medieval Women*. Berkeley: University of California Press, 1987.

———*The Resurrection of the Body in Western Christianity, 200–1336*. New York: Columbia University Press, 1995.

Calvert, Samantha Jane. "'Ours Is the Food That Eden Knew': Themes in the Theology and Practice of Modern Christian Vegetarians." In Rachel Muers and David Grumett, eds., *Eating and Believing: Interdisciplinary Perspectives on Vegetarianism and Theology*, 123–134. London: Clark, 2008.

Campos, Paul. *The Obesity Myth: Why American's Obsession with Weight Is Hazardous to Your Health*. New York: Gotham, 2004.

——— "Why Being Fat Isn't Bad for You: Weighting Game." *New Republic* (2003): 17–21.

Campos, Paul, Abigail Saguy, Paul Ernsberger, Eric Oliver, and Glenn Gaesser. "The Epidemiology of Overweight and Obesity: Public Health Crisis or Moral Panic?" *International Journal of Epidemiology* 35, no. 1 (2006): 55–60.

Capatti, Alberto, and Massimo Montanari. *Italian Cuisine: A Cultural History*. Trans. Aine O'Healy. New York: Columbia University Press, 2003.

Cawley, Martinus. "Vegetarianism, Abstinence and Meatless Cuisine." *American Benedictine Review* 38 (1987): 320–338.

Carnesecchi, C. *Cosimo I e la sua legge suntuaria del 1562*. Florence, 1902.

Centers for Disease Control and Prevention. "Physical Activity for Everyone." http://www.cdc .gov/physicalactivity/everyone/guidelines/adults.html.

Chambers, D., and B. Pullan, with J. Fletcher, eds. *Venice: A Documentary History, 1450–1630*. Toronto: University of Toronto Press, 2001.

Chapman, Thomas. "Journal." MS 56, Auckland War Memorial Museum.

——— "Letters and Journals to the Church Missionary Society," qMS-0425, Alexander Turnbull Library, Wellington.

——— "Papers." Vol. 2. MSS and Archives A-180, University of Auckland Library.

Chaves, Mark. "Secularization as Declining Religious Authority." *Social Forces* 72, no. 3 (1994): 749–774.

Climenhaga, A. W. *History of the Brethren in Christ Church*. Nappanee, IN: E.V., 1942.

Cocklin, Charles. "Let Us Be Careful." *Evangelical Visitor* 4 (July 1891): 194–195.

Cole, Charles Wolsey. *French Mercantilist Doctrine Before Colbert*. New York: Smith, 1931.

Colenso, W. "Contributions Towards a Better Knowledge of the Maori Race." *Transactions and Proceedings of the New Zealand Institute* 14 (1881).

"Communion Seasons." *Evangelical Visitor* 6 (December 1893): 362.

Conrad, Peter. "Medicalization and Social Control." *Annual Review of Sociology* 18 (1992): 209–232.

Correspondent. "Love Feast at Springfield, O." *Evangelical Visitor* 25 (November 1911): 5.

Coyle, Neva, and Marie Chapian. *Free to Be Thin*. Minneapolis: Bethany House, 1979.

Crandall, Christian S., Silvano D'Anello, Nuray Sakalli, Eleana Lazarus, Grazyna Wieczorkowska Nejtardt, and N. T. Feather. "An Attribution-Value Model of Prejudice: Anti-Fat Attitudes in Six Nations." *Personality and Social Psychology Bulletin* 27, no. 1 (2001): 30–37.

Creeds and Confessions of Faith in the Christian Tradition: Reformation Era. Ed. Jaroslav Pelikan and Valerie Hotchkiss. Vol. 2. New Haven: Yale University Press, 2003.

Crome, François. *Dialogue d'entre le malheustre et le manant contenant les raisons de leurs debats et questions en ses presens troubles au Royaume de France*. Ed. P. Ascoli. Geneva: Droz, 1977 [1593].

Crozet, Julien Marie. *Crozet's Voyage to Tasmania, New Zealand and the Ladrone Islands and the Philippines in the Years 1771–1772*. Trans. H. Ling Roth. London: Truslove and Shirley, 1891.

Dallaeus, Joannes. *De Jejuniis et Quadragemisa Liber*. Daventriae: Johannis Columbii, 1654.

Dameron, George. *Episcopal Power and Florentine Society, 1000–1320*. Cambridge: Harvard University Press, 1991.

Davidson, Henry, ed. "The Brethren Conference." *Evangelical Visitor* 1 (August 1887): 9.

—— "Church News." *Evangelical Visitor* 4 (September 1891): 264.

—— "Love Feast." *Evangelical Visitor* 5 (June 1892): 184.

—— "Our Visit East." *Evangelical Visitor* 4 (June 1891): 185–187.

—— "Temperance." *Evangelical Visitor* 4 (September 1891): 264.

—— "Untitled Submission." *Evangelical Visitor* 28 (June 1915): 4.

—— "Untitled Submission." *Evangelical Visitor* 6 (June 1893): 184.

d'Avila-Latourrette, Victor-Antoine. *From a Monastery Kitchen*. Rev. ed. New York: Harper and Row, 1989.

DeJong, William. "The Stigma of Obesity: The Consequences of Naive Assumptions Concerning the Causes of Physical Deviance." *Journal of Health and Social Behavior* 21 (1980):75–87.

De La Mare, Nicolas. *Traité de la police, ou l'on trouvera l'histoire de son etablissement, les fonctions et les prerogatives de ses magistrats; toutes les loix et tous les reglemens qui la concernent. On y a joint une description historique et topographique de Paris, et huit plans gravez . . . Avec un recueil de tous les statuts et reglemens des six corps des marchands, et de toutes les communautez des arts & métiers*. Paris, 1719–1738.

de Vogüé, Adalbert. *To Love Fasting*. Trans. John B. Houde. Peterson, MA: St. Bede's, 1989.

Dieffenbach, Ernst. *Travels in New Zealand*. Vol. 1. London, 1843.

"The Diet Industry a Big Fat Lie." *Business Week,* January 2008. http://www.businessweek.com/debateroom/archives/2008/01/the_diet_indust.html.

Doner, Sallie K. "Untitled Submission." *Evangelical Visitor* 22 (January 1908): 4–5.

Douglas, Mary. *Natural Symbols: Explorations in Cosmology*. London: Barrie and Rockliff, 1970.

—— *Purity and Danger: An Analysis of Concepts of Pollution and Taboo*. London: Routledge and Kegan Paul, 1978.

Dourte, Monroe. "Mastersonville, Rapho District, to C. O. Wittlinger, Grantham, Pennsylvania, June 17, 1971." Brethren in Christ Historical Library and Archives, Messiah College, Grantham, Pennsylvania.

———— "Love Feast at Mastersonville, Rapho District: 1898." Unpublished MS.

Doyle, William. *Jansenism: Catholic Resistance to Authority from the Reformation to the French Revolution*. New York: St. Martin's, 2000.

Drexel, Jeremias. *Aloe Amari sed salubris succi Ieiunium*. Munich: Cornelij Leyserij, 1637.

Durkheim, Emile. *The Elementary Forms of Religious Life*. Trans. Karen E. Fields. New York: Free Press, 1995 [1912].

Durnbaugh, Donald F., ed. *The Church of the Brethren Past and Present*. Elgin, IL: Brethren Press, 1971.

———— *Fruit of the Vine: A History of the Brethren, 1708–1995*. Elgin, IL: Brethren, 1997.

E., I. S. "Love Feast at Rosebank M. H., Waterloo, Ont." *Evangelical Visitor* 25 (November 1911): 5.

Ebersole, Aaron. "Untitled Submission." *Evangelical Visitor* 21 (November 1907): 4.

Eden, Trudy. *The Early American Table: Food and Society in the New World*. DeKalb: Northern Illinois University Press, 2008.

Elder, J., ed. *The Letters and Journals of Samuel Marsden*. London, 1932.

Elias, Megan J. *Food in the United States, 1890–1945*. Santa Barbara: Greenwood, 2009.

Elwood, Christopher. *The Body Broken: The Calvinist Doctrine of the Eucharist and the Symbolization of Power in Sixteenth-Century France*. New York: Oxford University Press, 1999.

Engle, Jesse. *A Treatise on the Lord's Supper: What It Is, Its Relation to the Passover and Love Feast and How Observed by the Brethren in Christ*. Louisville, OH: Baker, 1893.

———— "The Lord's Supper." *Evangelical Visitor* 2 (February 1889): 68–70.

Engle, S. G. "Love Feast at Philadelphia Mission." *Evangelical Visitor* 13 (November 1900): 437.

Erasmus, Desiderius. "Ichthyophagia." In *Collected Works of Erasmus: Colloquies*, 675–762. Trans. Craig R. Thompson. Toronto: University of Toronto Press, 1997.

Eyster, J. R., and Malinda Eyster. "Lovefeast at Intokozo, South Africa." *Evangelical Visitor* 22 (January 1908).

Fagan, Brian. *Fish on Friday: Feasting and Fasting and the Discovery of the New World*. New York: Basic Books, 2006.

Feast and How Observed by the Brethren in Christ. Louisville, OH: W. O. Baker, 1893.

Feeley-Harnik, Gillian. *The Lord's Table: Eucharist and Passover in Early Christianity* (Philadelphia: University of Pennsylvania Press, 1981)

Fillmore, Charles. "As to Meat Eating." *Unity* 19, no. 4 (1903): 194–201

Flandrin, Jean-Louis. "From Dietetics to Gastronomy: The Liberation of the Gourmet." In Albert Sonnenfeld, ed., *Food: A Culinary History*. New York: Columbia University Press, 1999.

Fontanon, Antoine. *Les édicts et ordonnances des rois de France*. Paris, 1611.

Fortin, John R. "The Reaffirmation of Monastic Hospitality." *Downside Review* 121 (2003): 105–118.

Foster, David. *Reading with God: Lectio Divina*. London: Continuum, 2005.

Foucault, Michel. *Discipline and Punish*. New York: Vintage, 1979.

Franklin, Alfred. *La vie privée d'autrefois: Textes choisies et présentés par Arlette Farge.* Paris: Librarie Academique Perrin, 1973.

Fraser, Laura. *Losing It: False Hopes and Fat Profits in the Diet Industry.* New York: Plume, 1998.

Freudenberger, Herman. "Fashion, Sumptuary Law, and Business." *Business History Review* 37 (1963): 37–48.

Frisch, Andrea. "In a Sacramental Mode: Jean de Lery's Calvinist Ethnography." *Representations* 77 (Winter 2002): 82–106.

Fussell, Betty Harper. *The Story of Corn.* Albuquerque: University of New Mexico Press, 2004.

Gaesser, Glenn A. *Big Fat Lies: The Truth About Your Weight and Your Health.* Carlsbad: Gurze 2002.

Gimlin, Debra L. *Body Work: Beauty and Self-Image in American Culture.* Berkeley: University of California Press, 2002.

Gordon, Ronald J. "Brethren Groups." Church of the Brethren Network, http://www.cob-net .org/docs/groups.html (November 9, 2011).

Gorski, Philip. "Historicizing the Secularization Debate: Church, State and Society in Medieval and Early Modern Europe, ca. 1300 to 1700." *American Sociological Review* 65(1) (2000): 138–167.

Gottfried, Robert. *The Black Death: Natural and Human Disaster in Medieval Europe.* New York: Free Press, 1983.

Grant, Edward. *A Sourcebook in Medieval Science.* Cambridge: Harvard University Press, 1974.

Grant, Mark, ed. *Galen on Food and Diet.* London: Routledge, 2000.

Greenfield, Kent Roberts. "Sumptuary Law in Nürnberg. A Study in Paternal Government." Baltimore: Johns Hopkins University Press, 1918.

Gregory, James R. T. E. "'A Lutheranism of the Table': Religion and the Victorian Vegetarians." In Rachel Muers and David Grumett, ed., *Eating and Believing: Interdisciplinary Perspectives on Vegetarianism and Theology,* 135–152. London: Clark, 2008.

Grey, George, ed. "Maori correspondence." Grey New Zealand Manuscripts (GNZMA), Auckland City Library.

Griffith, R. Marie. *Born Again Bodies: Flesh and Spirit in American Christianity.* Berkeley: University of California Press, 2004.

———— "There Seems to Be a Growing Interest Today in Religiously Based Diet Programs— What's Going On?" *Eating Disorders* 9 (2001): 185–187.

Grimm, Veronika. *From Feasting to Fasting: Attitudes to Food in Late Antiquity.* New York: Routledge, 1996.

Harris, Marvin. *Cows, Pigs, Wars, and Witches: The Riddles of Culture.* New York: Vintage, 1974.

Harte, N. B. "State Control of Dress and Social Change in Pre-Industrial England." In D. C. Coleman and A. H. John, eds., *Trade, Government, and Economy in Pre-Industrial England: Essays Presented to F. J. Fisher.* London: Weidenfeld and Nicolson, 1976.

Hatch, Nathan O. *The Democratization of American Christianity.* New Haven: Yale University Press, 1989.

Hecquet, Philippe. *La médecine théologique.* Paris, 1733.

Henisch, Bridget Ann. *Fast and Feast: Food in Medieval Society*. University Park: Pennsylvania State University Press, 1976.

Herlihy, David. *The Black Death and the Transformation of the West*. Cambridge: Harvard University Press, 1997

Hess, Linda. "The Brethren-in-Christ Love Feast." Academic paper for "Brethren-in-Christ Life and Thought" class, April 1972, Brethren in Christ Historical Library and Archives, Messiah College, Grantham, Pennsylvania.

Hoffmann, George. "Anatomy of the Mass: Montaigne's Cannibals." *PMLA* 117, no. 2 (March 2002): 207–221.

Hooper, Wilifred. "The Tudor Sumptuary Laws." *English Historical Review* 30 (1915): 433–449.

Howe, K. R. "Morgan, John 1806/1807?–1865." *Dictionary of New Zealand Biography*. http://www.dnzb.govt.nz/ (June 22, 2007).

Hughes, Paul, and James Larkin. *Tudor Royal Proclamations*. New Haven: Yale University Press, 1964.

Hunt, Alan. *Governance of the Consuming Passions*. New York: MacMillan, 1996.

Hursthouse, Charles. *New Zealand, or, Zealandia, the Britain of the South*. London, 1857.

Iacobbo, Karen, and Michael Iacobbo. *Vegetarian America: A History*. Westport, CT: Praeger, 2004.

Imellos, Stephanos, and Ekaterini Polymerou-Kamilaki. "Traditional Material Life of the Greek Populous." *Reports of the Centre of Folklore Research Athens Academy* 17 (1983): 64–66.

Isambert, Francois André. *Recueil général des anciennes lois françaises, depuis l'an 420 jusqu'à la révolution de 1789*. Paris, 1821–1833.

Jackson, S. M. "Fasting." In P. Schaff, ed., *The New Schaff-Herzog Encyclopedia of Religious Knowledge*, 4:281–284. 4 vols. Michigan: Baker, 1952.

Jakes, T. D. *Lay Aside the Weight: Taking Control of It Before It Takes Control of You!* Minneapolis: Bethany House, 2002.

Juster, Susan. *Doomsayers: Anglo-American Prophecy in the Age of Revolution*. Philadelphia: University of Pennsylvania Press, 2003.

Jutel, Annemarie. "Does Size Really Matter? Weight and Values in Public Health." *Perspectives in Biology and Medicine* 44, no. 2 (2001): 283–296.

Killerby, Catherine Kovesi. *Sumptuary Law in Italy, 1200–1500*. Oxford: Clarendon, 2002.

King, Peter. *Western Monasticism: A History of the Monastic Movement in the Latin Church*. Kalamazoo: Cistercian, 1999.

Kipe, H. Frank. "Report of Early Love Feasts in the Ringgold District of Franklin County, District of Franklin County, Pennsylvania, as Given by Mrs. William Wisler (Alice Hykes Wisler), December 1959, Supplimented [*sic*] by Information from Mr. William Wisler, Mr. Omar H. Kipe, Mrs. Omar H. Kipe," Academic paper for "Brethren in Christ Church History" class, December 1959, Brethren in Christ Historical Library and Archives, Messiah College, Grantham, Pennsylvania.

Knowles, David. *The Monastic Order in England: A History of Its Development from the Times of St. Dunstan to the Fourth Lateran Council, 943–1216*. Cambridge: Cambridge University Press, 1940.

Kremmydas, Vassilis. "Urban Dietary Patterns: A Paradigm from the Greek Island of Syros in 1837." *Historica* 14 (1998): 352–390.

Kwan, Samantha. "Framing the Fat Body: Contested Meanings Between Government, Activists, and Industry." *Sociological Inquiry* 79, no. 1 (2009): 25–30.

Kwan, Samantha, and Christine Sheikh. "Paradoxes in Evangelical Christian Weight Loss Discourses." Unpublished MS.

Kwan, Samantha, and Mary Nell Trautner. "Beauty Work: Individual and Institutional Rewards, the Reproduction of Gender, and Questions of Agency. *Sociology Compass* 3, no. 1 (2009): 49–71.

L'Alouette, François de. *Traité des nobles et des vertus don't ils sont forms.* Paris, 1577.

La Noue, François de. *Discours politiques et militaires.* Geneva: Droz, 1967 [1580].

Laffemas, Barthelemy de. *Advis sur l'usage des passements d'or et d'argent.* Paris, 1610. Bibliothèque nationale: Li 8.2.

——— *Le Merite de travail et labeur, dedié aux Chefs de la Police.* Paris, 1602. Bibliothèque nationale: 8° R. Pièce 8246.

——— *Les tresors et richesses pour mettre l'Estat en spendeur et monstre au vray la ruine des François par le trafic et négoce des estrangers.* Paris, 1598.

Lazarou, Chrystalleni, and Demosthenes Panagiotakos, and Antonia-Leda Matalas. "Dietary and Other Lifestyle Characteristics of Cypriot Children: Results from the Nationwide CYKIDS Study." *BMC Public Health* 9 (2009): 147–155.

Leake, Chauncey Depew. *Some Founders of Physiology, Contributors to the Growth of Functional Biology.* Washington, DC, 1956.

Lee, Heidi Oberholtzer. "'The Hungry Soul': Sacramental Appetite and the Transformation of Taste in Early American Travel Writing." *Early American Studies* 3, no. 1 (2005): 65–93.

Le Thresor de santé. Paris, 1607.

Lery, Jean de. *History of a Voyage to the Land of Brazil, Otherwise Called America.* Trans. Janet Whatley. Berkeley: University of California Press, 1990.

Lindemann, Mary. *Medicine and Society in Early Modern Europe.* Cambridge: Cambridge University Press, 1999.

Lindman, Janet Moore. *Bodies of Belief: Baptist Community in Early America.* Philadelphia: University of Pennsylvania Press, 2008.

Littré, Emile. "Carême." *Dictionnaire de la langue francaise.* Paris, 1872–1877.

Lorant, Stefan, ed., *The New World: The First Pictures of America, made by John White and Jacuqes Le Moyne and Engraved by Theodor de Bry.* New York: Duell, Sloan and Pearce, 1946.

Louis, Lewin. *Phantastica: A Classic Survey on the Use and Abuse of Mind-Altering Plants.* New York: Inner Traditions/Bear, 1998.

Luynes, Charles-Philippe D'Albert duc de. *Mémoires du duc de Luynes sur la cour de Louis XV.* 17 vols. Paris, 1860–1865.

McKinley, Nita Mary. "Ideal Weight/Ideal Women: Society Constructs the Female." In Jeffery Sobal and Donna Maurer, eds., *Weighty Issues: Fatness and Thinness as Social Problems,* 97–115. New York: Aldine de Gruyter, 1999.

McLeod, Hugh, and W. Ustorf. *The Decline of Christendom in Western Europe, 1750–2000.* Cambridge: Cambridge University Press, 2003.

McManners, John. *Church and Society in Eighteenth-Century France*. 2 vols. Oxford: Clarendon, 1998.

McNeill, Hinematau. "Te Hau Ora o Nga Kaumatua o Tuhoe: A Study of Tuhoe Kaumatua Mental Wellness." Ph.D. thesis, Auckland University of Technology, Auckland, 2005.

Malkmus, George, Peter Shockey, and Stowe Shockey. *The Hallelujah Diet*. Shippensburg: Destiny Image, 2006.

Markowitz, Sarah, Michael A. Friedman, and Shawn M. Arent. "Understanding the Relation Between Obesity and Depression: Causal Mechanisms and Implications for Treatment." *Clinical Psychology: Science and Practice* 15, no. 1 (2008): 1–20.

Marshall, W. B. *A Personal Narrative of Two Visits to New Zealand, in His Majesty's Ship Alligator, A.D. 1834*. London, 1836.

Martel, Heather. "Ferocious Appetites: Hunger, Nakedness, and Identity in Sixteenth-Century American Encounters." In Cynthia Kosso and Anne Scott, eds., *Poverty and Prosperity in the Middle Ages and the Renaissance*. ASMAR 19. Turnhout: Brepols, 2011: 303–321.

——— "Hans Staden's Captive Soul: Identity, Imperialism, and Rumors of Cannibalism in Sixteenth-Century Brazil." *Journal of World History* 17, no. 1 (2006): 51–70.

Martin, A. Lynn. "Old People, Alcohol, and Identity in Europe, 1300–1700." In Peter Scholliers, ed., *Food, Drink and Identity: Cooking, Eating and Drinking in Europe Since the Middle Ages*, 119–140. Oxford: Berg, 2001.

Matalas, Antonia-Leda, and Charles Franti, and Louis Grivetti. "Comparative Study of Diets and Disease Prevalence in Chian-Greeks, part 1: Rural and Urban Residents of Chios." *Ecology of Food and Nutrition* 38 (1999): 351–380.

Matalas, Antonia-Leda, and Louis Grivetti. "The Diet of Nineteenth-Century Greek Sailors: An Analysis of the Log of Konstantinos." *Food and Foodways* 5, no. 4 (1994): 353–389.

Matthaiou, Anna. "Dietary Taboos During the Ottoman Occupation." *Historica* 21 (1994): 259–288.

——— "Olive Oil and the Fast." In *Olive Tree and Olive Oil*, 112–138. Athens: ETBA Foundation, 1996.

Members Plan: Your Guide to a Christ-Centered Program. Brewster: Paraclete, 1998.

Mémoires pour l'Histoire des Sciences et des Beaux Arts (Mémoires de Trévoux). Paris, 1702.

Mennoti, Allessandro, Daan Kronhout, Henry Blackburn, Flaminio Fidanza, Ratko Buzina et al. "Food Intake Patterns and Twenty-Five-Year Mortality from Coronary Heart Disease: Cross-Cultural Correlations in the Seven Countries Study." *European Journal of Epidemiology* 15 (1999): 507–515.

Mentzer, Raymond A. "Fasting, Piety, and Political Anxiety Among French Reformed Protestants." *Church History* 76 (2007): 330–362.

Meredith, Paul. "A Half-Caste on the Half-Caste in the Cultural Politics of New Zealand." lianz.waikato.ac.nz/PAPERS/paul/Paul%20Meredith%20Mana%20Verlag%20Paper.pdf (June 19, 2009).

Merton, Stephen. "Old and New Physiology in Sir Thomas Browne: Digestion and Some Other Functions." *Isis* 57, no. 2 (1966): 249–259.

Méthode aisée pour conserver sa santé jusqu'à une extreme vieillesse, Fondée sur les Loix de l'oeconomie animale, et les Observations pratiques des meilleurs Medecins, tant anciens que moderns. Paris, 1752.

Miller, William Ian. "Gluttony." *Representations* 60 (1997): 92–112.

"Miscellany." *Evangelical Visitor* 21 (November 1907): 2.

Montanari, Massimo. *The Culture of Food*. Trans. Carl Ipsen. Oxford: Blackwell, 1994.

Montenach, Anne. "Esquisse d'une économie illicite: Le marché parallèle de la viande à Lyon pendant le Carême (1658–1714)." *Crime, Histoire et Sociétés* 5, no. 1 (2001): 7–25.

Morey, Adrian. *David Knowles: A Memoir*. London: Darton, Longman and Todd, 1979.

Morgan, John. "Letters and Journals." MS 213, Auckland War Memorial Museum.

Muers, Rachel, and David Grumett, eds. *Eating and Believing: Interdisciplinary Perspectives on Vegetarianism and Theology*. London: Clark, 2008.

Munn, Daniel Digby. "Ngati Manu an Ethnohistorical Account." MA thesis, University of Auckland, Auckland, 1981.

Murcott, Anne. "Family Meals—a Thing of the Past?" In Pat Caplan, ed., *Food, Health, and Identity,* pp., 32–49. Abingdon: Routledge, 1997.

Murphy, Terence D. "The Transformation of Traditional Medical Culture Under the Old Regime." *Historical Reflections/Réflexions historiques* 16 (1989): 307–350.

Newett, M. Margaret. "The Sumptuary Laws of Venice in the Fourteenth and Fifteenth Centuries." In T. F. Tout and J. Tait, eds., *Historical Essays by Members of the Owens College*, 245–278. Manchester: University Press, 1902.

Orbach, Susie. *Fat Is a Feminist Issue*. New York: Berkley, 1978.

Panagiotakos, Demosthenes, and Chris Pitsavos, Christine Chrysohoou, J. Skoumas, and C. Stefanadis. "Status and Management of Blood Lipids in Greek Adults and Their Relation to Socio-demographic, Lifestyle, and Dietary Factors: The ATTICA Study." *Atherosclerosis* 173 (2004): 351–359.

Pennsylvania, as Given by Mrs. William Wisler, (Alice Hykes Wisler), December 1959, Supplimented [*sic*] by Information from Mr. William Wisler, Mr. Omar H. Kipe, Mrs. Omar H. Kipe." Academic paper for "Brethren in Christ Church History" class, December 1959. Brethren in Christ Historical Library and Archives, Messiah College, Grantham, Pennsylvania.

Petrie, Hazel. *Chiefs of Industry: Māori Tribal Enterprise in Early Colonial New Zealand*. Auckland: Auckland University Press, 2006.

Pinkard, Susan. *A Revolution in Taste: The Rise of French Cuisine, 1650–1800*. Cambridge: Cambridge University Press, 2009.

Plaisted, Susan McLellan. "Mid-Atlantic Region." In Andrew Smith, ed., *The Oxford Encyclopedia of Food and Drink in America*. 2 vols. New York: Oxford University Press, 2004.

Polack, Joel. *New Zealand: Being a Narrative of Travels and Adventures During a Residence in that Country Between the Years 1831 and 1837*. London, 1838.

Poncet, Maurice. *Remonstrance à la noblesse de France, de l'utilité et repos que le roy apporte à son peuple:Et de l'instructio qu'il doibt avoir pour le bien gouverne*. Paris, 1592.

Pope, Harrison G., Jr., Katharine A. Phillips, and Roberto Olivardia. *The Adonis Complex: The Secret Crisis of Male Body Obsession*. New York: Free Press, 2000.

Puhl, Rebecca, and Kelly D. Brownell. 2001. "Bias, Discrimination, and Obesity." *Obesity Research* 9, no. 12 (2001): 788–805.

Puskar-Paskewicz, Margaret. "Kitchen Sisters and Disagreeable Boys: Debates Over Meatless Diets in Nineteenth-Century Shaker Communities." In Etta M. Madden and Martha L.

Finch, eds., *Eating in Eden: Food and American Utopias*, 109–124. Lincoln: University of Nebraska Press, 2006.

Raeff, Marc. *The Well-Ordered Police State*. New Haven: Yale University Press, 1983.

Rainey, Ronald. "Sumptuary Legislation in Renaissance Florence." Ph.D. dissertation, Columbia University, 1985.

Ramirez, Frank. *The Love Feast*. Elgin, IL: Brethren, 2000.

Rapport, Jeremy. "Eating for Unity: Vegetarianism in the Early Unity School of Christianity." *Gastronomica* 9, no. 2 (2009): 35–44.

"Ready Reference File: Vegetarianism." Unity Archives. Lee's Summit, Missouri.

Redon, Odile; Françoise Sabban, and Silviano Serventi, *The Medieval Kitchen: Recipes from France and Italy*. Trans. Edward Schneider. Chicago: University of Chicago Press, 1998.

Rees, Daniel, and English Benedictine Congregation. *Consider Your Call: A Theology of Monastic Life Today*. London: SPCK, 1978.

Robinson, Mary Kathryn. *Regulars and the Secular Realm*. Scranton: University of Scranton Press, 2008.

Rodin, Judith, Lisa R. Silberstein, and Ruth H. Streigel-Moore. "Women and Weight: A Normative Discontent." In Theo B. Sondregger, ed., *Nebraska Symposium on Motivation: Psychology and Gender*, 267–307. Lincoln: University of Nebraska Press, 1985.

Rolland, Nicolas. *Remonstrances Trés-Humbles au Roy de France et de Pologne Henry Troisieme de ce nom, par un sien fidelle Officier & subiect, sur les desordres & miseres de ce Royaume, causes d'icelles, & moyens d'y pouruoir à la gloire de Dieu & repos vniversal de cet Estat*. Paris, 1588

Roper, Lyndal. "'Going to Church and Street': Weddings in Reformation Augsburg." *Past and Present* 106 (1985): 62–101.

Rosser, Gervase. "Going to the Fraternity Feast: Commensality and Social Relations in Late Medieval England." *Journal of British Studies* 33, no. 4 (October 1994): 430–446.

Rothblum, Ester D. "The Stigma of Women's Weight: Social and Economic Realities." *Feminism and Psychology* 2, no. 1 (1992): 61–73.

Rothschuh, Karl E. *History of Physiology*. Trans. Guenter B. Risse. Huntington, NY: Kreiger, 1973.

Rozin, Paul, and A. E. Fallon. "A Perspective on Disgust." *Psychological Review* 94 (1987): 23–41.

Rozin, Paul, Janathan Haidt, Clark McCauley, and Sumio Imada. "Disgust: Preadaption and the Cultural Evolution of a Food-Based Emotion." In Helen Macbeth, ed., *Food Preferences and Taste: Continuity and Change*, 65–82. Providence: Berghahn, 1997.

Rubin, Jordan. *The Maker's Diet*. New York: Berkley, 2004.

Rusden, G. W. *History of New Zealand*. Vol. 1. London, 1883.

Sack, Daniel. *Whitebread Protestants: Food and Religion in American Culture*. New York: St. Martins, 2000.

Sadler, Hone. "A Clash of Cultures: The Traditional Funerary Practices of Maori from a Ngāpuhi Perspective." Presentation in the Department of Maori Studies, University of Auckland, September 16, 2008.

Salmond, Anne. *Two Worlds: First Meetings Between Maori and Europeans, 1642–1772*. Auckland, Viking, 1993.

Sarri, Katerina, and Anthona Kafatos. "The Seven Countries Study in Crete: Olive Oil, Mediterranean Diet or Fasting?" *Public Health Nutrition* 8, no. 6 (2005): 666–671.

Schmidt, Benjamin. *Innocence Abroad: The Dutch Imagination and the New World, 1570–1670*. Cambridge: Cambridge University Press, 2001.

Seasoltz, Kevin. "Monastic Hospitality." *American Benedictine Review* 25 (1974): 427–451.

Sekora, John. *Luxury: The Concept in Western Thought, Eden to Smollet*. Baltimore: Johns Hopkins University Press, 1977.

Shamblin, Gwen. *The Weigh Down Diet*. New York: Galilee, 2002.

Shaw, Frances J. "Sumptuary Legislation in Scotland." *Juridical Review* 24 (1979): 81–115.

Shaw, Teresa M. *The Burden of the Flesh: Fasting and Sexuality in Early Christianity*. Minneapolis: Fortress, 1998.

Shedd, Charlie. *Devotions for Dieters*. Nashville: W, 1983.

——— *Pray Your Weight Away*. New York: Lippincott, 1957.

——— *The Fat Is in Your Head: A Life Style to Keep It Off*. Nashville: W, 1972.

Showalter, Carol. *Members Plan: Your Guide to a Christ-Centered Program*. Brewster: Paraclete, 1998.

——— *3D: Diet, Discipline, and Discipleship*. Brewster: Paraclete, 1977.

Showalter, Carol, Maggie Davis, and Martin Shannon. *Your Whole Life: The 3D Plan for Eating Right, Living Well, and Loving God*. Brewster: Paraclete, 2007.

Sider, E. Morris. *Messiah College: A History*. Nappanee, IN: Evangel, 1984.

Simoons, Frederick J. *Eat Not This Flesh*. 2d ed. Madison: University of Wisconsin Press 1994.

Sister L. "Our Love Feast." *Evangelical Visitor* 3 (November 1890): 346–347.

Smith, Andrew. *The Oxford Encyclopedia of Food and Drink in America*. 2 vols. New York: Oxford University Press, 2004.

Smith, Christian. *American Evangelicalism: Embattled and Thriving*. Chicago: University of Chicago Press, 1998.

Sobal, Jeffrey. "The Medicalization and Demedicalization of Obesity." In Donna Maurer and Jeffery Sobal, eds., *Eating Agendas: Food and Nutrition as Social Problems*, 67–90. New York: Aldine de Gruyter, 1995.

Sorg, Rembert. *Towards a Benedictine Theology of Manual Labor*. Lisle, IL: Benedictine Orient, 1951.

Sotiropoulos, Maria. "The Pre-Holiday Fasting of the Orthodox Christian Church," *Theologia* 76, no. 1 (2005). http://www.myriobiblos.gr/texts/greek/sotiropoulou_nisteia.html.

Spencer, Colin. *The Heretic's Feast*. London: Fourth Estate, 1993.

Spencer, Rev. S. M. "Letters 1843–1868," NZ266.3 S74, Auckland City Library.

Sprague-Zones, Jane. "Beauty Myths and Realities and Their Impact on Women's Health." In Cheryl B. Ruzek, Virginia L. Oleson, and Adele E. Clarke, eds., *Women's Health: Complexities and Differences*, 249–275. Columbus: Ohio State University Press, 1997.

Staden, Hans. *The True History of His Captivity*. Ed. and trans. Malcolm Letts. New York: McBride, 1929 [1557].

Steckley, Leah. "My Experience." *Evangelical Visitor* 3 (October 1890): 307.

Stephans, J. L. *Incidents of Travel in Greece, Turkey, Russia, and Poland*, 1:16. 2 vols. New York: Harper, 1853.

Strachan, A. *The Life of the Rev. Samuel Leigh*. London: William Nichols, 1870.

Swidler, Ann. "Culture in Action: Symbols and Strategies." *American Sociological* Review 51 (1986): 273–286.

—— *Talk of Love: How Culture Matters*. Chicago: University of Chicago Press, 2001.

Taylor, Richard. "Journal." MS 302, Auckland War Memorial Museum.

—— *The Past and Present of New Zealand*. Wanganui, 1868.

"The Convention." *Unity Magazine* (September 1906): 214–215.

"The Unity Inn—901 Tracy Avenue." Unity Archives, n.d.

Theophano, Janet. *Eat My Words: Reading Women's Lives Through the Cookbooks They Wrote*. New York: Palgrave Macmillan, 2003.

Thompson, Becky. *A Hunger So Wide and So Deep: A Multiracial View of Women's Eating Problems*. Minneapolis: University of Minnesota, 1994.

Trexler, Richard. *Public Life in Renaissance Florence*. New York: Academic, 1980.

U.S. Department of Agriculture. *MyPyramid.gov: Steps to a Healthier You*. http://mypyramid .org (accessed April 13, 2009).

U.S. Department of Health and Human Services. *The Surgeon General's Call to Action to Prevent and Decrease Overweight and Obesity*. Rockville, MD: Office of the Surgeon General, 2001.

Vahle, Neal. *The Unity Movement*. Philadelphia: Templeton Foundation Press, 2002.

Vandereycken, Walter, and Ron van Deth, *From Fasting Saints to Anorexic Girls: The History of Self-Starvation*. New York: New York University Press, 1996.

Van Kley, Dale. *The Jansenists and the Expulsion of the Jesuits from France, 1757–1765*. New Haven: Yale University Press, 1975.

Verga, Ettore. "Le leggi suntuarie e la decadenza dell'industria in Milano, 1565–1750." *Archivio storicolombardo* 27, fascicolo 25 (1900): 49–116.

Vincent, John Martin. *Costume and Conduct in the Laws of Basel, Bern, and Zurich, 1370–1800*. Baltimore: Johns Hopkins University Press, 1935.

Vovelle, Michel. *Piété baroque et déchristianisation en Provence au XVIIIe siècle*. Paris, 1978.

Waitangi Tribunal. "Report of the Te Reo Maori Claim, 3.2.6." www.waitangi-tribunal.govt .nz/ . . . /2580F91B-5D6F-46F4-ADE0-BC27CA535C01.pdf (September 13, 2009).

Wakefield, Edward Jerningham. *Adventure in New Zealand, from 1839 to 1844: With Some Account of the Beginning of the British Colonization of the Islands*. London, 1845.

Weiner, Bernard, and Robert P. Perry, and Jamie Magnusson. "An Attributional Analysis of Reactions to Stigmas." *Journal of Personality and Social Psychology* 55, no.5 (1988): 738–748.

Welch, Evelyn. *Shopping in the Renaissance: Consumer Cultures in Italy, 1400–1600* (New Haven: Yale University Press, 2005.

West, Candace, and Don H. Zimmerman. "Doing Gender." *Gender and Society* 1 (1987): 125–151.

Wharton, James C. "Physiologic Optimism: Horace Fletcher and Hygienic Ideology in Progressive America." *Bulletin of the History of Medicine* 55 (1981): 60–63.

—— "'Tempest in a Flesh-Pot': The Formulation of a Physiological Rationale for Vegetarianism." *Journal of the History of Medicine and the Allied Sciences* 32, no. 2 (1977): 115–139.

Bibliography

Whatley, Janet. "Food and the Limits of Civility: The Testimony of Jean de Lery." *Sixteenth Century Journal* 15 (1984): 387–400.

White, John. "The Ancient History of the Maori, His Mythology and Traditions." http://www.nzetc.org.ezproxy.auckland.ac.nz/tm/scholarly/tei-corpus-WhiAnci.html (June 10, 2009).

Willet, Wallet. "The Mediterranean Diet: Science and Practice." *Public Health Nutrition* 9 (2006): 105–110.

Williams, Susan. *Food in the United States, 1820s–1890.* Westport: Greenwood, 2006.

Winger, A., and W. Winger, "Untitled Submission." *Evangelical Visitor* 24 (June 1910): 4.

Wittlinger, Carlton O. *Quest for Piety and Obedience: The Story of the Brethren in Christ.* Nappanee, IN.: Evangel, 1978.

Wolf, Naomi. *The Beauty Myth.* New York: Harper Collins, 1991.

Woloson, Wendy A. *Refined Tastes: Sugar, Confectionery, and Consumers in Nineteenth-Century America.* Baltimore: Johns Hopkins University Press, 2002.

Woolgar, Christopher, Dale Serjeantson, and Tony Waldron, eds. *Food in Medieval England: Diet and Nutrition.* New York: Oxford University Press, 2006.

Woon, Rev. W. "Extract from His Journal." June 30, 1851. South Taranaki Museum.

Zanelli, A. "Di alcune leggi suntuarie pistoiesi dal XIV al XVI secolo." *Archivio storico italiano* 5th ser. 16 (1895): 206–224.

Zanger, Mark H. "German American Food." In Andrew F. Smith, ed., *The Oxford Encyclopedia of Food and Drink in America,* 1:561–567. 2 vols. New York: Oxford University Press, 2004.

Zdekauer, I. *Leggi suntuarie maceratesi del 1563.* Siena, 1901.

Zook, Noah, and Mary Zook, "On Our Mission." *Evangelical Visitor* 13 (November 1900): 437.

Lightning Source UK Ltd.
Milton Keynes UK
UKHW040859101222
413706UK00001B/90